Lionel Caplan is Professor of South Asian
Anthropology at the School of Oriental and African
Studies, London.

CLASS AND CULTURE IN
URBAN INDIA

CLASS AND CULTURE IN URBAN INDIA

Fundamentalism in a Christian Community

LIONEL CAPLAN

CLARENDON PRESS · OXFORD

1987

Oxford University Press, Walton Street, Oxford OX2 6DP

Oxford New York Toronto
Delhi Bombay Calcutta Madras Karachi
Petaling Jaya Singapore Hong Kong Tokyo
Nairobi Dar es Salaam Cape Town
Melbourne Auckland

and associated companies in
Beirut Berlin Ibadan Nicosia

Oxford is a trade mark of Oxford University Press

Published in the United States
by Oxford University Press (USA)

British Library Cataloguing in Publication Data
Caplan, Lionel
Class and culture in urban India:
fundamentalism in a Christian community.
1. Fundamentalism 2. Christianity—India
I. Title
306'.6   BT82.2
ISBN 0-19-823402-3

Library of Congress Cataloging in Publication Data
Caplan, Lionel.
Class and culture in urban India.
Bibliography: p.
Includes indexes.
1. Sociology, Christian—India—Madras—Case studies.
2. Protestants—India, South. 3. Madras (India)—
Religious life and customs—Case studies. 4. Fundamentalist
churches—India—Madras—Case studies. I. Title.
BR1156.M33C37 1987   306'.6   87.11089
ISBN 0-19-823402-3

Processed by the Oxford Text System
Printed and bound in Great Britain by
Biddles Ltd, Guildford and King's Lynn

PREFACE

THIS book examines religious change within a minority community in a south Indian metropolis. The development I outline and seek to comprehend involves, in a word, the polarization of religious tendencies within the Protestant fold, occasioned by the increasing influence of fundamentalist practices and discourses on adherents of orthodox denominational congregations. This transformation is to be understood not simply in terms of the religious order itself, but against a wider backdrop of particular historical, cultural, and social conditions.

The data presented in this study were collected mainly in the course of two periods of field-work in Madras city, capital of the state of Tamilnadu. The first, of twelve months duration in 1974–5, was made possible by an award from the Social Science Research Council of Great Britain, and a grant of study leave from the School of Oriental and African Studies, University of London. SOAS also provided the funding for a second visit lasting seven months in 1981–2. During this latter period, the University of Madras and the Christian Institute for the Study of Religion and Society (CISRS) in Bangalore offered academic affiliation. I am most grateful to all these bodies for their generous assistance. I owe a special vote of thanks to Professors D. Sundaram and N. Subba Reddy of Madras University and to Dr Richard Taylor of CISRS for their personal interest in the project.

While in Madras my work was both facilitated and made pleasurable by the help and encouragement of countless individuals. It is a matter of genuine regret to me that only a tiny proportion of them can be mentioned here: Murdoch and Anne Mackenzie, Mahimai Rufus, T. J. David, L. Santappa Durai, Theodore and Thilaka Baskaran, John and Saroja Samuel, Peter and Dorothy Millar, John Kanagaraj, E. D. Devadason, Lalitha Manuel, Kala Rao, Brindavan Moses, A. D. Nathaniel, and the late Noble Rajamani. I owe a special vote of thanks to Anand Samuel and Franklyn Stanley who acted as my assistants at different stages of the field-work.

Some of the arguments presented in these chapters have already been published and rehearsed in a somewhat different form, and I am grateful to the following journals and publishers for permission to reproduce parts of these papers: *Contributions to Indian Sociology*, *Modern Asian Studies*, *Religion and Society*, Basil Blackwell, Oxford University Press (Delhi), and Macmillan.

I am beholden to my colleague David Parkin, for his sensitive comments on an earlier version of the introduction, and to Abner Cohen for his careful reading of the entire text.

My greatest obligation is to Pat Caplan, who shared the field-work experience, read the manuscript at several stages of its development, and offered constant encouragement and numerous insights gained from her own knowledge of south Indian society and culture. Our young children—like those of most anthropologists—had no choice about accompanying their parents to the site of field-work. Emma and Mark cheerfully put up with the disruption to their own lives on two occasions, and provided a fresh perspective on their new surroundings which would otherwise not have been available to me. I express my gratitude by dedicating this study to them.

In transliterating Tamil terms I have followed the system recommended by my SOAS colleague and first Tamil teacher John Marr. The only exception is that the Tamil letter normally rendered as 'c' is given as 's' where the letter seems to approximate more closely the English pronunciation. Words such as *sari* or *biriyani*, which have a wide currency throughout India, have not been given in their Tamil form, nor have caste and other proper names.

L. C.

CONTENTS

ABBREVIATIONS

Missions

AAM	American Arcot Mission (of the Dutch Reformed Church in America)
CMS	Church Missionary Society
IMS	Indian Missionary Society
LMS	London Missionary Society
NMS	National Missionary Society
SPCK	Society for the Promotion of Christian Knowledge
SPG	Society for the Propagation of the Gospel

Other

ADMK	Anna Dravida Munnetra Kazhagam (Breakaway from DMK)
AITUC	All-India Trades Union Congress
CISRS	Christian Institute for the Study of Religion and Society
CMCH	Christian Medical College Hospital
CSI	Church of South India
DMK	Dravida Munnetra Kazhagam (Dravidian Progressive Federation)
IAS	Indian Administrative Service
ICS	Indian Civil Service
IIT	Indian Institute of Technology
INTUC	Indian National Trades Union Congress
MBE	Member (of the Order) of the British Empire
MIPF	Madras Intercessory Prayer Fellowship
NCC	National Christian Council
NIMHANS	National Institute of Mental Health and Neuro-Sciences
OBE	Officer (of the Order) of the British Empire
OIE	Officer (of the Order) of the Indian Empire
RSS	Rashtriya Swayam Sevak Sangh (Nat'l Voluntary Service Org.)
SIUC	South India United Church

TNHB   Tamil Nadu Housing Board
TNHB Income Categories:
EWS   Economically Weaker Sections
HIG   Higher Income Group
LIG   Lower Income Group
MIG   Middle Income Group
TNSCB   Tamil Nadu Slum Clearance Board

INTRODUCTION

ONE of the most striking developments of recent times has been the extraordinary growth of fundamentalist forms of Christianity. In the West generally, and in the United States in particular, groups which preach the inspiration of the Holy Spirit have for a generation been the most successful in expanding the numbers of their adherents, invariably at the expense of the 'mainline' churches. Lately, through the charismatic movement, this kind of religiosity has begun to penetrate the hitherto impregnable walls of the orthodox congregations themselves.

An important corollary of this trend has been the extension of fundamentalist ideas and observances to the Third World, partly as a result of the considerable efforts and resources applied to international evangelism by these groups, though it has also been encouraged by local circumstances. The influence of fundamentalism has, therefore, reached into the very heartland of what had been, for some hundreds of years, the exclusive domain of the established mission organizations and the indigenous churches they created. This 'alternative' version of Christianity is purveyed by groups which are mainly Evangelical and Pentecostal. The latter, Wilson notes (1970), has since the Second World War become the most flourishing Protestant movement in many parts of Latin America, Indonesia, and Africa. I would add India to this list, although the Pentecostal presence there, like that of other similar sectarian influences, has only become apparent during the past two decades. This book examines the impact of this fundamentalist efflorescence on the Protestant community[1] and its 'traditional' church in the south Indian city of Madras.

According to most Christian thinkers, 'fundamentalism' suggests a belief, among other things, in the inerrancy of scriptures, in individual salvation, and in the eternal torment awaiting those who fail to accept the 'true faith'. These doctrines con-

stitute the legacy of conservative evangelicalism bequeathed to
their converts by the early missionaries, and one which most
Protestants in Madras today still regard as the basis of their
faith. But the recent fundamentalist arrivals on the scene lay
special emphasis on another Christian doctrine, albeit one hitherto muted in the orthodox church, namely that of the Holy
Spirit, and its special 'gifts' as set out in Paul's Letter to the
Corinthians (1 Cor. 12: 4–11). The gifts or powers most commonly conferred on true believers are those of speaking in
'tongues', prophecy, discernment of evil spirits, and healing.
The Holy Spirit and its gifts are, by common agreement, the
core of the new fundamentalism. Most Protestants in Madras,
though they remain anchored in the orthodox churches, nowadays flock to listen to fundamentalist preachers and seek the
help of such ritual specialists in dealing with the adversities in
their lives.

In this version of Christianity, the biblical miracles are seen
to be relevant for all ages, including the present one, and not
only for the days of the Apostles, as the orthodox Protestant
churches have for so long argued. The saving mission of Christ
is, therefore, increasingly understood in terms of its opposition
to the power of the devil, itself much downgraded in the doctrines of the main denominations (Russell 1977: 249). Fundamentalism therefore brings the conflict between good and
evil once again to the centre of the Christian stage. In offering
an alternative set of views and rites to those of the mission-
derived churches, it represents a potential challenge to the
dominant knowledge system and to those sections of the Protestant church and community who uphold it.

The changes which have occurred and are occurring within
Protestant Madras cannot be understood simply in terms of the
religious order itself, but against a wider backdrop of particular
historical conditions. In this study, religious practices and discourses are not separated from the exercise and implications of
power.

The functionalist preference, now much discredited, was for
regarding the social order (not always without good reason) as
reflected in and, on occasion, inverted by its religious institutions. In some writings on India, for example, a congruent
relationship was posited between Hindu gods and humans. On

the basis of his recent study of a major temple complex in south India, Fuller argues that no such correspondence exists: 'the world of the gods is not simply an "upward" projection of the world of human beings, as defined by the caste system' (1979: 474).

Most anthropologists nowadays no longer see religion as holding a mirror to social life. Many prefer to see it as rendering that life meaningful and acceptable. In this conception, religion is a way of enabling human societies and their component members to come to terms with the 'mysteries' of existence and mortality. It affords a vital mode of legitimation for individuals to cope with what Berger and Luckmann see as the precariousness of social reality (1971).

These formulations have a commonsense ring of truth about them, which most anthropologists who have studied and experienced religious activities in the field would find hard to quarrel with. But they none the less present certain theoretical difficulties. The idea of a universal need for ultimate meanings, and that it is the task of religion to provide them, leads Van Binsbergen to suggest that 'the dominant tradition in the anthropology of religion is upholding a rationalistic, volitional philosophical position which the mainstream of western thought has largely rejected ...' (1981: 222). In a different direction, this view of religion is somewhat static. It seems to assume a holistic system of beliefs and observances which provide meanings for equally integrated social wholes. In Madras, however, the orthodox churches and the fundamentalists offer quite *different* explanations for and responses to, for example, affliction; each appeals, moreover, to a *different* section of the community. An important reason for the attraction of fundamentalism among the majority of ordinary Protestants lies in the extent to which it accommodates popular beliefs—shared with Hindus—regarding traditionally recognized symptoms of evil in the world. Thus, a more dynamic conception of religion is required to cope with the complexities of the local situation.

Another difficulty is that this 'intellectualist' approach, as Kiernan points out, 'attempts to treat religion as a self-contained system of ideas divorced from social context' (1981: 138). It is perhaps worth reminding ourselves that Evans-Pritchard, who is sometimes regarded as the source of this emphasis in anthropological studies of religion, did not reject the significance of context. While he regarded as 'inadmissible' the tendency by 'sociological writers' to portray religion as a 'projection of the social order', and preferred to 'describe and interpret it as a system of ideas and practices in its own right', Evans-Pritchard did not treat religion as a wholly autonomous realm. He acknowledged how some features are 'influenced by' or 'coordinated to', or 'can be presented more intelligibly in relation to' social life (1956: 320). But, by and large, the eschewal of the reductionist tendency in functionalism has not only led most latter-day anthropologists writing on religion away from the search for correspondences between the religious and social spheres, but away altogether from any attempt to explore the links between them. Religious systems have come to be seen as constituting virtually independent cultural domains, to be understood in their own terms.

This touches on the vexed question of determinism. Within Marxism, those who still operate with what Worsley describes as the 'fallacious model of base and superstructure' (1981: 249), who continue to regard the latter as a simple reflection of the former, are today much discredited as purveyors of crude 'economism' or 'vulgar Marxism' (see Barrett *et al.* 1979: 10, 21). Structuralists have replaced the base–superstructure metaphor with a conception of the social formation as consisting of separate 'instances' or 'levels'—the economic, political, and ideological (Althusser 1970). Each is given a 'relative autonomy' from the others; a fragmentary view of the whole which encourages, as McDonnell and Robins point out, the development of a 'regional science' of any particular level, 'suspending consideration of its relation to other levels' (1980: 179). Thus, in superseding vulgar Marxism, the Althusserians posit an ideological realm virtually independent of the material conditions of existence. In the view of many, they have abandoned the ground of determination.[2]

But while this tendency is constantly challenged within Marxism, the same or similar tendency in mainstream anthropology has become the received view. The reason for the paramountcy of one or other paradigm here, as in any mode of enquiry, is a complex issue to which few practitioners have given much thought, though Crick has recently referred in a disarming way to the manner in which particular interests and orientations come, in time, 'to seem increasingly like a definition of the discipline' (1982a: 30).

Still, there have, all along, been some dissenting voices. Abner Cohen has consistently preached the virtues of a 'two-dimensional' perspective in our studies, a need to explore the dialectics between the material world and their symbolic representations. In his seminal analysis of a mystical order among the Hausa of Ibadan, Cohen (1969) demonstrated the rich and complex interplay of political and religious processes.

More recently, Van Binsbergen has bemoaned the anthropological predilection for religious activities and beliefs to be presented as 'totally divorced from processes of production, control and expropriation' (1981: 69). Asad, too, has criticized Geertz for his refusal to acknowledge that 'the religious world or perspective is ever affected by experience in the common-sense world' (1983: 250). He goes on: ' ... the meanings of religious practices and utterances are [not] to be sought in social phenomena, but ... their possibility and their authoritative status are to be explained as products of historically distinctive disciplines and forces. The anthropological student of religion should begin from this point and not ... from a notion of culture as an a priori totality of meanings, divorced from processes of formation and effects of power, hovering above social reality' (1983: 251). A not dissimilar plea is made by Keith Thomas in response to a review (by Hildred Geertz) of his study of magico-religious beliefs and practices in sixteenth- and seventeenth-century England. Thomas observes that 'if we wish to understand why men's basic assumptions change, it is insufficient to expose the inner logic of their systems of thought; we have also to take account of the relationship of those systems to the external social context ...' (Thomas 1975: 103; Geertz 1975).

These voices urge a break with both the crudities of reductionism or economic determinism, and the ahistoricism or de-contextualization of so much structuralist and interpretive analysis. Religion as an aspect of culture may be seen as neither determined nor determining, but as constantly being re-made and renewed, shaping and conditioning social processes as well as being shaped and conditioned by them (see Bennett *et al.*

1981: 10–12). The cultural developments to be considered in
this book will be discussed in relation to the urban class system,
and it will be helpful to clarify the way in which this concept is
understood and employed.

CLASS IN URBAN INDIA

Anthropological interest in the Indian class system has, to say
the least, been slow to evolve. While economists, political scientists, and historians have for some time debated its rural
character, social anthropologists (with some notable exceptions) seem to have 'deliberately avoided' such analyses in
their own studies (Béteille 1974: 33). In one attempt to examine
village society in terms of agrarian (*kisan*) rather than caste
(*jati*) structure, Jain suggests that while the latter may be ideo-
logically 'the over-determining part', it does not 'in any sense
constitute the whole of the relations of production between the
agrarian classes' (1977: 101). Despite the theoretical possibilities suggested by such a focus, and increasing signs of
awareness among social scientists generally (see Pouchedapass
1982), anthropological interest continues to be sporadic.

Such a generalization is perhaps marginally less true when
applied to the urban context, although Saberwal is understandably impatient with colleagues who appear to ignore
altogether the fact that the 'capitalist class ... has steadily
consolidated its dominance in urban areas ...' (1978: 11). After
all, many contemporary metropolitan centres—including the
locus of the present work—were initially created and subsequently developed by and for the benefit of British capitalism,
latterly becoming the *loci* of multinational as well as indigenously generated industrial growth.[3]

Thus, a number of studies have focused on urban contexts
shaped directly by—though by no means totally subsumed
within—the capitalist mode of production. If we can identify a
dominant concern in many of them, it turns on the notion of
change and continuity in traditional values and practices as
these are manifested in urban places. Since Pocock (1960) first
sought to dissolve the boundaries between urban and rural
sociologies in India, on the grounds that institutions of Hindu

culture recognize no such frontiers, scholars have turned their sights increasingly on the urban contours of these institutions.

Not surprisingly, kinship has received abundant attention. In particular, the joint family system and its ability to with-stand the processes of urbanization has been a recurring theme. Vatuk, in her study of two middle-class neighbourhoods in Meerut, addresses herself to Wirth's contention that urbanism brings about the demise of extended kin ties, and persuades us that, at least in the north Indian context she describes, such a proposition is not applicable (Wirth 1938; Vatuk 1972). Similarly, Singer (1972) seeks to challenge the view that joint families are 'incompatible' with a modern capitalist system— and demonstrates the significance of such links for a score of key industrialists in Madras.

No less interest has attended the fate of caste, and debates as to its structure and importance in urban centres continue unabated. Some argue that it has altered little, and see, in this, evidence of its resilience in the face of surrounding change; others that it is proving extremely adaptable, assuming new forms and roles (see, for example, Fox 1967; Conlon 1977). Another, more recent theme has been the 'retreat' of caste in the face of the growing importance of class as an indicator of identity in towns and cities. Berreman reports that in the modern, ethnically diverse north Indian city of Dehra Dun, 'middle class status' seems to take precedence over all else, 'even caste', in influencing behaviour (1972: 578-9). Likewise, among the Vellalar group in Madras studied by Barnett, 'a person's actions and life-style can come to reflect his socio-economic position more than his caste membership ...' (1973: 155).

What is significant in these observations is the recognition that class cannot be ignored in the urban context, although, for the most part, the class order itself has been bracketed, while other interests have been pursued. Of late, however, this order has become the focus of some attention. Peace's work on 'structured inequalities' in Jaipur (1980), Holmstrom's on industrial workers in Bangalore (1976; 1984), Wiebe's on slums and slum tenements in Madras (1975; 1981), Pat Caplan's on women voluntary 'social workers' in the same city (1985)—to name but a few—not only imply a class order, but deal directly with theoretical issues arising from its presence. Increasingly,

anthropologists are concerned—as I am in this study—to explore what Foucault (1980: 101) calls the 'micro-mechanisms
of power', which assist us in understanding the nature of the
urban class order, the manner of its reproduction, and its involvement with social and cultural (including religious)
processes.

The long-standing reluctance to employ a class model stems,
at least in part, from a widespread view which contends that
analyses through indigenous (emic) categories provide a more
authentic understanding of cultures than do those which utilize
outsiders' (etic) categories. Moreover, it is argued that in India
one of these native concepts, namely caste, subsumes and effectively obliterates all others. The former part of this equation
raises a whole variety of complex issues which are the source of
much debate in the contemporary literature, and we cannot
hope to examine them here. But it may be apposite to make
several observations which are relevant to the approach taken
in this study. The first intimates that the notions of 'emic' and
'etic' have served whatever usefulness they may once have had
in reminding us about the dangers of linguistic and cultural
imperialism. Burghart (1983: 278-9) considers the distinction
an 'unfortunate episode in anthropology', since it suggests that
'insiders' can never think analytically, i.e. as 'outsiders', about
their own culture, and vice versa. It is, moreover, moot whether
what is labelled 'emic' is nothing less than the observer's way
of constituting the 'other'. Secondly, if Western social scientists
of the 'eticist' persuasion bring too many of their own cultural
notions with them to the field—including ideas about class
better suited to an analysis of Western capitalist or post-
capitalist formations—the 'emicists' not only raise suspicions in
purporting to bring none, but threaten to lead us, as Parkin
observes, to 'extremes of cultural relativism and a refutation of
the relevance of seeking universals' (1982: xiii). Thirdly, in
dismissing virtually everything the members of a society do not
themselves perceive and articulate in discourse, they seem to
refuse the possibility that historical conditions may change in
ways and according to logics not always or necessarily accessible to indigenous ways of understanding (see Asad 1979:
624; Bloch 1983: 137). Social forces, as Johnson (1979: 55) puts
it, sometimes operate behind people's backs, or perhaps more

accurately, out of their minds. Finally, the idea that there is available *one* genuine, indigenous view of reality, on the basis of which an anthropological model can be constructed, ignores the possibility that there may be *several* renderings of the same reality. The observer, Bourdieu reminds us, might (unwittingly?) accept and reproduce the 'official' version, if for no other reason than that it overrides and represses all others (1977: 37). Those who have followed the long debate on whether or not all segments of any local caste organization accept the dominant (usually Brahmanic) view of hierarchy will recognize the problems inherent in offering a unitary, 'correct' model of 'how the system works' (see Dumont 1970; Berreman 1967; Mencher 1974).

Notwithstanding such cautionary notes, however, it should be unthinkable in any anthropological study not to take account of indigenous perceptions of the world, and how these are represented. The recent interest taken by (mainly Marxist) historians and sociologists in popular culture and what Burke (1976: 71) calls the 'history of the inarticulate' suggests some interesting lines of enquiry. I will return to these in a moment.

A micro-sociological study of class in an Indian metropolis confronts certain difficulties. Not the least of these is the extent of autonomy or agency attributable to the participants in the small-scale social context being examined. The 'world systems' approach has been criticized for paying insufficient attention to 'local specificities' and for failing to understand the 'role of class struggle and class alliances' within particular states (Patankar and Omvedt 1977: 2165). Nevertheless, it is important to bear in mind that the processes we are attempting to understand are articulated with, and in certain obvious senses incomprehensible without, reference to macro-cosmic events and structures. The establishment of a colonial presence in India; the arrival of Protestant missionaries on the subcontinent; the demands of industrialization; the struggle for India's independence; the growth and spread of new theologies within world Christianity; and the country's absorption into a post-colonial economic system dominated by Western capitalism—were and are vitally important global influences shaping the power dynamic in Madras. While these links are identified and their local significance acknowledged in the narrative, it is no part of this study, whose focus remains contextual and ethnographic, to attempt analysis of these macro-level structures themselves.

Another problem turns on the nature and meaning of 'class' in the Madras setting. Students of Western societies are, even now, not in agreement on the criteria for identifying the major protagonists in late capitalist formations. How much more complex, then, are these questions where such systems are comparatively new and shaped by a range of quite special historical conditions. Rather than make an arbitrary selection of one exogenous model which could prove wholly inapplicable to local circumstances, my own preference is to approach the problem by inquiring first after people's own notions of inequality in their urban environment.

This brings us to the second part of our equation concerning the widely accepted view that in India caste not only has pride of place in the indigenous hierarchy of concepts, but effectively smothers all other paradigms. This view is closely associated with Dumont, who quotes with approval the statement by Marian Smith that 'Indian society is structured in terms of caste but not in terms of class' (1953: 304). She clearly recognizes, writes Dumont, 'the subordination of the phenomena of class to those of caste ...' (Dumont 1970: 286). Burghart has recently drawn attention to the several discourses on inequality which comprise Hinduism, only one of which is the Brahmanic model of caste. The kingly hierarchy, which he identifies as another, comes closest to portraying the agrarian system based on tenurial rights *vis-à-vis* the monarch, though he does not present it as an indigenous rural class system (1978). Béteille (1974) and Jain (1977), however, as I have noted, do argue explicitly for such prototypes. The latter, moreover, insists that while these notions are widespread in India they have been effectively veiled by being incorporated in alternative modes of representation adopted by anthropologists. 'Whenever indigenous vocabulary is reported ... to denote classes of masters and servants in the village community the classificatory grid either of the caste system or of the administrative and revenue typology is imposed to order relationships designated by these terms' (1977: 109).

CASTE AND CLASS IN PROTESTANT MADRAS

Protestants, like most people in Madras, have clear notions of inequality based on other than caste categories. It is not that caste is absent among them. However, in a metropolis like Madras, to which people have come from all parts of the south and elsewhere in the country, from many disparate local caste systems, caste groups cannot be placed in a single agreed hierarchy. And since others cannot 'read' claims to status phrased in parochial terms, these claims must be asserted by reference to widely understood and recognized notions of *varna* or caste categories. Thus Protestants might identify themselves or others as Vellalars, a congeries of agricultural castes who rank next to the Brahmins in most parts of Tamilnadu, or as Nadars, originally 'toddy-tappers' who spread throughout the state and succeeded in raising their original quasi-untouchable position by collective action (see Hardgrave 1969). They may proclaim themselves (or admit to being) Harijans or Adi-Dravidas (i.e. native Dravidians)—both of which are euphemisms for 'untouchable'. These identities, however, are generally not referred to a hierarchical order integrated in interactional terms. In other words, they are not validated in an ongoing system of relationships in which rank is determined by accepted forms of ritually significant interaction (see Marriott 1968). Moreover, when we realize that a substantial minority of Christians in the city cannot or choose not to identify themselves or be identified by others in caste terms, it becomes apparent that a caste model alone does not adequately convey the full extent of social asymmetry and their understanding of it.

These Protestants, who are preponderantly Tamilians, have another image of their world which conveys, perhaps with greater accuracy, their experience of material and cultural inequalities. This indigenous model is generally represented as a trichotomous order, and the terms I encountered most commonly in its description were the Tamil equivalents of 'rich' (*paṇakkārarkaḷ*), 'poor' (*ēḻaikaḷ*), *and 'middle quality people'* (*natuttara makkaḷ*)—'middle class' when it is rendered in English. Other terms heard were 'big people' (*periya vaṅaka*) and 'small people' (*siṟiya vaṅaka*), 'those who have' (*irūkkappaṭṭa vaṅaka*) and 'those who don't have' (*illātappaṭṭa vaṅaka*). Driver reports that his 463 interviewees in Madras used eighteen different terms of 'social class identification' (1982: 230).

Most people I spoke to place themselves in the 'middle class', although perceptions of who occupies the strata above and below vary significantly. The well-educated and well-to-do oppose their own 'middle class' self-designation, on the one side, to greater families in the city, state, and nation. Since these Protestants are not represented among the large capitalists or 'big bourgeoisie' (i.e. among those whom they cite as 'the rich'), their references are to a tiny minority of industrial magnates who are mainly outside the Christian community. Beneath them is the generality of people—including the mass of their co-religionists—whom they define as 'lower middle' or 'poor middle' class. Not infrequently, they will refer to the occupants of this lower stratum by the term 'less educated people', or 'hut dwellers'.

Definitions go beyond simple location in the productive sphere. For these Protestants, to be 'middle class' is indicated not only by a high income and property ownership, but by a particular culture. This is defined by such attributes as a university education (usually a post-graduate or professional qualification), fluency in English and certain Western forms of behaviour, appropriate consumption patterns (housing, transport, leisure, etc.) and a world-view, including appropriate Christian beliefs and practices, which distinguish their purveyors from those beneath them. This segment of the middle class, however, has a great deal in common with those whom they designate 'the rich', sharing many aspects of life-style (though on a more modest scale) and value orientations, including a common interest in the success of capital.

The great majority of ordinary Protestants also regard themselves as 'middle class', but do so by comparison with a different set of 'others'. Above them are the 'rich' or the 'élites', by whom they mean their aforementioned co-religionists who have top jobs and good salaries, advanced education, plenty of jewellery and dowry for their daughters' weddings, and bungalows with many rooms—'bungalow people' (*paṅkaḷākkāraṇ*) is a common epithet for such a category. Below are the 'poor', without jobs or prospects, with no homes, regular meals, decent clothing, nor money for bus fares. The least well-off among this 'middle class' point outside the Protestant fold to the Narikuravas, a floating 'gypsy' population in Tamilnadu, as an example of the truly poor.

Accordingly, being 'middle class' in this context connotes having enough to meet the demands of a humble life-style. It means living in rented, simple accommodation, educating children in state or municipal schools (in Tamil), providing modest weddings for them, having a decent set of clothes for church, and, in general, maintaining the minimum standards expected by neighbours, friends, and kin. These include a range of appropriate behaviours and outlooks, not least particular religious dispositions.

Thus, both the material conditions of existence and certain cultural practices and understandings establish a clear division within the urban Protestant community. Though these Christians generally place themselves in the middle of a three-tier order, in effect the extremes of both wealth (the big bourgeoisie) and poverty (the lumpenproletariat and the gypsies) lie outside their community and their direct experience. In the context of everyday life, the hierarchy—for them as for the vast majority of urban dwellers—is essentially dichotomous.[4] It is this dual structure which forms the core of the urban class order. Peace (1980) identifies a similar dichotomy in Jaipur and, like him, I refer to the levels as 'lower' and 'middle' classes.

In a more general sense, each level comprises an alliance of different classes and forces (some might prefer to call them 'class fractions' or 'status groups'). Ultimately, however, the primary division with which I am concerned is between the dominant minority, the 'élites',[5] and all those (the rest) whom the former have the power to exclude, and thereby to constitute as subordinate; dominance, Parkin suggests, implies the 'capacity to nominate others as equal or unequal' (Parkin 1982: xlvi). In S. Hall's terms (1981a: 238) it is the most general opposition between, on the one side, 'the power bloc' and, on the other, 'the people' or 'the popular classes' (see also Turton 1984: 44).

This division clearly does not correspond precisely to any Western model of class which distinguishes the bourgeoisie either from those who perform manual work or from all who sell their labour. It does reflect, however, the situation of people in a Third World urban centre where ownership of the means of production resides principally with the state or multinational corporations, so that the indigenous capitalist class is only a tiny, highly compact, and barely visible minority.[6] In India the power bloc in most urban contexts (and this is the case in Madras) is seen to consist of small industrialists, senior managers, professionals, and top bureaucrats who 'serve' their capitalist 'patrons'. This model, which is anchored in indigenous notions of inequality but is not wholly constituted by them, recognizes that each class is internally fragmented (by occupation, education, wealth, life chances). The differences within them, however, are mitigated and, to an extent, overcome by common experiences, the possibility of kinship ties, some awareness of mutual interests, and, above all, a sharing of the institutions and meanings we label culture.

Such a model, therefore, takes us away from the static and sterile notion of class as an occupational or income category, or even a set of people standing in a particular relation to the means of production. It invites us, rather, to regard class as a cultural as well as an economic formation. This enables us to treat class struggle as being every bit as much about definitive meaning systems or appropriate religious views and observances as about material means, scarce jobs, or the control of property. It is no longer confined to 'some reified and isolated zone of "the economy"', as Worsley has remarked (1981: 249).

CLASS AND CULTURE

A class system so conceived, however, highlights for us the problem of the unity and particularity of culture. Much of functionalist anthropology assumed the existence within a society of an undifferentiated universe of shared meanings. Post-functionalist approaches, though distinct in so many ways, often give the impression that they, too, presuppose the integrity of the culture whose 'code' they are trying to break, whose 'text' they are attempting to read, or whose 'hermeneutic circle' of meaning they are hoping to enter. But, 'just how collective are collective representations?' asks Crick (1982*b*: 295). While anthropologists are being made increasingly aware of the need to acknowledge the possibility of age- or gender-specific models of cultural process, plural modes related to distinctions of class seem not to have found a place in our discourse. The concept of class culture, which emerges from our indigenous model of urban inequality, becomes a useful tool for analysis.

There is now so considerable a literature on the cultures of the urban dispossessed that Fox has identified the 'anthropology of poverty' as one of the three major foci of the discipline's urban branch. It may be, as he suggests, that this concentration of interest is a means by which anthropologists are able to preserve their traditional, intensive research methods derived from studies of small-scale societies, and reaffirm their concern with the 'romantic' (Fox 1977), although I suspect that motives are more mixed. There are several problems with this focus on 'cultures of poverty'. The one most relevant to this discussion is that they are too often presented in isolation, without reference to 'cultures of affluence'. For it is the latter which help to establish and recreate the conditions giving rise to the former. Urban anthropologists still seem insufficiently interested in those who wield the power not only to control resources and make or influence policy, but to create meanings and privilege certain modes of discourse (see P. Caplan 1985: 18). It is not simply a matter of 'studying up', as Nader (1974) recommends, of replacing a perspective on the 'have-nots' with another on the 'haves'. Both must be brought together. The need is to explore the manner in which dominant and subordinate cultures relate to and inform one another. Among those historians and sociologists who seek to give voice to popular cultures, there is a growing recognition that it is not enough to focus on such configurations alone, but that they must be examined in interaction with 'higher' or 'elitic' cultures (Burke 1983: 186).[7]

In this conception both superior and inferior are the producers of culture. The popular version may be understood in several ways. One, following the dictum of the *German Ideology*, sees the ruling class imposing its ideas on those whom it subordinates, so that all members of the society think in the categories of the 'power bloc'. Seen through such a lens, the culture of the majority is, at best, a mediated version of the dominant culture, a species of false consciousness. Even then, we are reminded by Merquior, the payment of lip-service to the super-

ordinate culture should not be too hastily regarded as a proof
of deep belief; 'for it may well be the case that the acceptance
of dominant values by subordinate classes results to a large
extent from the relative inarticulateness of *alternative* value
sets ...' (1979: 28, emphasis in original).

Another approach accords a greater degree of agency to 'the
people', seeing popular culture as an alternative world-view,
representing the 'authentic' experience of the subjugated majority. Ginzburg's (1983) historical study of folk religion in
Friuli in the Venetian republic demonstrates how popular ideas
and practices which focused on a category of ritual witchfinders
and curers (*benandanti*) were vehemently opposed by the church
and its supporters within the élite. This leads Hill, in a recent
review of the English edition, to suggest that the 'old notion'
that ideas percolate downwards from the top 'hardly seems
borne out' by this study (1984). On the other hand, Hall rejects
such an option on the grounds that it is too 'heroic', since it
suggests a significant degree of autonomy for the culture of
the subordinate majority, neglecting the 'absolutely essential
relations of cultural power ... which is an intrinsic feature of
cultural relations' (1981*a*: 232).

This constitutes a third approach, following or at least tending to accord with Gramsci's view of culture as a crucial terrain
on which the process of winning hegemony occurs (1971). Popular culture is then seen as the product of 'negotiation', the
outcome of attempts on the part of the subordinate class to
oppose, resist, or modify the dominant culture, even if it can
never quite escape its influence (see Parkin 1972: 80–92; Clarke
et al. 1980: 54–63). The relationship between these unequal
cultures—their struggle and co-existence—therefore becomes a
crucial focus of study. The precise nature of this relationship,
however, is not static or knowable in advance, but changes
over time. In the context of the Madras Protestant community,
no single paradigm—domination, autonomy, negotiation—
provides a wholly adequate way of conveying the cultural dialectic. What is clear, however, is that most aspects of lower and
middle class cultures, including religious dispositions, can only
be understood—and so will be examined—not in isolation from
but in their historical relationship with one another.

Although my analysis focuses on two major class alliances, I cannot thereby claim to provide an exhaustive account of the class structure in Madras, let alone the wider south Indian field. For one thing, there are categories of people (e.g. merchants) who would not easily fit into either designation, and to include such groups would have required additional fieldwork and/or a more extended discussion than is possible here. For another, to the extent that I confine myself in this study to the members of a minority community, I cannot devote adequate attention to the many and varied ties and affinities across the religious divide, among persons belonging to the same or different classes. Moreover, where institutional practices and values (such as certain religious beliefs and rites) are not shared, the detection of a particular relationship between class cultures in one community should not, quite obviously, be assumed for another. Thus, in as much as this study cannot hope and does not attempt to deal with the entire range of cultural possibilities throughout the extent of the class order, but with particular cultural complexes within a segment of each (i.e. the Protestant community), it is necessarily and inevitably limited. The concept of 'class culture' must, therefore, be annotated accordingly by the reader.

It might be objected that theoretical concepts developed for the analysis of large-scale structures and processes are out of place in the small-scale setting of a south Indian urban community. To apply notions like 'power bloc' or 'class order' to the minutiae of everyday life may seem excessive to some students outside the anthropological fold. None the less, such concepts emerge as abstractions from the observed realities of daily existence, and only retain their explanatory usefulness by being continually referred back to and tested against these realities. It is necesarry to enquire 'how things work at the level of on-going subjugation, at the level of those continuous and uninterrupted processes which subject our bodies, govern our gestures, dictate our behaviours etc.' (Foucault 1980: 97). It thus does seem important to know what constitutes 'dominance', 'subordination', and the 'cultural struggle' in a particular setting, such as Protestant Madras. The alternative is an anthropology of 'disembodied abstractions' (Bloch 1983: 170). I

therefore make no apology for the ethnographic emphasis of
this monograph.

THE STUDY OF INDIAN CHRISTIANS

The decision to conduct research among Indian Christians (or
for that matter any group) should require no justification, but
it may be worth noting several reasons for embarking on such
a project. First of all, as Ahmad points out, to achieve a genuine
and comprehensive sociology of India it is imperative to bring
as broad a selection of groups as possible under our purview
(1973). To this end, Ahmad himself has stimulated a substantial
and theoretically important anthropological literature on
India's Muslims (see also Ahmad 1976; 1981). But, to date,
very few monographs on Christians in India have appeared,
and none at all on Protestants in an urban milieu.[8] This book,
then, attempts to make an ethnographic beginning.

Second, Protestants lend themselves with particular aptness
to a study whose historical background involves processes of
urbanization and class formation. For they stem mainly from
humble origins—humble both in terms of caste and their place
in the system of agricultural production. A minority became
mobile partly as a result of missionary assistance (especially in
education) and patronage. It is these 'spiralists' who are today
part of the dominant class in Madras. This seems to contrast
with the situation found among urban Hindus. Peace is only
among the most recent observers to note that the origins of the
urban middle class are to be found among the higher castes, in
the case of Jaipur city, 'virtually without exception in the ranks
of the twice-born' (1980: 241). Indeed, the parallel is close
enough to suggest to Michaelson, writing about Bombay, that
'the standards of caste and class are not two separate and
opposing hierarchies of prestige, but are inter-locked in a multi-
variate stratification system' (1973: 235). The Christian case
reminds us that the two categories can be dissociated in the
actor's mind, and should be in the analyst's.

Finally, and most importantly, the study of a Christian community in India presents an opportunity to assess the nature,
degree, and context of Hindu influence on the descendants of
the original converts. It enables us to explore the extent to

which theodicies and ideas about affliction can be shared by people claiming distinctive religious affiliations. And it invites us to examine the differential impact of particular traditions within Protestantism itself on separate sections of the local community in changing historical circumstances.

Before introducing the unit of study, it is necessary to say a brief word about the Protestant community and church in Madras city. Christians are the largest minority in Tamilnadu, one of the four linguistic states into which south India was divided some two decades ago (the others are Kerala, Karnataka, and Andhra Pradesh). The Christian population in 1981 was nearly 2,800,000 or just under 6 per cent of the state's total. But, despite the increase in their numbers over the years, Protestants have remained a minority within the Christian fold. Since recent censuses do not provide a breakdown of Christians, we have to rely on other sources, which suggest that Protestants comprise between 30 and 35 per cent of the total (see McGavran 1979).[9] This would give us between 900,000 and 1 million Protestants in Tamilnadu in 1981.

Christians, like the country's other minority religious communities, although probably for somewhat different reasons, are over-represented in towns (see D'Souza 1966: 421). Despite claims that the community was almost completely rural (see, for example, Azariah and Whitehead 1930), by 1931 over 20 per cent were living in urban areas, against a national figure of 13.5 per cent (Misra 1962: 163). The proportion of Christians in towns has risen since that time, as has the rate of urbanization generally. According to the 1981 Census figures, approximately one-third of the population of Tamilnadu is now resident in urban areas; nearly 40 per cent of Christians live in towns and cities.

The association of St Thomas with Mylapore (San Thome) and the existence of a Persian cross on St Thomas's Mount dating to the seventh or eighth century provide evidence of a long-standing Christian presence in and around what is now Madras city. Numerous conversions to Roman Catholicism apparently followed the visit of Francis Xavier to Mylapore in 1544, and in 1690 Mylapore became the seat of a bishopric for the whole of the Bay of Bengal. The oldest places of Catholic worship—Luz church and San Thome Cathedral—were built in 1516 and 1557 respectively.

Protestants are comparative newcomers to the city. Although missionaries of the SPCK were in Madras by 1726, and the headquarters of several Protestant organizations were subsequently located there, conversions among the resident population were never very numerous. Houghton quotes one source as suggesting that the task of evangelizing Madras was 'well nigh impossible' (1981: 254). The Revd Westcott attributed the difficulties to the 'stirring life' of Madras, 'with its many occupations and distractions' added to 'the contaminating influences of abounding heathen idolatry and licentiousness', to say nothing of the 'presence of a large European and Eurasian population nominally Christian ...' (1897: 94). Indeed, another missionary suggested that missions in large towns seemed hardly ever to flourish. 'There is no comparison in difficulty between working in a town and in a village. In the latter the missionary is a great man, far above any country squire in influence. But in a large town the missionary ... is ... a nobody' (Sharrock 1910: 64).

The city's Indian Protestant population, which numbered around 3,000 in 1871, had risen to approximately 58,000 a century later, and today is perhaps 75,000 out of an overall Christian figure of 220,200 in a total population of 3.2 millions for Madras (1981 Census). Protestant numbers have expanded mainly as a result of migration by those already professing Christianity. These migrations, needless to say, affected the urban church. Up to the middle of the nineteenth century Indian converts worshipped—usually at separate times and often under separate pastors—in churches built for Europeans and Eurasians. Penny (1904 (vol. 3): 159) records that the East India Company's directors were opposed to such joint use of places of worship and this led to the first church being built for the sole use of an Indian congregation, which was consecrated in 1842.[10] By 1871, according to Houghton (1981: 6), there were thirty-four native congregations in the city. Based mainly on Penny's (1904) history of the church in Madras, I estimate that by the end of the nineteenth century approximately fourteen congregations worshipping in Tamil or other vernaculars belonged to the various denominations which were in 1947 to form the united Church of South India; an additional eight such vernacular churches were built up to the time of its creation, in the year of India's independence. Christians affiliated to the CSI provide the ethnographic focus of this study.

The CSI is today the largest Protestant church in the country, with 1.6 million members—or just under one-third of all Protestants in India (McGavran 1979: 186). Some twenty-five new places of worship have been built in Madras alone since 1947, to say nothing of the numerous congregations outside the city's boundaries but inside the metropolitan region. The church contains the largest non-Catholic following in Madras, with nearly half the city's Protestants in its membership.

The CSI federated the Presbyterian, Congregational, Methodist, and Anglican churches in what had been the Madras Presidency. Baptists and Lutherans were the only two major denominations which remained outside the union. The discussions and negotiations which led to the federation took place over many years and resulted in numerous compromises over ritual and doctrine. The historical episcopate, which cut across some of the most basic convictions of the Nonconformists, was incorporated in the ecumenical church. While all ordained ministers of these denominations were accepted directly into the CSI, new candidates for the ministry were to be ordained in the episcopal tradition by bishops who had themselves been sacralized in such rites. Diocesan bishops (there were fourteen in 1947 and several new dioceses have since been added), together with a number of appointed lay personnel, form the CSI Synod, and elect from their number a Moderator. Diocesan business is the responsibility of a Council, made up of clerical and lay representatives from the constituent pastorates. Councils have a say in the election of their own bishops, although the final choice rests with the Synod. Each pastorate is composed of one or more congregations, and is administered by an elected Pastorate Committee, which assists the minister.

THE UNIT OF STUDY

The field-work on which this monograph is based was conducted in two stages. During the first (1974-5), a year was spent among the mainly middle-class members of two 'élite' congregations (as they are generally called by both their members and others) affiliated to the Madras diocese of the CSI. In accordance with their locations in the city, I will refer to them as the CSI-Northern and CSI-Southern congregations/churches. The second trip, of seven months duration in 1981–2, was devoted principally to the adherents of another CSI congregation—this one situated in the western part of the city. The members of this pastorate are predominantly within the lower class. The 'ethnographic present' of this study, therefore, covers a period of some eight years. Here I outline briefly the history and composition of the three congregations.

The CSI-Northern church

This church, one of the grandest in Madras, was consecrated during the first quarter of the nineteenth century. It is situated on a major thoroughfare some two-and-a-half miles west of Fort St George, the original site of British settlement in the city, and was built for Presbyterians living in or near the capital. From its beginnings the congregation included many of the most prominent Europeans in the Madras Presidency. Membership rolls reveal ICS (Indian Civil Service) officers, university professors, surgeons-general, judges and solicitors, senior police and military personnel, etc. From time to time the governor himself was a regular attender and participant in the church's affairs.

A large proportion of the congregation was engaged in trade and commerce. Members were senior executives of banking houses, managing agencies, and business firms. The list of companies with which the church's adherents were associated reads like a *Who's Who* of European enterprises in south India during the colonial period. The most eminent figures in the congregation had interests in more than one sector of the economy, and also played an active role in the political and social life of the city.

The church's news-letters and other records from the colonial period reflect the day to day concerns and activities of the members. Their marriages were often grand affairs which 'included all the most distinguished members of Madras Society from their Excellencies [the governor and his wife], down'.

Several parishioners were almost invariably included in the periodic honours lists, and the awards duly noted by the church magazine.[11]

While persons associated with the highest strata within the Civil Service, the military, and the business community provided its most distinguished adherents, as well as its lay leadership, and were primarily responsible for the high reputation it enjoyed in the city, the congregation was by no means homogeneous as to rank. It also included others somewhat lower down in the European social order, i.e. middle level supervisory personnel, junior officers and executives, and their families. Beneath them were the technicians, proprietors of small businesses, teachers, and artisans. At the very bottom of the congregational hierarchy were a number of people without adequate means to make ends meet. The latter, who were explicitly recognized and referred to as the 'poor of the congregation' were, it would appear, mainly Eurasians (subsequently referred to as 'Anglo-Indians').

The chaplains were appointed by the church authorities in Britain, and their duties were not regarded as extending to the pastoral care of Indian Christians who were the concern of the missionaries. Brown (1948: 228) quotes an entry from a mid-nineteenth-century European diary which sums up the careful distinction maintained between the two kinds of pastor and those for whose spiritual welfare each was responsible:

Who is that in the smart gharry [carriage], with servants in livery?
That is the chaplain . . . who marries and baptises and performs service
   for the Europeans.
Does he go among the natives?
Not he; he leaves that to the missionaries, of whom there are lots
   here . . .

Although there are occasional references to Indian members in the church records as far back as 1896, they did not begin to form a significant proportion of the congregation until after independence. Even when other European churches in the city were absorbed into the CSI at the time of its inception, the congregation remained outside the united church. This was partly due to the fact that, whereas all foreign Civil Servants and military personnel left the country at independence, a

comparatively large number of businessmen and senior executives of European firms stayed on. Only during the 1950s,
when Reserve Bank and income tax policies encouraged the
exodus of expatriates, did the numbers of congregants fall dramatically. In 1959, with its European numbers at an all time
low (perhaps a score), the congregation voted to affiliate to the
CSI and, from that time, the indigenous membership grew
steadily. The first Indian was appointed to the Pastorate Committee in 1960, and today it is composed entirely of Indians.
Those affiliating to the church after 1960 were principally newcomers to Madras, entering the city from every part of India,
although predominantly from the south, in the course of career
mobility. Thus, many of the most prominent Protestants have
assumed the erstwhile pews of the Europeans in this as in other
élite churches of Madras.

The Tamilians among them trace their origins mainly to
districts in the southern and central parts of the state. Very few
are, in fact, of Presbyterian background (perhaps 10 per cent).
The majority were baptised in other Protestant churches, as
well as in several Keralite Christian faiths (e.g. Mar Thoma).
Congregational heterogeneity extends to caste affiliation as
well. While most members claim Tamilian group status (Nadar,
Vellalar, Kallar, etc.), some are also associated with castes
which originate in other south Indian states (such as the Syrian
Christians of Kerala and the Naidu of Andhra Pradesh) and
in north India. However, as many as four members in ten
cannot or prefer not to identify themselves in caste terms at
all. There are also a number of Anglo-Indian members. The
CSI-Northern has become, if anything, more cosmopolitan and
uni-class than it was during colonial times. For this reason,
among others, people from all over the city join the congregation; while most adherents live within comparatively easy
reach (by vehicle), it cannot be regarded as a neighbourhood
church. In many respects, the CSI-Northern has preserved its
earlier European character. Worship continues to be in English
and was, until very recently, led by a European minister.
Though an increasing number of CSI forms of worship have
been adopted, there is still a strong attachment to Presbyterian
rites, despite the fact that only a tiny proportion of the membership had such an attachment in the past.

The CSI-Southern church

The beginnings of this church can be traced to the last decade of the nineteenth century when a missionary of the SPG purchased a few acres of land on the sparsely settled south side of the Adyar river—which formed the city's southern boundary at the time—and built a small school there in memory of his sister. The school catered for the children of poor families in the neighbourhood, and the salaries of the teacher, as well as the upkeep of the buildings, were met out of the modest income from mango and cashew-nut trees in the compound. During the next half-century, services were occasionally held in the school for the benefit of the mainly poor residents of the neighbourhood who had been converted. The pastor of an Anglican church several miles north of the river went there periodically to offer communion.

The dramatic expansion of Madras city's population during the 1940s, and the extension of the city's boundaries south of the river, led to increased settlement in the area, and the growth of new garden suburbs. This part of Madras became recognized as one of the capital's most salubrious colonies, noted for its wide, tree-shaded avenues, and its (by Madras standards) 'cool' sea breezes. Following independence, a number of state and central educational and research institutes were located in the area, which attracted highly qualified personnel from many parts of the country. Today, it is undoubtedly one of the more desirable sections of the city, settled overwhelmingly by those in the upper reaches of the urban class order. Such a population contains, as we might expect, a proportionate number of Protestants. Indeed, by 1951 their numbers were sufficient to require the recommencement of Sunday worship in the school, which had ceased during the war period.

The original adherents of the congregation were poor fisherfolk and unskilled farm, workshop, or domestic labourers. By all accounts, they were mainly Harijans who lived in villages and low-cost housing enclaves near the school compound. Those who affiliated after 1951 were mainly from the middle class, who soon came substantially to outnumber the former group, and to dominate most aspects of congregational life. Their first concern was for the erection of a new church, both large enough to cater for an expanding number of Protestant settlers in the suburb and expressive of their standing in the community. Accordingly, in 1959, the congregation purchased a plot of land close to the residential concentrations of these élites and, much to the annoyance of the original congregants, at some distance from the school compound.

The time needed to agree the plans and raise the necessary funds for the new church (an original, modernistic, and not uncontroversial design) encouraged the building of a temporary structure on the site, and in 1967 it was consecrated for worship. The pastorate was thereafter composed of two quite separate congregations. The new arrivals in the area had, in effect, established their own uni-class church and, since they greatly outnumbered those who worshipped in the original school, effectively controlled the Pastorate Committee. The new church building was completed in 1980.

Although the CSI-Northern and CSI-Southern congregations are alike in regard to the class of their memberships, they differ in other respects. Unlike the former, which draws its votaries from all parts of India (although mainly from the south), the latter congregation is composed almost exclusively of Tamilians. In caste composition it differs too. Nadars are a majority, with Vellalars the next largest group. Virtually no one in this ritual body denies or cannot claim a caste designation. Because the Anglican missionaries were especially active among the Nadars, most CSI-Southern congregants are of Anglican background, although other orthodox Protestant denominations (e.g. Lutherans and Congregationalists) are also represented among them. But despite the fact that the church has its origins in the Anglican fold, and that its current membership stems primarily from this denomination, it resembles much more the newer, post-independence, urban congregations which recognize no ritual attachments other than to the CSI. Hence they tend to utilize only the CSI order of service.

Sunday morning worship is principally in Tamil, although most of the evening services are in English for the benefit of Protestant students and staff of nearby educational and research institutes who come from other parts of the country (although few take any part in church affairs). Unlike the CSI-Northern congregation, this is very much a local, neighbourhood unit: few members live more than a short walk or drive away.

The CSI-Western church

The history of this church commences at the beginning of the present century with the establishment of a prayer hall, by Methodist missionaries, for their votaries settled in one of the older and most densely populated areas on the western side of Madras. To this day, the church continues to serve the locality, its membership drawn mainly from the lower class families living in the immediate environs.

The congregation was first served by a local catechist, but, as it grew, was placed in the charge of a fully ordained (Indian) minister. After worshipping for two decades in the hall, a new (and in the Methodist manner, architecturally bland) building was erected on mission-owned land a short distance away, and mainly with mission funds. The church was absorbed, along with the greater part of the Methodist establishment in south India, into the CSI at the time of the latter's creation. From the beginning, services have been held only in Tamil and the pastors have been almost without exception Indians. From the time of its absorption into the united church, the CSI's order of service alone has been followed.

Virtually all adherents of the CSI-Western church are Tamilians who trace their origins to villages in the northern districts of the state, close to Madras. Their caste and previous denominational affiliations reflect this geographical concentration. Regarding the latter connections, these tend naturally towards mission bodies which were active in these areas. We find the Wesleyans most strongly represented in the congregation, with the American Adventists, the Arcot missions of the Reformed Church in America, and the Missourie Lutherans also prominent in congregants' backgrounds. About a fifth of the present membership are either converts to Christianity themselves, or the children of such converts. About half of them, and a similar proportion of the congregation as a whole, are Harijans by caste. The remainder make claims to Vellalar or other Tamilian caste status.

To sum up, then, the congregations whose members comprise the unit of study have distinctive histories and characters. They

are differently composed in terms of the areas of origin, denomination, and caste of their adherents. Two of the churches
draw their memberships from a quite separate class stratum
than does the third. But, while the congregational affiliation of
Protestants is important and will be discussed in the course of
the narrative, what I want to emphasize here is that the unit
of study is not the religious congregation—or this set of three
ritual groups—*per se*, but the example they provide of Protestants belonging to different levels of the urban class order.

It might be objected that, by selecting my principal informants from the membership rolls of religious congregations,
I have biased the unit of study in favour of those with a strong
Christian commitment, whose life and values may very well be
shaped by this factor. In response to this caveat I can only
point out that in Madras city (and, I suspect, elsewhere in
south India), it would be very unusual for a Protestant of
whatever class—whether a 'strong believer' or not, whether
practising regularly or not—to remain completely unattached
to a congregation. This is partly to do with the widespread
wish to marry, baptize children, and be buried according to
Christian rites. It is also because without such an attachment
one would appear in the eyes of others to be entirely without
religious faith (*nampikkai*), a notion which people find difficult
to comprehend. Care was taken to meet and interview all
persons on the membership lists, even those who attended services only at Christmas.

The unit providing much of the descriptive and quantitative
data which appear in the text consists of some 300 households,
with a total universe of some 1,500 men, women, and children,
divided almost equally between middle and lower classes. These
households comprise virtually the entire population of Indian
Christians belonging to the three congregations. The Anglo-
Indians who form a small minority of members of the CSI-
Northern pastorate are excluded from the discussion, since they
do not regard themselves as Indian Christians, and are not so
regarded by the latter. In the course of the narrative I refer to
the principal adults in these domestic units as 'focal householders', to avoid the sometimes misleading notion of a 'household head'. It is meant to indicate that, by and large, decisions
and responsibilities within the household are shared, in most

cases by a married couple acknowledged by others as the key figures. I should note at this point that the quantitative data which appear in the text are not meant to provide numerical 'proofs' for my interpretations, or to lend the analysis a spurious scientific flavour. The lower and middle class 'samples' I refer to are not samples in the statistical sense but rather, to borrow a phrase from Owen Lynch (1974: 1658), 'respondent groups' whose particular experiences and characteristics illustrate, complement, and lend support to the general observational data.

Because of the complexity of the urban milieu, and the aims of the study, members of the three congregations provided only a portion (though a very crucial and substantive portion) of the complete range of material gathered. Numerous Christians—and not a few non-Christians—in all walks of life were consulted and interviewed, sometimes at great length and more than once: officials of the CSI Synod and the Madras diocese, clergymen, lay preachers, popular fundamentalist prophets, representatives of various religious and secular institutes and associations (including trade union leaders), and others. Moreover, in keeping with the anthropological commitment to 'participant observation' as an additional and vital means to obtain experience of and insights into the richness and variety of local cultures, church services were regularly attended, as were a plethora of 'occasions'—among them weddings, death anniversaries, club evenings, diocesan-sponsored conventions and seminars, house churches, small prayer cell meetings, and hugely attended gatherings at which local or visiting charismatic figures appeared to preach and heal.

Finally, I made an attempt to become familiar with at least a tiny proportion of the many books, journals, and newspapers produced by a highly literate and self-conscious community, not to mention the numerous works by foreign observers of the Indian Protestant scene, especially the missionaries. By these and other means, the difficult problems of anthropological field-work in a large city, and among a disparate and dispersed community, were, if not entirely overcome, at least brought within manageable proportions.

OUTLINE OF THE BOOK

The next chapter introduces the Protestant community in south India. It traces the growth of foreign missions and outlines the patterns of conversion among the indigenous population, the majority of whom were from the low castes and rural poor. The gradual erosion of denominational structures established by the missions is related both to circumstances inside the mission field itself, and to the emergence of socio-economic differentiation within the Protestant community.

Chapter 3 then turns to the economic aspect of Protestant class divisions in Madras. After noting the distinctive patterns of migration associated with those entering different levels of the occupational structure, it concentrates on the material advantages enjoyed by the middle class as against their lower class co-religionists. Educational achievements, careers, income, and property-holding are compared. The domestic group is seen as a crucial setting within which people in each class experience and share their different material circumstances, and therefore within which analytical distinctions, such as manual/ non-manual work, formal/informal sector employment, or capitalist/non-capitalist, are mitigated if not dissolved.

The following chapters turn to the cultural dimension of hierarchy. Chapter 4 examines forms of consumption within the community. Two distinctive modes are identified: one, associated with the lower class, directs expenditure mainly to subsistence and the maintenance of existing kin and neighbourhood bonds. That of the middle class additionally deploys resources on luxury goods to make visible statements about rank and inequality. More significantly, they are seen to invest heavily in extending their range of contacts and accomplishments, through engagement in selective leisure activities, as well as by particular church affiliations and activities. By these means they acquire vital forms of knowledge which serve the retention of privilege.

Marriage is then discussed in Chapter 5. After considering marital arrangements, the rites and ceremonies accompanying a union are discussed. The role of 'dowry' in these alliances is then related both to the urban class and caste orders. Distinctive matrimonial sub-cultures are seen to exist within each class, a factor contributing to the reinforcement and re-production of the boundaries between them.

Chapter 6 asks how, in the particular context of Protestant Madras, individual subjectivities are formed. The focus is on those discourses and practices which promote or inhibit consciousness of caste and class. While recognizing that people are constantly 'addressed' in their daily lives by a host of formal and informal agencies and circumstances, particular attention is paid to the voices of the church and the dominant segment within the community. Individual Protestant consciousness comes to be seen as an important sphere of ideological struggle, with many and varied outcomes, and not as something determined entirely and inevitably by primordial links or the disposition of material conditions.

The last two chapters trace the growth and assess the impact of fundamentalist beliefs and observances. Chapter 7 first outlines the emergence of a strongly pietistic tradition within the Protestant fold, then points to the differential appeal of the 'social gospel' introduced in the early part of this century: its rejection by the majority of ordinary Christians and adoption as the favoured discourse by church leaders and intellectuals, and later by the new élites. The discussion then turns to ideas about misfortune—which lower class Protestants share with Hindus of the same social position—and notes the hostility to this popular knowledge on the part of the dominant segment within first the missions, and later the indigenous church and community.

The eighth chapter examines the ways in which fundamentalism subsumes and authenticates these popular theodicies, and offers a means of confronting misfortune. The ritual procedures surrounding the charismatic prophets, the main purveyors of fundamentalist doctrines, are then sketched. These figures and the religious ideologies they promote are seen as a threat to orthodoxy, a form of popular opposition to the dominant segment within the church and community, which may help to account for the recent interest shown by certain sections within the orthodox church in appropriating elements of this discourse.

2

PROTESTANTS IN SOUTH INDIA

Mission, Conversion, and the Erosion of Denomination

INTRODUCTION

PROTESTANT Christianity was brought to south India by Western missionaries. This chapter first outlines the growth of missions and identifies the specific forms and wider contexts of conversion. It then examines the denominational structure which emerged as a consequence of missionary efforts. Finally, it considers the effects on this structure of, on the one hand, ecumenical tendencies among mission organizations and, on the other, nascent class differentiation within the indigenous Protestant community. The latter, it is suggested, arose as a consequence of unequal access to mission benefits and was exacerbated by changes in the economic and political climate of south India in the late nineteenth and early twentieth centuries.

THE GROWTH OF MISSIONS

Protestant mission activity in south India began in the first decade of the eighteenth century, with the creation of a Lutheran station in the Danish territory of Tranquebar on the coast south of Fort St George, the site of present-day Madras. It was not until a century later, however, that the East India Company was compelled by the British parliament (under pressure from the Evangelicals) to recognize the principle of introducing Christianity in its own territories.

Following an amendment of the Company's charter in 1833, Christian missionaries were no longer required to obtain a licence to enter the country, and this effectively opened the door to a wide range of Societies based not only in Britain, but in continental Europe, North America, Australia, and elsewhere. Whereas, according to Ingham (1956: 125–32), there were in 1833 fifty-six foreign missionaries, representing six Societies, operating in south India, Richter (1908) refers to a census of Protestant missionary activities conducted in 1853 which suggests that there were at that time approximately 350 missionaries in the area. By the end of the nineteenth century, their population had nearly doubled, while the number of Societies, according to the Report of the Decennial Indian Missionary Conference of 1902, had increased eightfold. The ranks of missionaries continued to grow during the first half of the present century: the National Christian Council Review of September 1954 suggested that there were over 2,000 in the country in 1947—although no separate figures are given for peninsular India. Their numbers only began to abate with the approach of independence.

The result of this expenditure of personnel and resources was the emergence of a substantial and expanding Protestant community in south India. In 1855 some four-fifths of all Protestant Indians were in the Madras Presidency, and by the beginning of this century the proportion was still as high as two-thirds. The distribution as between north and south is not very different today.

Of late, the very basis of the missionary enterprise—to convert the world to Christianity—has come increasingly under question from Christian intellectuals, including many missionaries themselves (see Forrester 1980: 144). Those who journeyed to India during the first century and a half of Protestant activity, however, were in little doubt about the goals they had come to realize. It was an undertaking, as Beidelman says of the mission project in East Africa, to extend their own vision of the cosmos to an alien and (increasingly) subject people (1982: 4). While the earliest Protestant missionaries in south India (many of whom were German) distanced themselves from the East India Company, their replacement in the second quarter of the nineteenth century by arrivals from Britain gradually transformed the relations between rulers and missions (Frykenberg 1985: 322). By the middle of the century, the widespread assumption was of a divine purpose in the Western penetration of the Indian subcontinent, and that the missions were there to play a part in its fulfilment (see Ballhatchet 1961: 344–5). The views of the Revd J. A. Sharrock, a superintending missionary with the SPG in Trichinopoly at the end of the nineteenth century, are probably not untypical of missionary thinking at the time:

> We have taken their country and we owe them this debt; or, rather
> God has given us this country and demands from us that we shall do
> our duty ... The Church exists to evangelize the world and God has
> given India to us instead of to Holland, Portugal or France ... And
> we may be sure of this that if we English fail to do our duty, God will
> take—and rightly so—our empire from us and give it to some worthier
> nation (1910: 25-6).

Baago characterizes the outlook in this period as 'a curious
blend of Calvinist theology and political imperialism' (1966:
329). The Western missionary presence in India, therefore,
cannot be divorced from the wider colonial context.[1] In one
antagonistic view,

> The growth of the Protestant Church during the period of British raj
> in India was due mainly to the great patronage and support the
> church was getting from the Government of India. Instances of land
> grants and financial aid to build churches, missionary centres, hos-
> pitals, educational institutions, are numerous ... in almost every
> Indian state we can find big churches and missionary buildings erec-
> ted entirely with government aid (Niyogi 1956: 41).[2]

Even a sympathetic missionary and historian of the Indian
church, like Hough, acknowledges that the missionary enterprise was not only intimately connected with the beginnings
of the Anglo-Indian empire, but 'extended along with it from
one end of the country to the other' (quoted in Richter 1908:
128). In this regard there was little difference between the
missions associated with the 'established' churches in Europe
and those whose Nonconformist parent bodies had earlier challenged political and religious orthodoxies. Nor was it entirely
a Western phenomenon. Matsuo, discussing the missionary activity of the Japan Congregational Church in Korea in the
early part of this century, reports that 'the mainstream within
[the church] regarded the Japanese imperialistic rule of Korea
as an expression of God's will . . .' (1979: 584).

PATTERNS OF CONVERSION[3]

The proselytizing activities of the various missionary organizations led to the emergence of a religious community
drawn, for the greater part, from the lowest ranks of the economic and caste orders in south India. The early Protestant

evangelists[4] had hoped to attract the Brahmins to Christianity, and through them the generality of Hindus.[5] But even with the most painstaking efforts of argument and persuasion they failed to make any real headway among members of the highest caste. There were, to be sure, some missionary successes. In a discussion of Presbyterian growth in Madras, Nelson makes a point of referring to a 'noteworthy event', namely, 'the baptism of a Brahmin and his wife with four children!' (1975: 30). Such noteworthy events were, however, few and far between. The Methodists in the Kaveri region of the Tamil country, for example, converted a total of eight Brahmins between 1850 and 1900 (Oddie 1978), while of the 9,700 adherents of the LMS stations in Nagercoil and Neyoor (Travancore) in 1862, only six were Brahmins (Murdoch 1895: 47). In Tinnevelly district in the same year—where both the Anglican CMS and SPG were extremely active—there was apparently only one Brahmin in a population of 44,361 indigenous Christians (ibid.). And it is unlikely that other missionary Societies in the south had very many more in their midst.

Conversions from amongst the highest non-Brahmin castes were more numerous. Pickett, though he provides no figures, speaks of 'considerable numbers' of Vellalars in the Anglican church in Tinnevelly (1933: 28). In other areas (e.g. Tanjore) they were concentrated enough to provide the principal leadership of the local Protestant community until late in the nineteenth century, though of course this does not necessarily imply numerical preponderance. Figures provided by Oddie for the large-scale movement of non-Brahmins into the Anglican ranks in the Andhra country, in the first decades of this century, suggest that the higher castes among them (Reddy, Kapu, Kamma, and Telaga) together formed only ten per cent of the total mission population (1977: 80).

The Brahmins, and other high castes who became Protestants, by and large 'declared for Christ' singly or in small family groups, i.e. as individual converts, generally in defiance of other members of their local and caste groups and often, therefore, at the cost of their most intimate social ties. While all conversion is obviously individual, what is meant here by 'individual conversion' is that the circumstances of becoming Christian were fundamentally uninfluenced by considerations of wider group conversion and support. Even the most cursory reading of missionary reports and correspondence reveals how much time and care were devoted to the winning of every individual convert. Not surprisingly, the higher the caste and educational attainments of the potential proselyte—the two tended to go together—the greater the 'challenge' to and the more concerted the effort expended by the missionary. Hudson's (1970) account of the 'life and times' of the nineteenth-century Vellalar convert, H. A. Krishna Pillai, who eventually became a major Tamil literary figure, reveals the considerable resources and energies invested by the CMS in converting and keeping within the fold their high caste votaries.

But while missionary hopes had initially focused on the upper reaches of the caste hierarchy, their greatest successes were among groups lower down in the order. These converts, more-over, came to Protestantism not singly but in 'mass movements', a development which, at least at first, aroused the missionaries' suspicions, and which they did not whole-heartedly welcome. Pickett, in his seminal study of the 'mass movement' phenomenon in India, estimates that as many as four-fifths of Protestant converts entered the faith in this way (1933: 315). While the term 'mass movement' is by no means unambiguous, it connotes both large numbers and, more im-portantly, that the converts belong to the same caste within a region, so that the adoption of the new religion is more a collective than a personal act. Further, it does not usually entail any significant changes in traditional social norms and relationships among the converts, or necessarily a disruption of ties between them and members of Hindu groups in the region, or with those belonging to the same caste who do not become Christians. As Pickett suggests, its characteristic features are 'a group decision' and the consequent 'preservation of the con-verts' social integration' (1933: 22).

By the middle of the nineteenth century, the three British mission organizations working in the southern-most tip of the subcontinent—the CMS, SPG, and LMS—together had con-verted 51,000 people, some 70 per cent of the Protestants in the Madras Presidency at that time, mainly from the Nadar (or Shanar) caste. In the latter part of the century, large-scale conversions of outcastes began, especially in the northern parts of the Presidency. Between 1881 and 1901 the numbers of

Protestants in five districts of the Telugu country alone rose from 78,000 to 225,000, and virtually all the converts were 'untouchable' Malas and Madigas (Richter 1908: 231). Similar mass movements took place around this time among the Paraiyans and other outcaste groups in the North Arcot district. According to Richter (1908: 233) between 1880 and 1905 four in every five converts in the Madras Presidency were outcastes, who came, within a few decades, to comprise a majority of those adhering to the Protestant faith. The significance of these differential conversion patterns will become apparent when caste identities and marriage institutions are discussed in Chapters 5 and 6.

THE ATTRACTIONS OF CONVERSION

Any attempt to identify definitively the motives for conversion is fraught with difficulty. The literature on conversion in south India is essentially that left by missionaries, or by Indian Christian descendants of the original converts. The views available to us, therefore, are those of interested outsiders, whose aims in recording and interpreting these experiences, as well as their understandings of them, necessarily differ from those of the proselytes themselves.

Another difficulty is that the decision to adopt Protestantism—especially in mass movement areas—was frequently taken by a handful of people on behalf of larger groups. Many became Christians for no other than what Pickett refers to as 'social' reasons, i.e. following passively the lead taken by others (1933: 164-5). Thus, conversion in the south Indian context did not necessarily follow the familiar Western ideal of 'moving from conviction of sin to a personal experience of Christ' (Grant 1959: 19).

A third caveat relates to the effects of missionary conversion 'strategies' on particular 'target' populations.[6] Any comprehensive discussion of Christianization would require us to analyse these in detail, as indeed the missionary factor in general. For our present purposes, mission programmes and ideologies will be regarded as part of the total environment within which decisions about conversion were taken.

The aim here is not to participate in the somewhat sterile debate as to whether the principal motives were 'temporal' or 'spiritual'. To the extent that such a distinction is analytically useful, we must remember that most missionaries and students of Indian Christian society recognize not only the importance of both but their inseparability. Like people elsewhere in the missionized world, prospective converts in south India seem to have viewed missionary offerings as undifferentiated, as Guiart puts it, 'a package deal' (1970: 123). Furthermore, the initial reasons for conversion may have had little bearing on the individual's subsequent commitment to the new religion, and even less on that of his or her descendants. To begin, then, I want to identify some of the 'environmental' influences favouring a change of religious loyalty during the century and a half following the arrival of Protestant missionaries in British south India.

It has been widely observed that large-scale conversions often followed the occurrence of natural disasters. During periods of famine, drought, or plague, mission Societies 'worked at high pressure and saved thousands from perishing' (Pathak 1967: 104). Many recipients of their charity and concern were moved to embrace the missionaries' faith. Furthermore, children orphaned by these disasters were, during much of the period of colonial rule, given into the care of the missions, since the government was unwilling to assume responsibility for them. In the course of time, these children were usually baptized and raised as Christians (see Chapter 5). It was probably no coincidence that the dramatic increase in the numbers of converts between 1877 and 1900 coincided with a period of plague and famine which racked the country. Sharrock estimates that the Tinnevelly Anglican missions 'gathered in' 30–40,000 catechumens as a result of the 1877 famine alone (1910: 49).

It is also generally agreed that mass movements tended to occur among persons who were, on the whole, poor and without prospects. In Pickett's terms, they 'felt themselves oppressed and exploited', and were in 'economic distress' (1933: 60, 140). For example, the Nadars who embraced Christianity were not from the wealthier landowning section of the caste ('Nadan'), but palmyra tree climbers and marginal agriculturalists who lived near 'subsistence' level (Hardgrave 1969: 38–51). Conversion, for people in dire economic circumstances, could not be divorced from a desire to alleviate the harsh poverty of their lives. For it often meant access to land, agricultural assistance, or other benefits in the gift of the missionaries.

The latter provided homes for many of their votaries, allocated food and clothing to those in need, sold them cheap grain, and gave occasional low interest loans. They also aided destitute widows and bore the costs of marriages and funerals where necessary. They established institutions for orphans, the deaf and dumb, and the blind. Some missions ran industrial training schemes to provide converts with the means to earn a livelihood, as well as offering employment in various parts of their own organizations. Indeed, groups of *prospective* converts occasionally entered into correspondence with several mission Societies with a view to comparing the benefits each could offer; the most attractive might then be invited to set up a station in their area! (Pickett 1933: 324). In Travancore CMS and LMS missionaries sometimes served as district judges, and one reported a tendency among litigants to become Christians, presumably in the hope of influencing the decisions in their favour (Mullens 1854: 111). Bishop Hollis reminds us that while, to many Westerners, the missionary in India was a 'self-sacrificing' individual, to the potential convert he was a 'representative of power, a figure of awe-inspiring wealth and privilege' (1962: 43-6).

Perhaps their single most important resource was the missions' near monopoly of educational facilities in the south during the eighteenth and much of the nineteenth centuries.[7] Christian education policy in India was part of a general pattern found throughout the missionized world. For its part, the Government of India, like colonial regimes elsewhere,[8] was content to abandon its own responsibilities in this field to the missionaries. Thus, in 1852, mission schools in the country contained four times as many pupils as government schools (Ingham 1956: 66).[9]

The mission role in higher education was no less significant. By the end of the nineteenth century all of the four women's colleges in the south and over half the men's (21 out of 38), containing in all 5,300 students, were mission supported and run (Manickam 1929: 28). In 1885, Madras Christian College, the largest missionary institute for higher education in the country, had more students than all the other government and private colleges in Madras city combined (Gehani 1966: 8).

The benefits to Indian Christians of this considerable missionary investment in education were of two principal kinds. In the first place, some converts and many of their descendants profited from the teaching opportunities available in these institutions. There was a deliberate policy to employ Indian Christians in this extensive network of schools. It appears that, in the early part of the nineteenth century, Christians with the necessary qualifications were not always available. But, as more and more achieved the requisite standards, their proportion in the teaching body rose steadily.

The significance for the converts of mission education, however, lay only partly in the employment it provided for several thousand teachers at any one time. In the context of their depressed caste and economic backgrounds, the Indian Christians must be seen as among the principal beneficiaries of these educational opportunities, although they were, of course, not the only ones to profit. Converts were naturally encouraged to attend mission establishments, were charged lower fees than their non-Christian co-pupils, and where circumstances demanded, were excused payment altogether. In the diary of an elderly parishioner reprinted several years ago in the CSI-Northern congregation's magazine it is noted that at the American Madura Mission's college (c.1914) 'fees were only Rs 60 per annum of which Rs 50 was met from a fund for Christian students'. In Chapter 3 I will examine the extent of Christian involvement in schooling; here I want merely to indicate how conversion in south India may very well have been encouraged by the assumption of privileged access by Christians to mission-run education, with all its potential benefits.[10]

Quite apart from the resources, like education, which missionaries controlled, they were often able to intercede with authorities in government on behalf of their adherents, to obtain specific favours such as employment, or simply to stop the harassment and discrimination which lesser officials sometimes inflicted on those without wealth or influence. They were instrumental in winning for Christians in Travancore the right to rest from labour on Sundays (Mullens 1854: 111), and in obtaining for those who were traditionally denied the use of public wells the legal right to do so.

But if converts were drawn by the ability of many missionaries to intercede with the authorities, the attraction of Protestantism must also have lain, especially as the nineteenth century wore on, in its close links to the raj. As in so much of the colonized world, Christianity was the religion of the conqueror, and conversion was not infrequently seen as the first step towards acquiring a share in this power and privilege (see Ifeka-Moller 1974). Some converts perceived European dominion in terms of the superior power of the Christian deity.

Yet, despite the likely practical benefits of conversion, there were drawbacks as well. For one thing, there was the frequent hostility and occasional physical danger facing many new Christians, especially in the early years of the nineteenth century (see Frykenberg 1976). During the same period, the East India Company, fearful of jeopardizing its trading advantages by antagonizing the Hindu community, imposed various constraints on the converts. The Madras Regulations of 1816 deprived Indian Christians of their rights to inheritance and to remarriage if their spouses remained Hindus. Restrictions were also placed upon their appointment to many government posts. According to a contemporary missionary, 'all managers in public offices must be Hindoos ... the [Native Christian] is excluded not only from responsible Civil and Military employments, but also from attaining the highest station—that of manager—under the European Heads of offices . . .'.[11] They were also not employed in certain sections of the army, and barred altogether from promotion in the infantry.

While most of these disabilities were removed during the course of the century, they were unlikely, while in force, to have stimulated conversions, if material or status advance was the sole aim of changing faith. Yet they were overlooked by many thousands who became Protestants during this period. Again, while the prospect of economic improvement may have encouraged a tendency towards Protestantism, such betterment did not in most cases accompany conversion (Pickett 1933: 140). Yet neither the mass movements nor individual conversions ceased because of this. And finally, we have to remember that the overwhelming majority of impoverished and underprivileged Indians who came into contact with missionaries did not choose to abandon their (Hindu) faith. Thus to cite exclusively the material advantages of affiliation to Protestantism gives us only a partial understanding of the process of conversion. We must look for influences of a different kind as well.

THE WIDER CONTEXTS OF CONVERSION

It is sometimes suggested by those either closely involved in or strongly sympathetic to the proselytizing activities of missions that village Hindus were often profoundly influenced by Christian groups in the same area for whom conversion appeared to have wrought an improvement in their 'moral' behaviour. Bishops Azariah and Whitehead attributed the numerous conversions of caste Hindus in the villages of the Andhra country during the early twentieth century to the 'witness of the changed lives of the outcaste Christians' (1930: 61). After embracing Protestantism the latter were reported to have become more hygienic, thoughtful, trustworthy, sober, thrifty, and hardworking. For Oddie, writing about a similar situation, something like the reverse of Sanskritization had occurred. 'These and other changes in the attitudes and behaviour of Christians of untouchable origin ... clearly created more favourable attitudes towards Christianity and a growing conviction among caste Hindus that, if conversion could improve the lives of people as degraded as the Malas and Madigas, it might be of some benefit to themselves and their own community' (1977: 87).

It must be acknowledged that converts who accepted Protestantism singly or in small family groups might have been influenced by the spiritual and intellectual attractions of the missionaries' faith. Certainly, coming as they did mainly from the higher reaches of the caste hierarchy, as I noted above, they had more to lose in terms of their position in society. Referring to a small circle of Vellalars who came under the influence of CMS missionaries in mid-nineteenth-century Tinnevelly, Hudson remarks how, for young men of high caste, intelligent and educated, conversion 'was a vigorous, exciting, liberal, idealistic and daring thing, appealing to [those] who took religious values seriously' (1970: 349). For many young intellectuals, baptism was 'the only course open' once they had accepted the arguments of the missionaries and reached the 'point of belief' (1970: 413).

Another possibility—which emerges from an examination of the literature on nineteenth-century south India—is that many component groups were disenchanted with their place in society. The dissatisfaction was most strongly felt among the poor and low castes, who perceived that the rapid changes occurring at the time were passing them by. The general ferment found expression in various movements through which people sought, in different ways, to achieve a new dignity and self-respect by redefining existing social and religious categories. Christianity, Forrester reminds us, was only one among a number of options which these groups explored (1980: 80-1). Kaufmann notes the 'volatile shifts' in religious affiliation typical of this period. She also points to numerous instances of 'tactical conversion' to Christianity, and suggests that these might best be understood in terms of the recurrent conflicts over ritual and ceremonial privileges and access to 'sacred space' which characterized the wider Hindu society. The notion of permanent commitment to a single religious tradition was alien to most south Indians, she argues, so that the Hindu-Christian boundary was not seen as inviolate, nor were the lines separating the different Christian confessions. 'The most recent Christian converts were most likely to adopt Christian affiliation briefly and intermittently, and often in pursuit of specific gains in status within local—and essentially Hindu—ranking schemes' (1977: 387).

In brief, then, conversion to Protestantism must be accounted for by a complex of factors. Despite the close association of the Protestant enterprise with the might of European colonialism, especially from the middle of the nineteenth century, people in the villages and towns of south India were by no means the passive recipients of evangelism, but, rather, active agents in assessing and acting upon missionary attempts at proselytization.

DENOMINATIONALISM

While Protestant expansion was rapid, it was by no means haphazard. Partly to concentrate their limited resources, and partly, no doubt, to preserve some measure of harmony among the various organizations, each Society tended to focus its efforts in a limited number of areas. While the larger urban centres were regarded as 'common property', the rules of 'comity' required that one mission should respect and refrain from entering the territory of another. While clashes did occur between Societies, necessitating the creation in 1902 of a Board of Arbitration to settle disputes, the agreement appears to have been generally respected. Indeed, numerous instances are reported of mission organizations readily handing over their stations and their converts to others when financial or other considerations made it impossible for them to maintain their operations in a particular area.[12]

The outcome of this policy was that south India was carved up among various denominational bodies, such that an area— sometimes only a few villages, at other times corresponding to a large administrative division—was acknowledged to be the domain of a particular mission Society. Thus, to take only the Tamil-speaking parts of the peninsula, much of south Travancore was the province of the LMS; Tinnevelly district was divided between the Anglican CMS and SPG; large sections of the North Arcot area became the preserve of the American Arcot Mission (of the Reformed Church); a substantial portion of Madurai district was evangelized by the American Board of Foreign Missions (Congregational); Danish Lutherans were concentrated around Tanjore and Trichinopoly; Scottish Presbyterians and Wesleyan Methodist missions focused their activities in different parts of the northern district of Chingleput; American Adventists were concentrated near the Presidency's capital; and so forth. Denominational affiliation for the average Indian Protestant was, therefore, seldom a matter of personal choice or conviction, but fortuitously determined by residence.

The missions succeeded in establishing their manifold divisions in the south, and in creating among most of their converts a strong and faithful following. Pickett has remarked that, where missions had to compete with one another for adherents, 'intense denominational loyalty' was cultivated (1933: 323).

He notes, too, that frequently only the mission was the focus of identity, so that people described themselves as 'LMS/CMS/SPG Christians', without necessarily being fully aware of their denominational links. The result, according to Lucas, was that there were 'Indian Wesleyans and Indian Lutherans . . . the fossilized remains of conflicting creeds and ecclesiastical controversies . . .' (quoted in Gehani 1966: 438).

The establishment of rigid denominational boundaries was, of course, not unique to South Asia. The belief existed from earliest times that church structures were part of its gospel, and this took the form of extending to the missionized world the patterns of the West (Warren 1965: 73).[13] Biggs points to the hardening of these divisions during the eighteenth and nineteenth centuries, and notes how their exportation abroad led to the emergence of strong international groups focused on the home mission, thus making the barriers between the various denominations within a single overseas territory difficult to surmount (1965: 221). Even within the boundaries of a particular denomination, there could be a variety of national divisions which prevented any meaningful union of effort. The most glaring example of this in south India was the Lutheran community, whose adherents were (and still are) divided among eleven foreign mission bodies (R. D. Paul 1958: 87).

Denominational separateness was also fostered by geographical isolation—the result of comity—and the creation of a paternalistic environment which sometimes catered for the converts' every need (see above). Missions even established Christian villages where converts might be separated from the surrounding community. For example, in the first half of the nineteenth century in Tinnevelly, Anglican missions designed and created Christian villages around mission stations, some of which bore (and still bear) biblical place names such as Nazareth and Jerusalem, while others celebrated the new faith with Tamil designations, such as Suviseshapuram (Gospel village) or Megnanapuram (Salvation Village) (see Devapackiam 1963). Bishop Caldwell lived for much of his adult life in such a place 'where the mission bungalow was surrounded by church, parsonage, schools, dispensary, lace-rooms, etc. The roads were laid out and good houses were built for Christians who formed almost the whole of the village' (Sharrock 1910: 51).

Denominational boundaries were further strengthened by
the very character of mass movements. In general, large-scale
conversions from within particular castes resulted in the adherents of one mission in a single area coming predominantly
from the same caste. Thus Ponniah (1938: 29–30) noted how
the Tinnevelly diocese of the Anglican church was effectively a
'one-caste church', since the vast majority of its members—68
per cent—were Nadars. Given the tendency for many converts
to be related and for marriage within the caste to be practised
even after adoption of the new religion, the boundaries of the
mission were effectively co-extensive with those of the endogamous group. Moreover, in the first century and a half of
Protestant mission activity, traditional modes of production
and the absence of proper roads and railways imposed a limited
'demography of marriage' on the mass movement areas of south
India.

Thus, it is possible to characterize the eighteenth and early
nineteenth-century Protestant milieu—and, to an extent, the
period during and immediately following any mass movement—as consisting of relatively isolated communities of converts, poor and dependent on their missionary benefactors.
Each mission community was, moreover, united by multiplex
ties. Members tended to share a common caste position and a
similar place at the bottom of the economic order; they were
related by kinship and marriage and, of course, constituted
separate religious collectivities, each with its own particular
doctrine and rituals. Many of these religious groups, in the
early period of their establishment and growth, approached the
closed character of a sect. Forrester implies much the same
thing when he employs the term 'caste-sect' in referring to such
tightly knit units (1980: 84).

But, however much stress is laid on the religious cleavages
imposed by the missionaries on Protestants in south India, it is
important to take account of the circumstances which, in the
course of time, mitigated and even blurred the lines separating
the different denominations, as well as the loyalties of their
adherents. In the next section I want to note briefly the influences at work within, on the one hand, the missionary fold
itself, and, on the other, the Indian Protestant community.

THE EROSION OF DENOMINATIONS

Given that Christians were a tiny minority on the subcontinent, the Indian context encouraged a less than rigorous concern for denominational exclusivity among the missionaries themselves. As Sundkler notes, 'the differences which once had loomed so large, in England or America, appeared in another light against the background of Hinduism' (1954: 24). Missionaries of all denominations were united in their zeal for intense evangelism to bring the light of Christianity to those lost in 'heathenism'. They shared, though in varying degrees, a common outlook which can be characterized as pietistic (see Chapter 7). Expressing what must have been a widespread feeling among those in the 'field', one missionary manual 'earnestly recommends' the young missionary setting out for India 'to forget denominational questions at home' (Murdoch 1895: 496).

A not too fastidious regard for denominational niceties was manifested in several ways. In the first place, missionaries of one denomination were found in the employ of missions of quite different persuasions. At the very outset of the Protestant enterprise in India, the English mission, under the auspices of the Anglican SPCK, was staffed and run almost exclusively by German Lutherans. Indeed, they were not only ordained as Lutherans, but were guided by Lutheran principles both in their missionary practice and church government. It was not until the second decade of the nineteenth century, following the arrival in the country of the first English bishop, that a more stringent policy was adopted by the mission (see Sherring 1875: 454–5).

Secondly, where finance, comity, or simple expediency required it, missionaries of one denomination were not averse to transferring their own stations and converts to those of another. Such transfers were a not uncommon feature of early missionary 'colonization'.[14]

Finally, missions whose theologies, histories, status, and influence in their countries of origin were in no sense uniform nevertheless shared, in the Indian context, a set of problems which, they soon realized, could form the basis for joint meetings and discussions. As early as 1836 an Indian Missionary Society—a co-operative venture of existing mission organizations—operated to evangelize areas 'unoccupied by other Protestant missions'.[15] The first conference of south Indian Protestant missions was held in 1858, and it was followed some 15 years later by an all-India assembly of missionaries. These meetings, which became a regular feature of missionary life, created a forum for the exchange of ideas and the resolution of common problems and inter-mission disputes. They also provided an important stimulus for the establishment of inter-denominational co-operation in a number of fields. Thus the Madras Christian College, which was set up by the Free Church of Scotland mission in the first half of the nineteenth century, in time came to involve the Methodist, Anglican, and other missions as supporting bodies. Similarly, Vellore Christian Medical College and Hospital, originally the creation of the American Arcot Mission, was transformed into an inter-denominational enterprise—which enabled it to grow to its present size and stature (see Chapter 6). Other ventures resulting from the co-operation of different mission bodies were the Christian Literature Society, the Bible Society, St Christopher's Teachers' Training College and, of course, the Indian YMCA–YWCA organization.

This coming together of the various Protestant missions in the nineteenth century undoubtedly created a climate for the church unions which have been such a striking feature of south Indian Protestantism in this century. The amalgamation of Presbyterian churches in 1904 was followed in 1908 by the South India United Church (SIUC), which confederated the Presbyterian, Congregational, and Reformed churches. Forty years later, the Church of South India created an even more integral union of Wesleyan Methodists, Anglicans, and the SIUC (see Chapter 1). However, the establishment of these ecumenical churches cannot be understood only in terms of common missionary or church interests. Such developments were both possible and desirable because of the erosion of the earlier commitment to denominationalism among Indian Protestants themselves.

For one thing, the mood generated by the nationalist movement did not fail to influence many Protestant intellectuals, who came to see denominations as artificially and unnecessarily divisive of the community. One expression of this consciousness was the establishment of the National Missionary Society, an organization of Indian Christians which sought freedom from foreign domination of the Indian church by utilizing indigenous personnel and funds for its evangelistic work. As Sundkler suggests, the work of the NMS brought home to at least the educated section of the community 'its essential unity in spite of the denominations imported from the west' (1954: 35).

Equally significant for its effects on the pattern of exclusive denominational groupings was the growing socio-economic differentiation within the community. This was occasioned, in part, by the limited benefits which the missions were ultimately able to offer, and the unevenness of their availability to votaries. Not all missions or stations within the same mission could provide comparable opportunities for schooling, training, or employment. Inequalities of education, skills, and income arose, therefore, within and between mission congregations. The existence of an indigenous clergy, for example, who were both better educated than and highly respected by most ordinary adherents of the missions, provided an important core of potentially mobile individuals. The gradual expansion of administration, commerce, and industry in south India, during the late nineteenth and early twentieth centuries, intensified the differences as the more advantaged and socially ambitious Protestants began migrating to urban centres in various parts of the south in search of educational and occupational betterment. This kind of mobility, therefore, made it likely that many individuals would, in the course of a lifetime, come into contact with missionaries of various backgrounds, and thereby alter their perceptions of denominational identity. Nadars, for example, who were previously LMS adherents in south Travancore and Anglicans in Tinnevelly, became (American Board of Mission) Congregationalists in Madurai, Lutherans in Tanjore, Baptists in Burma, and so forth.

The effect of mission employment is a case in point. Whereas most missions attempted, naturally enough, to confer jobs on their own votaries, they were compelled, if these lacked the necessary skills and qualifications, to hire Protestants from other backgrounds. In the more advanced educational and medical establishments especially, recruitment policies had to stress ability without too much regard for denominational pro-

clivities. Thus, well-educated Protestants of one tradition were
employed by missionaries of another, which circumstances inevitably led to easy familiarity if not formal affiliation with the
employing agency's denomination. One SPG missionary even
complained that because his own mission trained far more
college students than it could itself employ, they went off to
teach in 'Dissenting Schools'. And, 'as they get their salaries
from Non-conformist Missionaries they have not the courage
to refuse to attend their places of worship and partake of Non-
conformist communions'.[16] Moreover, co-operation among
various missions in establishing joint ventures (see above)
meant that Protestants of various backgrounds were increasingly brought together in these multi-denominational
contexts.

Mobility, therefore, led to the same individuals forming attachments to several denominations in disparate places; to siblings being born in different mission areas, and being baptized
or confirmed in diverse denominations; to the same individual
being baptized in one, confirmed in another, educated by a
third, and perhaps being affiliated on a long-term basis with
yet a fourth. Finally, because marriage unions increasingly
took place across denominational lines (see Chapter 5), it was
common, if at the time of marriage each partner lived in a
different region, for the woman to join her husband and also
to adopt his current denominational attachment. Thus, it was
not unusual, as Bishop Neill has pointed out, for 'families [to
be] divided ... among half a dozen Christian confessions . . .'
(1972: 168).

This widespread interaction with both missionaries and adherents of various persuasions was, undoubtedly, in part responsible for the somewhat cavalier manner in which upwardly
mobile Protestants came to regard these religious boundaries
and certainly contributed to the comparative ease with which
they were ignored or put aside. The very notion of denominational affiliation itself was rendered ambiguous by the
character of the Protestant milieu in south India. To the extent
that baptism, confirmation, education, employment, and marriage created multiple links, many individuals, at least within
the more privileged sector of the community, grew attached to
and at home in more than one denomination. This situation

no doubt contributed to the success of the church union movement this century.

CONCLUSION

Protestant missionaries were, in one obvious regard, part of the imperialist entourage, for their influence extended under the protection, if not always the enthusiastic patronage, of European rulers in India. In another sense, they might be regarded as the more fervent colonizers, for in seeking to bring their own version of truth to the consciousness of indigenous peoples, they 'demonstrated a more radical and morally intense commitment to rule than political administrators or businessmen' (Beidelman 1982: 6). Local reaction to mission proselytization was mixed. While conversion numbers were not insignificant among the highest castes, on the whole they came to Christianity sporadically as individuals or in small family groups. The overwhelming proportion of converts entered the Protestant fold in mass movements from the lowest castes and economic strata.

The denominational organization which the mission Societies erected was eventually eroded from two directions. Despite their own traditional doctrinal and organizational differences, missionaries in south India found themselves sharing a common pietistic outlook and similar goals of evangelism which made inter-mission co-operation seem worthwhile. For its part, the Protestant community—or at least that part of it touched by nationalist sentiment and benefiting from the opportunities for education and skilled employment provided by the missions—began to question the very structures introduced by their Western benefactors. Those entering or aspiring to enter the emergent middle class, since they required unhampered access to the various opportunities becoming available in the changing economic climate of the late nineteenth and early twentieth centuries, could not tolerate rigid barriers of this kind. Thus, increasing mobility eroded many of the sect-like features the early mission-based congregations had acquired. Within barely a century of its establishment in British south India, Protestantism had become ecumenical in mood if not in formal structure. Though many retained a strong denominational attachment, awareness grew of a wider religious identity, defined partly in contrast to other religious traditions (i.e. Catholicism, Hinduism, Islam) and partly in terms of a common core of doctrine and ritual, which was to make possible church unions in this century.

Those members of the community—in effect, the majority—who could not or did not take full advantage of missionary education and other material benefits remained, for much of this period, attached to their missions, excluded from the kinds of possibilities for mobility described above. Their first experience of different denominations occurred only in this century when migrations commenced to centres like Madras, in response both to severe conditions in the rural areas and increased possibilities for urban employment. In time, they were also to encounter the fundamentalist sects, whose influence spread dramatically in the metropolis in the late 1960s, a development I will examine at length in the later part of the book. The next chapter considers the migration patterns of these Protestants, and locates them within the class structure of Madras.

3

THE MATERIAL DIMENSION OF INEQUALITY

Migration, Education, and Household Economy

INTRODUCTION

THE changing economic climate in south India and the emergence of Madras city as a centre of trade and commerce, administration, health services, education, and latterly industry, have encouraged considerable migrations to the metropolis during this century. Three-quarters of the city's population increase in the sixty-year period to 1961 can be accounted for by in-migration (Chandrasekhar 1964: 31). Poverty and famine conditions in the surrounding districts of Chingleput, North Arcot, and South Arcot brought many belonging to the poorest sections of village society, generally the outcastes, who were invariably the worst affected, to seek work.[1] Thus, Ransom observed how members of these groups provided the bulk of manual labour in the Presidency capital (1938: 3). But, outside a few large cotton mills, employers of industrial labour were few prior to the Second World War.

Between 1941 and 1951 the city's population grew by an unprecedented 61.8 per cent, and migration accounted for all but a tenth of this increase (Chandrasekhar 1964: 29). While the figures were inflated due to an extension of the municipal limits,[2] and an influx of wartime refugees from South East Asia, they were primarily related to the city's rapid industrial expansion which began in this decade and continued at a vigorous pace for some twenty years.

I begin this chapter by outlining briefly the emergence of Madras as an industrial centre, and trace the migration patterns of Protestants now in the city. The discussion then turns to their occupations, and points to certain factors—including access to education—which help to account for employments and opportunities for mobility. I also consider the applicability of dualistic economic models to the urban Protestant context. The household is identified as the crucial site within which such analytical divisions are mediated and dissolved. The primary aim of the chapter is to identify the nature and extent of material inequalities between class levels within the Protestant community. For the reader who finds such subject matter tedious to follow I provide a comprehensive outline of the chapter's findings in the conclusion.

MADRAS CITY

Established in 1639 as a factory by the East India Company, the city soon became the capital of an eponymous presidency (encompassing much of British south India), and the *locus* of administration and services for the entire area. Following the assumption of power by the Crown in 1858, the city's importance grew steadily. Alongside a considerable increase in the Presidency's administrative and military expenditures, railways and major roads began to converge on the city, a steamer service from and to Europe was inaugurated, a new harbour built, and the headquarters of all important banking and commercial firms in the south were located there, as were a host of advanced educational institutions.[3] This kind of growth necessitated and encouraged the development of other infrastructural elements, such as hospitals, telephone services, tramways and buses, newspapers, etc.

The period up to the Second World War, however, was not one of significant industrial expansion. In 1936 there were only 124 factories employing over 20 operatives, and, according to Hodgson, 47 of these were printing presses! (1939: 239). The major employers of labour were the cotton spinning and weaving mills (11,000) and the railway workshops (5,000)—both of which had been established during the latter part of the nineteenth century. The majority of industries, however, were small and existed mainly to supply local needs. Even the port, though the Presidency's largest, handled a disproportionately small part of its trade (Baker 1975: 217).

While the war stimulated the city's economy somewhat, it was the post-independence policies of state and central governments which made Madras and its environs (now the Madras

Metropolitan Area) an important industrial region. As a result of these policies the area of greater Madras today contains one of the largest concentrations of engineering industries in the country. There are over 1,400 registered factories manufacturing, among other things, transport equipment, electrical machinery and appliances, chemicals and chemical products, petroleum and petrochemicals, machine tools, tractors, and railway coaches. Madras is also the centre of a large and flourishing film industry. While much of this development has been internally financed, there has been some overseas capital investment. In addition, a number of foreign companies have continued to operate branches in the metropolis, or established local subsidiaries.[4]

At the same time as these alterations to Madras's traditional economy were occurring, the city continued to expand as a centre of services and administration, as it became the capital city of Madras state and then the more recently established state of Tamilnadu. This expansion created openings at all levels of the urban economy, and attracted migrants—including, of course, Protestants—from all parts of south India. They entered the metropolis, in growing numbers, to seek employment in the industries emerging in and around the capital, or otherwise pursue opportunities which arose in the wake of this growth.

MIGRATION

Certain sections of old Madras have, since the establishment of a missionary presence in the city, been the *loci* of Protestant settlement, and probably still contain its largest concentrations. (People joke that it is impossible to throw a stone in Vepery without hitting a church.) But as the city expanded along the coast as well as further inland, gathering in its urban embrace what had been portions of rural Chingleput district, Protestants came to be found in most parts of the capital.

In the area of Madras settled by members of the CSI-Western congregation (who form the core of my lower class sample), population densities are nearly 16,300 per square kilometre, a figure exceeded only in a few of the very oldest sections of the metropolis. This quarter, a web of narrow lanes, is skirted

on the east by Anna Salai (formerly Mount Road), one of
Madras's busiest thoroughfares and a national highway, and is
bifurcated by major railway lines (including a suburban service) which creates endless congestion at level crossings. To the
visitor from less densely settled sections of the city the impression is of incessant noise and activity—from vehicle horns,
hawkers, bullock cart drivers, market traders, and countless
people scurrying about their business. Nevertheless, to its Protestant residents—as I suspect to many others—the area has
many advantages. It is well served by transport to most parts
of the city and its suburbs, there are amply stocked shops and
outdoor food markets, several schools and churches, including,
of course, their own place of worship. Not least, for most of
them, there are close relatives nearby, including the dead in
local graveyards which can be easily visited. Though many
have moved residence several times in their lives, very few
seem anxious to leave the area. They are, by comparison with
middle-class co-religionists, a fairly stable population.

A significant proportion of them are two or more generations
removed from the original urban migrant. This suggests a fairly
long-standing association with the city on the part of many
lower class residents, mainly those from the northern districts
of Tamilnadu closest to Madras. In response to a query about
native place (*sonta ūr*), such persons as often as not reply simply
that they are 'Madras people'.

The majority, nevertheless, entered the city in their own
lifetimes, on the whole as young adults during the period of
rapid population influx in the decades 1941–61. (The average
age of householders in the lower class sample is 47.0 for men,
and 42.6 for women.) Like those who came to Madras earlier
in the century, these migrants moved directly from their native
villages to the capital. The metropolis provided an attractive
alternative to the rural areas which were seen to offer no prospects. Many recall that there appeared to be plenty of work
around when they first migrated.

What is striking in their migration histories is the extent to
which this movement was not an individual phenomenon but
involved groups of siblings. The brothers and sisters of a rural
household tended to become urban migrants as a unit, though
they did not usually move together, but serially. So, if we

take all the siblings of focal householders in the CSI-Western congregation, and inquire where they reside at the moment, we find that nearly two-thirds are in Madras city, a fourth are in another urban centre (usually in Tamilnadu), and only one-tenth live in villages. Looked at from a slightly different perspective, that of the household, we find the following: in one quarter of the households all the siblings of the focal couple are in Madras; in half the households, the focal couple's siblings are all either in Madras or some other urban location. In only a quarter of households, therefore, does the focal couple have one or more rural siblings. Let me illustrate the process of sibling migration by an example.

Anand, the eldest of four children in a village in Chingleput district, came to Madras shortly before independence to seek work. With the assistance of a distantly related fellow villager he managed to obtain a job in a small garage helping the mechanic, though within several months he changed to a more promising post in the maintenance section of the Public Transport Corporation. Two years later he assisted in arranging the marriage of his sister to a workmate, and she came to settle in the city. A year after that Anand managed to get his younger brother a place as a trainee driver with the PTC, and the latter came to live with him in Madras. Four years later their youngest sister arrived to begin a teacher's training course in Madras, supported by her three siblings. She lived with her elder sister until her marriage to a city resident. Their widowed mother stayed on in the village for a short period but then came to live with her youngest daughter. All four siblings are now married and settled in Madras.

The introduction of migrants to the city was facilitated by (usually close) relatives and fellow villagers who preceded them. These provided guidance and advice, assistance in obtaining jobs (often in the form of personal recommendations to employers), and accommodation. Thus, the networks and patterns of association reported for migrants to the cities of the subcontinent by Rowe (1973) and others were no less in evidence among these Protestants.

Women, as the above example suggests, came for different reasons than men. A small proportion (some one in ten) migrated to begin a job already arranged, but none arrived to look for work on their own. A few entered Madras to train as teachers, and a handful joined relatives in the city to continue education. But most—approximately seven in ten—moved to the capital to join their newly wedded husbands already settled there.

Migrants entering Madras to work in the lower reaches of the occupational hierarchy were, on the whole, inclined to remain permanently in the metropolis. After marriage there were and are no compelling attachments to rural homes to which they might return with some regularity. Nor is the end of a working life in the city followed by a resettlement in the native place, even when relationships there remain extant. Most elderly Protestants in the CSI-Western congregation have spent the greater part of their adult lives in the city, and find both their material possessions (such as they are) and their emotional ties mainly in the urban place. Moreover, since their children have grown up and are now employed in Madras— or hoping to be—and it is upon the latter that the elderly depend for support and assistance, the possibility of emigration seldom if ever arises.

The movement of Protestant élites into the city occurred mainly after independence, in the majority of cases after 1960. In contrast to lower class householders, only a tiny proportion of middle-class respondents are the descendants of persons who entered the Presidency capital more than two generations back. Their origins are distinct as well, having come mainly from southern districts of Tamilnadu and, less frequently, other states in the south, such as Kerala or Andhra Pradesh.

But if most middle-class Protestants are relative newcomers to the metropolis, they have long been part of the urban milieu. Only a handful came to Madras direct from village homes. On the whole, they trace their peasant forebears at least three to four generations back, at which time removal to a town and the change from an agricultural to a non-agricultural occupation took place. There are indications that they share a long-standing commitment to urban life (if to no special urban place) with class counterparts among the non-Christian population. Gould points out how, among business and professional élites in Lucknow, 'divorcement from the village has gone so far that less than half the genealogies revealed any rural ties at all . . .' (1970: 72).

The desire for advanced education was frequently a major factor bringing persons belonging or aspiring to the middle class into the capital. Some 40 per cent of male focal house-holders and a quarter of females first came to Madras to attend college or some specialist training institute. This is explicable in terms of the concentration of higher educational and other specialized facilities in the capital and their comparatively high quality.

The largest proportion of men in the middle-class sample, however, first entered Madras in the course of career ad-vancement. This movement was encouraged by two more or less contemporaneous occurrences. One was the exodus of Europeans from all positions of pre-eminence in the country at the time of independence,[5] and the other was the success of the Dravidian movement in puncturing the near-monopoly by Brahmins of whatever positions of responsibility were available to indigenous personnel (see M. R. Barnett 1976). This created new opportunities in administration, the professions, trade, and commerce for sectors of the local population hitherto under-represented in the senior echelons of these occupations.

Men in the middle-class sample recount how they came to the metropolis to establish a business, to begin new employment already contracted for, or—the majority—as the result of a transfer by their employers. Even the few who came in search of a job were not escaping from crushing poverty and un-employment, but aiming to better their already by no means uncomfortable situation.

Most women migrated either at the time of marriage, to join husbands already in the city, or with their husbands who were moving to the city for career consideration. Only a few mi-grated initially for their own employment purposes, and those who did were mostly unmarried. Since, generally, married women who are working allow their husbands' careers to take precedence over their own, they accompany their migrating spouses to the city, and there seek new employment. This in-cludes women with professional qualifications, such as doctors.

Those entering Madras to work in the lower reaches of the occupational order were, as I noted, inclined to remain permanently in the city. This is in sharp contrast to middle-class migrants, most of whom have migrated to the capital more than once. A not untypical migration history is that of *M. S.*, a member of the CSI-Southern congregation, and a retired senior state government official. Educated in schools in Tinnevelly and Trichinopoly, he first came to Madras in 1935 at the age of 18 to attend the engineering college in Guindy. On completion of his degree in 1940 he joined the public service (engineering branch) and soon after he was posted to Dindigul in Madurai district, where he spent four years and during which time he was married to a woman from Tinnevelly; he was then posted to Vellore for three years; to Chittoor in Andhra Pradesh (two years); back to Dindigul (two years); to Mangalore (two years); Salem (two years); Coimbatore (three years); and finally Madras, to which he returned with his family in 1964 at the age of 47. On retirement, eight years later, as Chief Engineer of the department, he established a small manufacturing firm in the city. His wife's first contact with Madras was in 1964 when, at the age of 45, she migrated with her husband and children.

This kind of circulation underlines an important feature of migration among the middle class, namely, that it involves movements between the metropolis and lesser cities and towns, and moreover, is not necessarily a once-and-for-all step, but may involve several 'entries' and 'exits'. It is important to stress how the metropolis, by its special characteristics, attracts and selects migrants in quite a different way from other, less dominant, urban localities. Because Madras is the hub of the region's commercial and industrial life, the headquarters of most large companies operating in the south, its educational, medical, and legal centre, a seat of government and *locus* of administration, as well as the 'cultural capital' of the Tamil world, the top cadres of virtually all occupational categories are situated there. This means, of course, that entry into the highest echelons is really only possible by migrating to the city, even if, as I have shown, the migration may not be permanent, but may involve circulation among several urban centres until career advancement results in the migrant's return to the capital. Gould, referring to other urban centres in India, notes how persons high in the occupational order 'gravitate toward the ultimate metropolitan structures' (1970: 67–8).

EDUCATION

Several general points emerge from a perusal of the various writings on the education of Christians generally, and Protestants in particular, during the decades prior to independence (see Chapter 2 n. 7). The first is that they were encouraged to pursue educational opportunities provided by the missionaries, and that large numbers did so—indeed, as I noted in Chapter 2, some people even converted in order to gain access to these facilities. Secondly, many Protestants developed a high regard for education, and this led to a gradual improvement in educational levels over the years, with each generation surpassing the previous one. Thirdly, this positive attitude to formal schooling was not confined to the education of males, although this is not to say that daughters were necessarily given the same encouragement as sons.[6] Finally, and perhaps most significantly, not all sections of the community were able to take equal advantage of whatever opportunities did exist. This not only generated socio-economic differentiation within the community during the nineteenth century, but continues to be a major factor perpetuating and sharpening urban class divisions in the present.

Some 60 per cent of the men and just half of the women in the lower class sample completed secondary school, and one tenth of the men (but hardly any women) went on to do the one year pre-university course (PUC) or attend college for a brief period. Well over half the women matriculates (who are usually 16–18 years old) trained as teachers, as indeed did the majority of those who studied only as far as middle school (eighth standard) which they tend to complete at 13–15 years of age.[7]

The principal difference between this and the previous generation (i.e. the parents of focal householders) seems to lie in the achievement of near-universal literacy, in so far as very few adults in this generation have not attended an educational institution. In general, however, while about half the focal householders have been educated beyond their parents' level, an equal number have only either just maintained the standard or failed to attain it.

Whatever the advances made by the present generation of lower class householders, there has not been a breakthrough into the kinds of educational spheres presently occupied by middle-class Protestants. How can we explain this? I have previously suggested that entry by Protestants into the middle class was dependent largely on mission schooling (Caplan 1977). In view of the fact that focal householders belonging to the lower class have also gained access to mission education—56 per cent of the men and 65 per cent of the women attended church or mission schools—it is clear that such access was a necessary but not a sufficient condition for social mobility. Several other factors appear to have been of vital significance as well.

One concerns the language of education. These householders studied mainly in Tamil, which placed serious limits on their ability to compete for entrance to university—and especially to those courses leading to a professional qualification, where fluent English is required. Differential access to this medium of instruction and communication related partly to mission policies on vernacular education. Some missions promoted Tamil medium schools more vigorously than others. One Society with a significant presence in that part of Madras near the CSI-Western church, and to which many congregants had been affiliated in the past, had a policy of teaching only in Tamil up to eighth standard, at which point pupils were encouraged to train as teachers for the mission's own schools. There were often disagreements within a single Society concerning the merits of vernacular as opposed to English education (see Pathak 1967: 60–1). The outcome of such debates in a particular region could well influence the ability of children to compete successfully for places beyond middle or high school. Those taught in Tamil in their early years often found it extremely difficult to cope with the switch to English at high school or college level, unless they lived in households or moved in circles where English was known and frequently spoken.

In the context of present-day Madras, the medium in which children are educated remains a complex and occasionally controversial matter. Most larger secondary schools in the city (whether church, i.e. ex-mission, private non-Christian, or

state/municipality run) provide some choice as between English and vernacular teaching up to matriculation. Nevertheless,
it is commonly accepted that only a handful of schools, mainly
in the private (including Christian) sector, in which the standards of teaching in English are high, produces the overwhelming proportion of university entrants. In particular, these
few schools provide the majority of successful candidates for
the most sought-after courses, i.e. medicine, engineering, law,
and certain sciences.

Given this situation, we can appreciate the significance of
the fact that the offspring of focal householders in the lower
class either attend less well-regarded private (including some
Christian) schools, or, as in the majority of cases, those which
are run by the state or municipality. Wiebe describes the quality of education available in the latter as 'dismal' (1981: 125).
Two-thirds of children in the sample, moreover, are being educated in Tamil medium, as were four-fifths of their parents.
While it is increasingly possible nowadays for someone with an
exclusively vernacular education to proceed to university, the
range of courses available is extremely limited. The irony is
that those who study in Tamil, which figured so prominently
in the Dravidian political and cultural revival, are seriously disadvantaged beyond matriculation, since universities in the state
cannot ignore the dominant position of English in the field of
higher education. The medium of study, now as in the past,
affects significantly opportunities for access to the most highly
prized forms of training.

Another constraint was and remains financial. In the colonial
period it was not simply a matter of affording the fees—since
missions did waive these where necessary. Rather, since secondary schools were few and far between, and situated mainly
in small urban centres, there was the outlay on boarding and
other 'accoutrements' of schooling, as well as the family's ability
to forgo the potential labour value of children sent to be educated. In post-independence Madras, the costs of the most
reputable secondary schools and of higher education generally,
presents a severe financial challenge to most Protestants.
Charges for tuition, books, transport, uniforms, examinations,
and hostels are within the means of only the most affluent.
Even if such financial obstacles can be overcome, the alleged

practice of demanding (unofficially) large 'capitation' fees
or 'donations' from the parents of aspiring entrants, further
contrives to exclude lower class Protestants from the most
sought-after schools and professional colleges. Indeed, these
householders frequently complain of what they see as the cal-
lous disregard with which their pleas for special consideration
by the more reputable Protestant educational institutions are
met. Whatever the validity of these accusations, the feeling is
now widespread that these institutions serve only the middle
class. Kurien suggests that 'their very excellence has ... made
them the coveted places for the richest and the highest' (1974:
179).

Then, again, discrimination by central and state authorities
in favour of both 'scheduled' (i.e. 'untouchable') castes and
those designated as 'backward', by reserving for them an ever-
increasing percentage of university places, has meant that these
Protestants are further handicapped. Christians, whatever their
caste background or status, belong to what is considered a
'forward community'. Hence, those in the lower class have to
compete against not only middle-class co-religionists, but the
most advantaged sections of the wider society, for a decreasing
proportion of places.[8] The exclusion of Christian Harijans from
the category of scheduled castes, on the grounds that their
adopted religion does not recognize untouchability, is a source
of grievance to the Protestant church and community. But,
while submitting countless petitions and complaints to the
authorities, the leadership has not sought to alleviate the
impediments of these Harijans (or indeed, the economically
disprivileged within the community) by reserving for them a
proportion of places within its own educational system. Generally, then, Protestants from depressed caste backgrounds,
who belong mainly to the lower class, have had to carry the
dual burdens of their traditional caste status and their poverty.
These together have seriously inhibited their chances for educational advance.

Quite apart from obvious differences in individual scholastic
ability, therefore, a variety of circumstances combined to filter
only a small minority of Protestants into the upper reaches of
the educational system. But even that degree of fluidity which
existed in the not too distant past within the Protestant en-

vironment seems no longer to obtain. In the increasingly competitive urban milieu, those with privileged access seek to retain
their hold on the limited fund of educational resources. While
education has historically played an important role in mobility,
there has been, as Saberwal suggests, a 'hardening of social
arteries' (1978: 243).

I have discussed in some detail elsewhere the considerable
educational attainments of focal householders in the middle-
class sample (Caplan 1977), and here it is only necessary to
draw attention to a few of the more pertinent findings. Two-
thirds of men and virtually all the women are better educated
than their fathers and mothers. About half the male focal householders have degrees in science, medicine, or engineering, while
four-fifths of the women have gone beyond high school, the
majority to obtain a Bachelor's degree or better. Indeed, a
higher proportion of women than men in the middle-class
sample have a post-Bachelor's qualification.

The children of these householders are being educated in
the city's most select schools, invariably private, fee-paying
institutions in which the medium of instruction is English. In
Madras city, certain Catholic schools have in the past decade
or two become the most favoured, mainly on the stated grounds
that they maintain 'good discipline'. This is a coded statement
meaning that they have not accepted financial aid from the
government, and are thereby not obliged to reserve places for
members of various disadvantaged groups, who are normally
blamed for 'lowering standards'. By contrast, most Protestant
institutions now receive grants-in-aid, and while a few still
enjoy considerable reputations in the city, most have been losing ground to the more select Catholic schools, even among
Protestants.

The competition for places in élite schools is intense, and
middle-class parents must use every available means at their
disposal to gain entry for their children. Their networks are
fully stretched to ensure that the appropriate recommendations
are forthcoming. An extremely high ratio of their post-
secondary school age children are, or have been at university,
and the evidence available on their career patterns suggests
that the largest proportion (especially among the males) is set
on obtaining professional qualifications, particularly in science,

medicine, and engineering. This tendency is greatly encouraged by the possibilities for work abroad for persons so qualified (see Chapter 4).

Protestants of the lower class recognize the advantages of schooling and especially of higher study, yet cannot help but be aware of their own handicaps in the educational stakes. While it would be misleading to speak of a culture of limited ambition, they do adjust their sights to accord with their perceptions of the opportunities available. None the less, there is considerable willingness to follow courses of study—often at the sacrifice of much time, money, and effort—which result in further practical skills and qualifications. Nowadays, young men enrol in courses on diesel mechanics, automobile engineering, air-conditioning, radio and television, electronics, and the like; women seek increasingly to acquire secretarial skills. On the whole, the new abilities thus sought pertain to and reflect an acute appreciation of the appropriate occupational niche to which these individuals may realistically aspire. In the next section I examine the kinds of occupations pursued by urban Protestants.

OCCUPATIONS

The earliest Protestant settlers in Madras appear to have been mainly servants engaged by Europeans (Orr 1967: 367; Grafe 1969: 47). Indeed, the siting of a number of Tamil churches within a stone's throw of important European churches of the same denomination is explicable largely in terms of the desire to provide facilities for worship for Indian domestic staff. In time, however, the range of occupations in which Christians were engaged expanded, so that by the end of the nineteenth century Westcott was able to note that they were also employed 'in subordinate positions in public offices, or in similar duties' (1897: 94). Still, a survey of the material conditions of church members in the city, published in 1906, recorded that the majority belonged to the 'servant and cooly classes', or had no work at all (quoted in Houghton 1981: 352).

Developments in Madras in the first half of this century expanded further the variety of employment possibilities, as is evident from occupations listed in the marriage registers of the

CSI-Western congregation between 1911 and 1951. During
this period about one-quarter of the men were either in domestic service or menial jobs, one-third were in clerical work,
one-tenth were teachers, and nearly one-quarter (many more
of the latter listed in the registers after 1941 than before) were
in employment requiring technical skills. Of the women who
were working at the time of marriage (a majority), almost all
were teachers, and a few were in some aspect of nursing. This
contrasts with the tendency for middle-class women not to enter
employment until after marriage.

Notwithstanding the trend towards greater participation in
paid employment among women of the lower class, it remains
largely confined to delimited fields in which, for historical
reasons to do with missionary policy, Protestant women have
already played an important part. For many years, they have
been engaged in educational and medical activities, forming a
disproportionate number of female teachers and nurses. Among
working women in the lower class sample, the proportion of
nurses has decreased as against the previous generation, while
that of teachers has risen, although most are now employed
outside the Christian school system.[9] An increasing though still
small number now work in offices and factories, and a few other
hitherto unfamiliar occupational contexts.

The necessity of finding paid employment, however, does not
make these women less accountable for the smooth running of
the household. Though other members may assist with children,
and, as is the norm in most Indian homes, men will usually
shop in the market-place, it is the women who assume the
primary responsibility for day to day domestic arrangements.
An article in the magazine published in 1970 on the occasion
of the Golden Jubilee celebrations of the CSI-Western parish
was on this very theme of 'Christian working women at home'.
I quote a lengthy excerpt because it not only identifies and
celebrates the seemingly endless demands made on these
women, but by glorifying their selfless sacrifices authenticates
the role they are called on to play in maintaining the household.

She has to prepare meals, get children ready for school and husband
for the office, and rush out of the house to jump on a bus, remain
standing until she reaches her office ... Tired after her 'working day'
she slinks back home catching the bus in the rush. At home there

starts another cycle of preparing meals and soothing frayed tempers
... She has to look presentable and fresh and await the arrival of the
bread-winner. In fact he needs her kind thoughts, words and deeds
more than anybody in the household ... When she has leisure (does
she ever have?) she has to stitch, mend and wash garments, prepare
special dishes, please the visitors and make her house neat and tidy.
Here is how she manages:

1. Prayer
2. Avoiding self-pity
3. Keeping everything in its place
4. Controlling her temper
5. Training the children to help
6. Calling her children and husband by endearing terms
7. Remembering 'cleanliness comes next to Godliness'
8. Keeping a cheerful countenance
9. Never forgetting that work is prayer
10. Keeping her work problems away from home.

Despite the considerable part these women play as 'productive'
workers, they are not thereby excused their prime responsibility
for everyday domestic activities which, as Pat Caplan notes,
are crucial 'in the perpetuation, reproduction and formation
of life-styles or cultures associated with class' (1985: 83).

Turning to the men, while a number of individual histories
reveal upward mobility, overall, despite an extension in the
range both of jobs now held and skills acquired, there has been
only a very modest improvement in the status of occupations
pursued as between the previous generation and this one. The
fathers of many of the male focal householders who are today
'coolies' (day labourers) in Madras were either agricultural
workers in the rural areas or held menial jobs as, for example,
domestics, watchmen, or messengers in the metropolis. The
most significant change has taken place in the technical sphere,
as focal householders have entered factories and workshops in
quite substantial numbers, especially in the immediate post-
independence period of rapid industrial expansion. While fewer
than one in ten 'fathers' were in skilled manual occupations,
over a quarter of male focal householders are so employed—as
masons, mechanics, turners, fitters, and so on. Furthermore, the
kinds of employment being entered by their own sons suggest a
reinforcement of this tendency towards greater involvement in
technical occupations. To appreciate this trend we have to

mark the avenues to employment accessible to these Protestants.

The range of occupations available has been shown to relate closely to their educational levels. Alternatively, the less privileged tend to adjust their educational ambitions to what they perceive as the realities of the opportunity structure. But education is no longer, if it ever was, the sole means of establishing eligibility for employment. Despite continuous upgradings of minimal requirements for most kinds of work, suitably qualified candidates regularly exceed the number of jobs available. For the most part, then, success in obtaining employment is crucially dependent on other factors as well. Merit and ability are certainly not discounted. Companies regularly advertise for, especially, skilled workers in the technical field. The only householder presently working in the Middle East is a telephone engineer who was installing equipment in one of the city's major hotels when he saw a notice in the lobby directing candidates for particular categories of technical employment to interviews being conducted on behalf of a large multinational company. He went to the appropriate suite, introduced himself and explained that he had not seen the initial newspaper advertisement, was interviewed on the spot, and walked out with a job offer.[10] There are also increasing numbers of employment exchanges in the state claiming a modicum of success in placements, and several householders reported being hired after attending interviews arranged by these offices.

Some have also benefited from a number of job reservation programmes. While they are unable to claim the same privileges as Hindus from identical backgrounds under the schemes which discriminate in favour of scheduled castes and 'backward' classes (see above), they can and do profit from others. Thus, a number of posts in the public sector are put aside for ex-servicemen, and a few householders had obtained their present jobs under this particular rubric. There are also reservations for the handicapped, through which at least one man in the congregation obtained his clerical employment. Moreover, many government and some private establishments have a policy of favouring the children or spouses of former employees. So, for example, the job of a port employee compelled to retire because of ill health was given to his son, while

on the death of a clerk employed by the Tamil Nadu Housing
Board, his job (or a very similar one) was offered to his eldest
daughter.

The majority of householders, however, acquired their employment through an intermediary. Most commonly, the person interceding was a parent who spoke on their behalf to
colleagues in the same or related departments or institutions.
Other relatives also appear in informants' accounts of their
first employment experience. One reported how a job in the
railways was conferred following the recommendation of a
mother's brother; another found a sweeping job in the municipality with the help of a sister's husband already working
there; a third obtained unskilled work in a factory through the
intervention of a sibling. What is clear and acknowledged is
that close relatives should assist one another in the search for
employment, since the assumption is that without someone to
intercede on your behalf the chances of finding a job are slim
indeed. No similar obligation attaches to caste as such, although obviously among those sections of the Protestant community practising caste-specific marriages, relatives inevitably
share a single caste label.

A few householders cited neighbours, friends, or patrons as
their gateway to employment. One elderly congregant recalled
how a missionary had spoken on his behalf to the managing
director of a large British firm. Another, who had spent many
years in the unofficial entourage of a state politician, had been
finally rewarded when the latter arranged a clerical job with a
large public corporation. A third, who was a cook in the private
service of the director of a scientific institute in Madras spoke—
successfully—on behalf of his son to his employer who found
the young man a job tending the lab animals. Most such
patrons/brokers have a very finite quantity of favours they can
bestow, and are careful how they utilize these limited resources.
The telephone engineer referred to above, for example, has
received numerous requests from relatives, neighbours, and
fellow congregants to help them find work in the Gulf, but he
has quite plainly felt it necessary to deflect their pleas (with
promises to see what he can do) so that he could utilize whatever limited influence he possessed to secure a job for his own

son. While I was in Madras in 1981 the young man flew out to join his father and take up his new post.

While these networks can be dense, they are extremely limited in reach and influence. To appreciate what I mean by this we need only consider the case of several children of focal householders in the lower class sample who managed to obtain a university degree against considerable odds. They have been unable to find work of any kind, let alone work appropriate to their educational status. The reasons given by these unemployed graduates, their parents, and others for this failure is the absence of 'someone to help'. Genealogies present a striking picture of status homogeneity, and marriage arrangements, as I show in a later chapter, ensure that members of this class are carefully insulated from co-religionists within the dominant stratum. Very few of these householders therefore have close relatives or other primary links among the middle class to whom they might turn for support in any serious attempt at occupational mobility.

The contrast with the middle class in respect both of occupational status and avenues to employment is worth noting. Householders in the middle-class sample work exclusively in the formal sector, and entirely in non-manual occupations which are, in the great majority of cases, of an executive or professional character. They are heavily represented in higher education. Women, in particular, have been able to benefit from the spread of female educational establishments in Madras during the past few decades, and have been well-placed to occupy a significant number of the higher posts—requiring advanced qualifications and requisite experience—which have been created. They are or have been headmistresses of and senior teachers in prominent schools for girls, principals of teachers' training institutes, professors of English, French, medicine, engineering, and economics, and lecturers in a wide range of subjects in both Protestant and non-Protestant (i.e. Catholic, Hindu, Muslim, and publicly funded) establishments of higher learning.

In the medical field, too, which engages about 13 per cent of middle-class women in the sample, the present generation is employed at higher levels than its predecessor (i.e. as doctors rather than nurses) which require longer periods of training and, of course, bring greater rewards in terms of income and status. Those without professional qualifications tend to obtain employment in clerical and lower supervisory posts in various organizations (e.g. insurance companies) within the formal sector.

The men are or have been located principally at top executive levels in the Civil Service and military services. They fill(ed) posts of deputy-secretaries, ICS/IAS officers, assistant police commissioners, chief engineers, senior customs superintendents, high-ranking naval officers, and so on. In the world of commerce and industry they belong(ed) to the management cadres of both private firms—some of them old established European companies still partly foreign-owned—or public corporations mainly created in the post-independence period.[11]

These men are employed by organizations which, with certain obvious exceptions such as those run by the church, are not Christian. Indeed, most of them work mainly with colleagues of other faiths. The majority, therefore, do not as a rule gain access to their positions through any kind of Protestant network operating within the urban occupational structure. Nor is caste the crucial factor in obtaining employment and/or promotion. There were and are, to be sure, organizations or parts of organizations, both public and private, with reputations as domains of particular castes, most commonly Brahmin, but not necessarily so. Members of the two élite congregations studied sometimes claimed to have resigned from a company because they saw no future there for anyone who was not a Nadar (or Vellalar or Brahmin), or that they would never apply to a certain firm because as Syrian Christians (or Vellalars or Nadars) they would not be considered for a position. But such comment notwithstanding, the great majority not only interact at their place of work with members of a variety of groups, but do not regard their own caste affiliation (or, in the case of some persons, lack of it) as of significance in shaping their careers.

Perhaps half of those with whom I discussed the details of hiring procedures indicated that their jobs had been conferred following a formal application and interview, and on no other basis. An equal proportion acknowledged openly and without embarrassment that they had obtained their first position through an intermediary. Nevertheless, it must be appreciated that the kinds of employment which they were helped to obtain almost invariably required specific skills and educational attainments not possessed by the generality of job-seekers and are, therefore, 'labelled' as high status positions, available only to a select pool of qualified or experienced candidates. Not uncommonly, the person who interceded was a kinsman, for close relatives at this level, no less than within the lower class, accept obligations to assist one another in obtaining work. But as often as not, the one who 'put in a good word', or 'spoke to the managing director' was linked by other than blood or marriage. These élites recount how jobs were secured through the good offices of a fellow church-goer, a former professor, an ex-classmate at university, a business acquaintance, a neighbour, a friend and bridge partner, a brother Mason or Rotarian. Just as associational networks aiding urban migration are more heterogeneous among the middle than the lower class (Caplan 1976), those assisting careers are similarly disparate, and not confined only to kin or those sharing a common caste background. The considerable investment by middle-class households in developing appropriate contacts, ultimately redounds to the advantage of those making their way into the upper echelons of the occupational hierarchy (see Chapter 4).

As a career proceeds there is less and less reliance on the kinds of mediation required at lower occupational strata. At the levels within which most of these focal householders circulate, the requisite education, technical knowledge, and experience play an increasingly important role in determining the disposition of personnel. Corporate interests and goals, at least within the private sector, frequently outweigh, even if they do not entirely eclipse personal considerations.

FORMAL AND INFORMAL SECTOR EMPLOYMENT

One common way of categorizing employments is in terms of their locations within the 'formal' or 'informal' sectors of the urban economy. Approximately three-quarters of focal householders in the lower class sample work in the former. This means that, on the whole, they are in stable employment in large-scale establishments, with union affiliation, some form of pension scheme or provident fund, and protected by labour legislation. They are attached to both private and public organizations, in manual as well as non-manual occupations. Thus, a sweeper working for the Madras Corporation, a clerk in the state bureaucracy, a turner in a foreign-owned factory, or a teacher in a Christian school are, by these criteria, part of the 'formal' sector. In terms of Breman's fourfold classification of the urban work-force, these Protestants are part of the 'labour elite' (1976: 1940). However, as Worsley points out to those who use similar terms like 'labour artistocracy', it may be stretching such concepts somewhat when they are intended to describe 'the army of wretchedly paid low level public servants'—messengers, porters, cleaners, road workers, and the like (1981: 241).

The rest belong to the 'informal' or 'unorganized' sector. In this regard, focal householders in the sample, and probably the lower class within the Protestant community generally, is untypical of the Madras working population as a whole, since approximately 69 per cent of the latter are estimated to be employed in the city's informal sector (Blomkvist 1983: 9). The term has often been used, without precision, 'to cover everything that does not belong to the formal sector' (Breman 1976: 1871).[12] Protestants within the informal sector mainly comprise what Breman and others have termed the 'subproletariat'. These are the poorly paid employees of small firms and workshops, without unions or legislation to protect them, and lacking security of employment. Casual workers hired by large establishments in the formal sphere are also included here, as are self-employed craftsmen, musicians, and technicians, salespersons who work on commission, shop assistants, typists, secretaries, untrained teachers, domestic servants, 'coolies', and independent evangelists.

Furthermore, (and despite their ubiquity they are seldom if ever assigned a place in these schemata) there are those who are waiting for their first job, or who have been unemployed over a long term. A handful of male focal householders (including one who has not worked in 17 years) and a significant proportion of their children—15·per cent of sons of working age—are without employment of any kind. Though nearly half their daughters of working age are not in employment, they do not necessarily declare themselves 'unemployed'. Only a few who have left their jobs or been made redundant actually do so. The rest are said simply to be 'at home'. All such persons share, in differing degrees, a present and/or future of insecurity and uncertainty.

The concept of a dual economy has been attacked for several reasons, perhaps the most common being that it posits a too rigid distinction between the formal and informal sectors (for a summary of the arguments see Lloyd 1982; Holmstrom 1984). The distinction between them is by no means precise and immutable. For one thing, the differences in income are probably as great within each sector as between them. Several persons engaged in the unorganized sector are significantly better off (at least in the short term) than others in the organized sector. Free-lance musicians working in the film industry, for example, earn among the highest incomes in the sample. Then, the boundaries between the spheres can be and are traversed with some regularity. I know of several cases where casually employed coolies secured permanent positions, or a tenured teacher resigned his job in preference to accepting a transfer, and turned to occasional tuitions as a source of livelihood. A few work in both spheres at once, as for example when an electrician employed by a state-owned firm does private work in the evenings.

Most importantly, however, we must remember that such category divisions are of the observer's making, models of significance for Western-oriented social scientists. But such labels have little if any status in indigenous ways of thinking about varieties of employment. Protestant householders, for example—and I suspect most members of the lower class—classify and regard work not primarily in terms of whether it is part of the organized or unorganized sector. It is evaluated, rather, in a particular biographical context; a job, any job, where there was none before; a permanent job where previously there was occasional employment and insecurity; a better-paying job in place of a poorly paid one; a job with accommodation in place of one without; or one near home in preference to a distant posting; and so on.

Significantly, too, those who occupy different sectors are not regarded as a species apart. Participants in what we may regard as separate spheres share neighbourhood and domestic life in common. This is true of the middle class as well. Those who own the means of production and others who 'serve' capital in the capacity of executives, managers, or senior bureaucrats belong to the same households. The domestic unit, therefore, must be seen as a crucial site within which what may be considered objectively distinctive sectors, productive modes, or occupational classes are experientially dissolved, in the sense that they do not enter the consciousness of actors themselves. The next section looks at the composition of Protestant households.

HOUSEHOLDS

Though Christians regard themselves as part of a wider family (*kuṭumpam*), their most intimate ties are to a household (also *kuṭumpam*), the primary co-residential and commensal unit. The average domestic group to which CSI-Western congregants belong consists of 5.08 persons, which is very close to the official figure (5.25) for the residential quarter as a whole, and somewhat higher than the average (4.07) for households in the middle class.

Dwellings

These household numbers assume a more poignant significance when viewed in the context of housing. The dwellings in which lower class Protestants live are of five principal types.

1. MUD HUTS with roofs of straw, which, while looking like the houses of the rural poor, are the hallmark of the urban slum. Built at minimal cost, comprising a single room without electricity, toilet, or washing facilities, they are vulnerable not only to inclement weather conditions, but the vagaries of official policy on urban slums.[13] Just over one in ten sample households occupy such a dwelling, both as owners and tenants.

2. TENEMENTS, usually one-room flats with toilet, washing, and cooking facilities, in three or four storey blocks (see Wiebe 1981). They are built by the Tamil Nadu Housing Board or Tamil Nadu Slum Clearance Board for people belonging to 'Lower Income Groups' or 'Economically Weaker Sections'. Slum clearance flats are frequently built on or near the site of an existing hutment, expressly for its long-standing residents.

Most of the sample households living in such tenements—
13 per cent of domestic groups occupy this kind of accommodation—were previously in such settlements. Most pay
rent to the housing authority, though some have purchased
their flats under long-term mortgage repayment schemes.

3. QUARTERS, generally built of brick or other permanent
materials, comprising one or sometimes two room(s), as well as
cooking and washing/toilet facilities. Most such dwellings are
provided, at low, income-related rent, by employers—usually
public organizations such as the railways or police—for their
low-ranking employees. On leaving employment this accommodation must be vacated. Approximately 35 per cent of
sample households live in such tied dwellings.

4. APARTMENTS in multi-occupancy houses. Not infrequently,
they are in dwellings of a traditional design found in many
older parts of Madras. This consists of a single-storeyed row
of terraced houses—each of which is as deep as 30 metres—
stretching from one street to the next parallel road. Internally,
the effect is of tiny, separate 'apartments' on both sides of a
long narrow corridor. The arrangement provides little privacy,
since the divisions between apartments are *ad hoc*, usually consisting of lengths of material or, at best, thin wooden partitions.
Although each dwelling unit has its own cooking arrangements,
as many as ten may share outdoor washing and toilet facilities.
Just under a third of lower-class Protestant households occupy
this type of accommodation.

5. HOUSES, usually consisting of three rooms or more. These
are permanent structures, sometimes with tiny gardens, none
the less situated in the midst of a heterogeneity of less comfortable or spacious dwellings. They are mainly owner-
occupied. Ten per cent of lower class sample households live in
such houses. They are primarily those whose senior members
or their immediate forebears were early residents in the area,
and built these dwellings some time ago. This attests both to
the relatively low costs of land and building when the area was
less densely settled, and to the financial advantages enjoyed,
only a few decades ago, by workers with permanent employment in the formal sector.

Several points emerge from this outline of the spatial settings
in which these lower class Protestants reside. In the first place,

some three-quarters of the households pay rent for accommodation, and most of the owner-occupied dwellings have been purchased through a public housing scheme for the urban lower class. Secondly, very nearly half the domestic units occupy only one room, while about a third have two; the accommodation of only a small minority comprises three or more rooms.

Thirdly, there is no systematic relationship between type of accommodation and employment. Workers, whatever the nature of their employment, live in all five types of housing mentioned. Moreover, they share the same streets and slum settlements, tenement blocks and multi-occupancy houses, not only with other Protestants, but with members of other religious communities as well. They live cheek by jowl, know one another as neighbours and friends, and share certain crucial aspects of life-style and values generated by common material circumstances.

By contrast, the homes of Protestant élites are generally situated in pleasant surroundings, often in garden suburbs first created by European settlers, or in one of the numerous attractive colonies built since independence on the city's outskirts—like the suburb inhabited by members of the CSI-Southern church. The houses of the middle class often stand in their own grounds, surrounded by well-tended lawns. Internally they are comfortably furnished, with separate sleeping and reception areas, and with their own 'modern' kitchen, dining, and washing facilities. There is no sense of crowding here, no lack of space for study, or privacy when required.

Just under half of the middle-class sample households own the dwellings they live in, and despite ceilings on urban property holdings, several own a second or even third house which they let out. The great majority of dwellings were built or purchased by their current occupants. This is partly due to the recency of their migration to Madras, as I have already shown. It is also attributable to the growing availability of long-term, low-interest mortgage loans from various housing societies, or public agencies such as the Tamil Nadu Housing Board, which tends (somewhat at cross purposes with its original intention) to favour the well-to-do. Blomkvist notes how the TNHB offers better and more expensive public housing to persons in higher income brackets, a policy he thinks may be unique in India (1983: 18, esp. n. 3).

With the dramatic rise in land values as well as the costs of construction in the capital over the past two decades, the ownership of a home regarded as worthy of élites nowadays requires considerable resources. In one area south of the Adyar river, inhabited by several members of the CSI-Southern congregation, the price of one 'ground' (60′ × 40′) had risen between 1975 and 1981 by over three times, from approximately Rs 15,000 to Rs 50,000. Even a modest independent house requires 2-3 grounds, and in 1981-2 cost upwards of Rs 250,000 to build.[14] Yet a decision to construct a dwelling is indicative not only of financial viability, but of having reached a particular phase in a working life. The constant movement of a person from one posting to another, consequent on the pursuit of a career in government service or large-scale industry, demands a willingness to accept a series of temporary residences in various parts of the south or even outside it (see the case of M. S. above). By and large, the spatial mobility experienced in early and middle adult life make it difficult to establish roots in the form of a home in any one place. It is generally in the later stages of a successful working life, when (if) the individual reaches the summit of a career— in the process migrating to the capital—and in the certainty that there are unlikely to be any further transfers out of the city, that the purchase or construction of a home becomes a real possibility. A member of the CSI-Northern church observed that 'Near retirement you start thinking of a house— previously it was not possible because of transfers. You couldn't just build a place in Madras and leave it.'

Apart from the comparatively small minority of businessmen, self-employed professionals, or certain categories of government employee, whose responsibilities do not render them liable to transfer out of Madras and who can, therefore, acquire a home there at any point in their working lives (assuming no financial constraints), most of those following careers had bought or built their dwellings during the decade prior to and in some instances at the time of retirement.

Household composition

Just over 60 per cent of households in the lower class sample
are nuclear in composition (this includes a handful which are
'sub-nuclear', consisting, for the most part, of widows and their
unmarried children). In explaining the predominance of nuclear households, people frequently quote the scriptural in-
junction that 'A man shall leave father and mother, and shall
cleave unto his wife' (Gen. 2: 24; Matt. 19: 5; Mark 10: 7).
But an alternative—though by no means contradictory—ideal,
while not explicitly or consistently voiced, celebrates extended
family living, in as much as it acknowledges and positively
values the links obtaining among close kin, especially parents
and siblings—whether or not they actually reside together.
Only seven per cent of households were 'joint' at the time of
field-work.

Domestic units not infrequently include, for varying periods
of time, persons who are outside the core nuclear or joint unit.
One in three households in the sample are at present aug-
mented in this way. If we remember that the normative household is both patrilineally and virilocally based, then certain of
these relatives are lineally 'appropriate' and, from the stand-
point of household residents themselves, not regarded as additions to the group. Indeed, it would be inaccurate to describe
a married man's widowed parent (especially one who has never
resided elsewhere) as 'supplementary'—simply because the
death of a spouse or advancing years has shifted the brunt of
domestic responsibilities to the younger generation. Similarly,
the inclusion of a focal male's younger unmarried siblings is
unexceptional and the obligations involved are assumed as a
matter of course.

Other relatives are incorporated, however, who would not
traditionally be found in a domestic unit because they are not
qualified by the criterion of lineality. Households in the lower
class sample include, for instance, (reckoning from the female
focal householder) one or both of her parents; her siblings of
both sexes, and where the latter are married, their spouses and
children; her mother's brother's daughters and, in one instance,
her husband's mother's brother's daughter. With some regularity, too, households incorporate married daughters of the
focal couple and their husbands. Indeed, one group includes

two daughters along with their spouses and children. No stigma attaches to such arrangements: I certainly never heard any adverse comments about them, although by ordinary Indian standards they are unorthodox.

A distinction, therefore, may be drawn between those 'additional' relatives who are, by virtue of their lineal ties, appropriate for inclusion in the household, and those who are not. Obligations to persons in the first category are accepted as imperative, and vindicated by the weight of tradition in the wider south Indian society. Responsibility towards those in the latter category, mainly matrilateral kin, is undertaken with no less sense of duty, but is justified in terms of values based principally on affect and expressed in notions of love and compassion. Occasionally, moreover, these values may be linked explicitly to Christian ideas of morality, filial duty, and so forth.

The positive cultural evaluation accorded such a tendency both is encouraged by and, in its turn, encourages a wide spectrum of possible responses to the precariousness of economic life experienced by so many Christians of the lower class. A few, by no means uncommon, examples of household accretions will underline the point:

1. A woman, her husband and small children were compelled to give up their rented accommodation when he lost his teaching post with a private school, and received only minimal severance pay. When it became clear that he could not find another job, they were invited to join her sister's household which contains the latter's husband (who, like his wife, is employed) and their own two young children.

2. After marriage, a daughter (along with her new husband) remained in her parental home because, she explained, her husband's parents (with whom they would normally be expected to reside) do not live in Madras, and his present job is not yet secure or well-paid enough for them to set up a household of their own.

3. On reaching retirement, a man was compelled to vacate the quarters provided by his former employer. He and his wife, a former teacher, moved in with their daughter and her family, who have a small but secure income. The elderly couple contribute their own occupational (there are no state) pensions.

4. On the death of her parents, a woman brought her three unmarried sisters to live with her. Only one works and contributes a small amount; another is unable to find a job; while the youngest still attends school. The focal couple made it plain that they will assume responsibility for the marriages of the three girls.

It may be seen from these examples that households belonging to the lower class maintain flexible membership over time, a measure of readiness to incorporate close kin, having more regard for the needs of particular individuals than their lineal qualifications. However much scriptural or other cultural models are accepted as authoritative blueprints for domestic structures, material circumstances can intervene critically to influence their actual shape.

A roughly similar division between nuclear and joint units exists within the middle as within the lower class. Moreover, they are explained and assessed similarly. We can therefore, speak of a common set of ideals reinforcing, reflecting, and, to an extent, shaping domestic arrangements within the Protestant community as a whole. But such a conclusion would blur the rather different kinds of organizational features operating within the formal structure. Let me illustrate what I mean by reference to two recurrent processes affecting and distinguishing the nature of domestic groups in each class.

As I noted above, because of the highly localized nature of their occupations, householders in the lower class are unlikely to reside apart from their domestic groups. By contrast, individuals in the middle class are compelled, from time to time, to live away from the unit for varying periods, in furtherance of their careers. Since the focal couple in approximately one-third of the sample households are both working, the possibility that one spouse will be or has been transferred out of Madras at some stage is by no means remote. At the time of field-work in 1974-5 there were a handful of domestic units from which one of the focal householders was absent (including one woman who had gone to the USA for an advanced course in medicine, and another employed by the state medical services who had been promoted and transferred to another city). Even more commonly, unmarried sons leave the city as part of the process of 'spiralism', and may spend many months and sometimes several years resident away from the group. As often as not, young men of this class are working and resident in another town at the time of marriage. Unmarried daughters, by contrast, seldom live away from their domestic group, partly because they tend not to begin working before marriage and partly because it is considered inappropriate for a young woman to be independent of parental supervision. When circumstances compel daughters to live apart—as when, in the past, they came to Madras to attend an institution of higher education—arrangements are made for them to live either in hostels or with relatives, who act *in loco parentis*. Despite all such separations, of course, the individuals concerned remain members of the domestic unit. The point is that the bland notion of 'household' can conflate and so fail to identify the rather different residential patterns at different levels of the class order, based on distinctive forms of career development.

A similar observation can be made in regard to the way households compose and recompose themselves over time. It was noted how the precariousness of material life frequently leads to household arrangements within the lower class which, by urban Indian standards, are somewhat unorthodox. A number of middle-class domestic units, though not nearly so high a proportion, also contain, for greater or lesser periods, matrilateral (and, therefore, lineally 'inappropriate') relatives. But here the predisposing factor is not economic necessity. It involves, rather, a readiness to assist relatives in meeting specific and usually ephemeral problems generated by belonging to a privileged class, and contributes thereby to the retention of a position within that class. In his discussion of a similarly placed élite in Sierra Leone, Cohen observes how the organization of Creole family and household 'is geared to the full mobilization of capacities and resources for the production of professionals and civil servants' (1981: 67).

A number of domestic groups in the middle-class sample include the married daughters of focal householders whose executive husbands are working in parts of the country where the schools are considered unsuitable, and who therefore prefer to remain in Madras with their children, so that the latter can benefit from the better facilities in the capital. A few households contain the grandchildren of the focal couple, attending schools in Madras while both their parents are working elsewhere. Relatives residing in other parts of the state also send children here to study (in schools and universities) and, for such purposes, one domestic unit includes a son-in-law's unmarried sister and another sister's son. Households also contain a focal woman's sister and her daughter, whose husband/father is an army officer and temporarily posted to a remote part of the country, and a mother's brother's unmarried son who is in Madras for a management training scheme. Household composition among the middle class is clearly influenced not by the compelling demands of material insufficiency, but by a desire to continue to secure the best possible advantages in the educational and occupational fields.

INCOMES AND PROPERTY

The sole basis of livelihood for the overwhelming majority of lower class householders consists in the incomes earned from urban employment, or from pensions due to those previously employed. As we might expect, then, the range of earnings reflects the variety of occupations pursued by Protestants of this class. To provide a comparative context for the sample figures, we might utilize the income banding scheme devised by the Tamil Nadu Housing Board for assessing eligibility to various forms of housing. It identifies four income strata:

Higher Income Group (HIG)—earnings over Rs 1,500 per month
Middle Income Group (MIG)—earnings between Rs 601 and 1,500 per month
Lower Income Group (LIG)—earnings between Rs 351 and 600 per month
Economically Weaker Section (EWS)—earnings below Rs 350 per month.

Unfortunately, these bands have not been revised for a number of years (they were being utilized during both 1975 and 1981). Consequently, they do not reflect the rise either in the cost of living (or housing), or in incomes generally.

The average earnings of focal householders in the lower class sample is Rs 540. Approximately 44 per cent of men and 42 per cent of women fall within the MIG band, although with few exceptions they tend towards the lower end of the scale, i.e. under Rs 1,000. The majority (56 per cent of men and 58 per cent of women) earn LIG or EWS incomes. A far greater proportion of women (43.5 per cent, as against 27 per cent of men) earn less than Rs 350: over one-third have incomes under Rs 250. This reflects the facts that women are less educated than men, more restricted in the occupations they can pursue, and more likely to find themselves in unskilled and non-supervisory employment, without promotion prospects.

The overall level of earnings suggests, however, that these Protestants are better off than the generality of Madras residents. According to the Structure Plan for Madras Metropolitan Area: vol. 2 (1980), some 73 per cent of incomes in the city fall within the EWS band and a further 16 per cent within the LIG band (see Blomkvist 1983: 9-10). In terms of annual per capita income, too, these Protestants generate approximately twice the average Madras figure of Rs 1,151 (Tamilnadu Statistical Handbook 1980: 14). Furthermore, because so high a proportion of focal householders in the sample work in the formal sector, they enjoy many 'fringe' benefits—superannuation, pensions, access to loans, paid leave—which, while not readily expressible in money terms, are, as Worsley puts it, 'scarcely marginal additions to real income' (1981: 241).

A majority of domestic groups have more than one person receiving an income: in 35 per cent there are two earners; in 21 per cent three or more. Multiple sources obviously enable some households to accumulate quite respectable earnings, and, in 1981–2, one in five of these domestic groups could claim totals of over Rs 1,500 per month (i.e. incomes within the HIG band). Generally, such levels of earnings are short-lived, however, since unmarried sons and daughters, or 'additional' household members in employment usually leave the domestic unit sooner or later.

I indicated earlier the greater likelihood that members of the domestic unit outside the focal couple itself will be either in jobs within the unorganized sector, or without employment altogether. My informants nowadays speak of a steadily contracting set of employment opportunities for young people in the lower class. Young men, and especially those without specific technical skills, find it increasingly difficult to obtain work and, if they do, are compelled to accept long periods as temporary employees, i.e. without the protection of labour legislation or the benefits available to permanent workers. On numerous occasions I was told that permanent status should have been granted (often was promised) after completion of a stipulated trial, training, or apprenticeship period; but when the time came, temporary status was merely renewed. Firms, especially in the private sector, seem increasingly reluctant to allow workers to make the transition into permanent employment with the security of tenure this implies. The advantages to these enterprises of having a pool of casual, non-unionized, and low-paid labour needs no elaboration. This kind of occupational relegation is now being experienced to a far greater extent than before, or so it appears to these Protestants. Focal householders note the difference between this situation and their own experiences of finding work and acquiring security a decade or two ago. There is a growing feeling that their children are unlikely to exceed, if indeed to match, their own achievements.

Wider trends in the economy help to explain these by no means unwarranted fears. The considerable economic activity of the quarter century beginning with the Second World War has no echo in the contemporary period. But by any measure, according to Shetty (1978), the performance of the economy since the mid-sixties has been unsatisfactory. The tendencies which have most directly affected ordinary Indians are what he describes as 'very negligent' employment growth, with 'absolute stagnation' in private sector employment (ibid.: 213); a quadrupling of unemployment during the decade 1966–76; large increases in the cost of living for the lower income groups (ibid.: 215); and a general 'deepening' of the 'character of urban poverty' (ibid.: 211). Other economists have reported that real wages in manufacturing industries for the lowest paid have 'gone down severely' since 1961 (Sau 1981: 81). In the same period, expenditure on labour in the public sector has decreased to 12 per cent from 36 per cent in terms of the value of annual production (Iyer 1982: 17).

Such developments in the wider economy filter into the local setting and are experienced directly as insufficient job opportunities, fewer chances for secure employment, inadequate and unstable earnings, and the like. These Protestants, like the lower class generally, are unable to defend themselves against such forms of exploitation. Therborn observes how conditions like this serve as 'ideological mechanisms' of fear and harassment (1980: 98).

Focal householders in the middle-class sample earn an average monthly income of Rs 2,340—at 1981 figures.[15] This is approximately 4.3 times that of their co-religionists in the lower class sample, and accords with Peace's data on a similar group in Jaipur whose 'incomes exceed lower class ones by a factor of four or five' (1980: 255). Women's earnings are considerably less than men's, averaging between one-third and one-half the latters'. This reflects the lower status jobs they do.

Turning from individuals to domestic groups, there are 1.58 earners per middle-class household (as compared with 1.76 for lower class units). This gives us an average household income of Rs 3,100 (1981–2) or 3.2 times the lower class average. Middle-class domestic groups have a per capita income of Rs 630 per month against Rs 187 for those in the lower class sample (i.e. 3.3 times greater).

Middle-class households are equally dependent on their urban incomes. With a growing commitment to city life in general, and Madras in particular, these élites are increasingly investing their income in property. Parkin's comment on the relation between occupation and property ownership in Western societies serves equally to describe trends evident in Madras as, no doubt, in other metropolitan centres. Inequalities are not generated principally through the inheritance of great wealth, but 'much more commonly by way of accumulation of modest wealth on the part of those in well rewarded occupations. Thus to characterize the occupational order as the backbone of the reward structure is not to ignore the role of property, but to acknowledge the interrelationship between the one and the other' (F. Parkin 1972: 24). In Madras, all segments of the middle class are brought together by common interests in property and the success of capital. Virtually every domestic group in the sample now holds some assets in the form of urban land, bank savings, industrial shares, government stocks and bonds, insurance policies, and, of course, house

ownership.[16] In an acknowledgement of middle-class accumulation, as well as inflation, the government in early 1982
announced its intention to raise the limit for wealth tax from
Rs 150,000 to Rs 250,000, and estate duty from Rs 50,000 to
Rs 250,000 (excluding the value of a house up to Rs 100,000).

CONCLUSION: SUMMARY AND COMPARISON

The Protestant community, no less than any other, was affected
by changes which occurred in the environment of late
nineteenth-century south India. A near-uniformly indigent
body of rural converts and their immediate descendants became differentiated as to education, occupation, and wealth.
A substantial minority began movements to urban places and,
in time, to the metropolitan centre of the Presidency. To conclude the first part of the book, and by way of summarizing
the discussion in this chapter, I want to reiterate some of the
more significant distinctions between Protestants associated
with different levels of the urban class order.
    I have examined the nature of Protestant migration and
suggested that both the underlying motives for and patterns of
this movement reflected the existing differentiation within the
community. Lower class householders trace their origins to
villages mainly in districts adjacent to the capital, whence they
came directly to the city. Householders of the middle-class have
entered the capital more recently—mainly during the past 20
years—though from a heterogeneity of locations throughout
south India. The latter are, none the less, much longer separated from their rural origins, having moved by a process of
'step migration' from urban place to urban place.
    The principal Protestant migrations occurred in response
to infrastructural growth and economic developments in the
metropolitan region during the second and third quarters of
this century, and especially following independence. For the
majority, migration represented a gamble on an urban future,
the only apparent alternative to poverty and famine, and the
bleak prospects offered by life in the rural areas, especially
of north Tamilnadu. Constrained by inadequate educational
qualifications, economic resources, and personal influence,

these Protestants could only seek and hope to find work in the more humble reaches of the occupational structure.

A minority, whose forebears had been able to take full advantage of mission schools and colleges (where, mainly, English was the medium of instruction), and who are themselves even greater beneficiaries of this educational system, entered Madras either to fill positions in the most senior echelons of existing and newly established organizations, or to pursue qualifications which would enable them to do so. These careers were becoming available for the first time—in independent India—to indigenous personnel, as a result not only of expansion on a variety of fronts (administrative, commercial, industrial) but of the removal of European élites from their pre-eminent place in society. The success of the Dravidian movement was an additional factor assisting their entry into the top ranks of the opportunity structure.

The occupations these Protestants pursued may be categorized in a number of ways: manual or non-manual; part of the formal or informal sector; and whether or not involving the ownership of capital and employment of labour. While the identification of these various classificatory schemata enhance awareness of the complexities of urban economic organization, they are inadequate in three senses. In the first place, they convey a notion of rigidity between the divisions which may distort the reality. Secondly, they are outsiders' categories which, though helpful for description and understanding, do not necessarily enter the consciousness of subjects, and fail adequately to reflect their own perceptions of the employment situation. Occupations, career prospects, and job opportunities are not evaluated in terms of their affiliation with particular economic spheres. Protestants of the lower class have what may be described as a contextual view, grading employments in terms of whether they are seen to offer an immediate improvement (whether in income or security) on previous or present job circumstances. Middle-class evaluations focus much more on future career prospects, and on appropriate status benefits in the long term. Both are realistic assessments of conditions in the employment market.

Finally, and emerging from the foregoing, persons engaged in formally distinct sectors are kin, affines, neighbours, and friends. And they are, moreover, co-householders. Those who are themselves capitalists and others who support capitalism as managers and executives are so linked, as are less privileged workers in various labour spheres. This has two direct consequences. The first is that disparate personal employment circumstances and the incomes they generate are shared within and, therefore, 'experienced' by domestic groups. Holmstrom has noted that although industrial workers engaged in the formal sector earn twice as much as comparable employees in the informal sphere, differences in family incomes are much less. This confirms his impression that such incomes are often 'spread thin among casual or temporary workers or unemployed relatives within the household' (1984: 271).

Domestic arrangements at both levels of the class order seem to confirm the propensity noted by many writers—including Vatuk (1971) on India—for urbanization to be accompanied by an increasing stress on matrilateral relatives among peoples with a patrilineal bias in their traditional kin groups. Among Protestants in Madras the strength of a woman's ties with matrilateral relatives is manifested not only in more frequent contacts but, with considerable frequency, in their sharing the same domestic unit.

The reason could lie, as I noted, in the existence of an alternative set of values, identified as Christian, to which the importance of love and compassion in non-lineal ties can be related. Moreover, we cannot ignore the material circumstances which compel households to absorb lineally diverse relatives. These may help to overcome difficult and even desperate economic conditions within lower class households, or, alternatively, serve to guarantee a domestic unit's place within the privileged élite.

Urban occupations provide the main source of income and access to property. Not only does a much smaller proportion of the lower class own property in the form of a house and land in the city, but the extent and value of the property owned is considerably less than that held by middle-class households. Furthermore, to recall Frank Parkin's important distinction, these assets are *possessions* rather than *capital* (1982: 183). By contrast, virtually all middle-class domestic units have property both in the sense of possessions and in the form of savings or industrial bonds and shares from which they derive income. The latter thus have a growing stake in the success of capital, not simply in their capacity as senior executives, top bureaucrats, professionals, or small industrialists, but increasingly as owners of urban property-as-capital.

Protestants belonging to the middle class in Madras most typically articulate a three-generation mobility model—which is sometimes referred to as the 'butler line': from domestic servant in one generation to mission school teacher in the next, to senior executive, engineer, etc. in this. Such a model faithfully represents the overall process of mobility which they have experienced, even if the time span is somewhat telescoped. In a significant minority of cases, the third stage in the mobility process occurred a generation ago. But in most instances the movement has occurred in the present generation of adults. They are better educated and employed than their parents. The occupations they perform demand more advanced technical knowledge, carry wider responsibilities, bring higher incomes, and are held in greater esteem. Distinctions between the generations, in brief, are such as to constitute a substantial difference of position in the class order.

The growth of a middle class within the Protestant community must be of some significance for students of Indian society, since it seems to qualify the widely held assumption that traditional élite communities invariably monopolize the top echelons of the urban class order. Thus, in his study of Bangalore, Gist noted that high castes are 'oriented' towards high status occupations (1954: 130), a point echoed by others (see Béteille 1969: 232). Most writers seem agreed, moreover, that it is the acquisition of the relevant educational qualifications which is the key to this process. Since, on the whole, it is the castes at the top of any local hierarchy which have enjoyed most the fruits of advanced education, the equation between high caste and high class follows naturally.

Many Protestants now in the middle class, however, managed to acquire higher education despite their association with castes at the lower end of the traditional ritual hierarchy (and many had no affiliation at all). This is attributable mainly to their privileged access to mission schooling and employment, but, as we have seen, other factors must also be taken into account if we are to comprehend more fully the complex social processes of mobility into the dominant class. The language of learning, the association of siblings in the migration process, and the extent and influence of networks were a few of the ingredients identified as of significance in this 'spiralism'.

Even then, caste is not altogether insignificant in the process. It cannot be regarded as coincidental that while those of out-caste origin constitute a majority of the Protestant population in south India, probably very nearly half the community in Madras, and a similar fraction of the lower class sample, they form an extremely tiny proportion of the middle-class (hardly three per cent of the sample). Even if some of those with mixed caste affiliation (see Chapter 6) are in fact Harijan or part-Harijan in origin, this would not significantly alter the balance. While all converts were, in principle, given equal encouragement and opportunity to take advantage of mission educational facilities, outcastes were not singled out for special consideration or 'positive discrimination', and so found it difficult to compete successfully with others whose circumstances were generally more favourable. Ironically, in independent India, Protestants of such backgrounds were denied the benefits and concessions granted by the Constitution to other (Hindu) Harijans, thus making their position no less difficult than it had been in the past.

But, if it was possible until quite recently for a small minority of Protestants emanating from a variety of depressed (though not untouchable) backgrounds to make their way into the middle class, such mobility is incomparably more difficult today. The growing scarcity of opportunities in the economy, as the rapid developments of the immediate post-war and post-independence periods have ground to a halt, has encouraged a near siege mentality among those already within the dominant class. They cling desperately to the most lucrative and prestigious kinds of employment, as to the degrees and courses providing access to such employment. They do so in the face of the most intense competition from non-Christians of the same class, as well as co-religionists who would aspire to improve their life chances. Protestants belonging to the lower class, even if they acquire the necessary educational qualifications, cannot now compete successfully against those who command the heights of the opportunity structure, since their networks of informal relationships are limited mainly to persons of their own standing. There has been, as Saberwal suggests, 'a decline in the mobility role of education' (1978: 243). The already narrow avenues of advancement which once existed appear to have contracted even further, as the middle class has closed ranks to defend existing privileges. This kind of closure, Giddens suggests, facilitates the formation of 'identifiable classes' (1982: 159). The process is marked and aided, moreover, by an intensification of the cultural divide between the classes. It is to the cultural dimension of this opposition that our attention now turns.

4

THE MESSAGES OF CONSUMPTION
Goods, Leisure, and Ritual Affiliation

INTRODUCTION

In the north Indian city of Jaipur, Peace remarks, there is not only a clearly defined system of class stratification, but it has a 'considerable degree of rigidity and "closedness". The division between middle class and lower class is firmly established ...' (1980: 259). In Madras, too, we can detect within the Protestant community the existence of very nearly closed circles of privilege, on the one hand, and relative privation, on the other. Among these Christians, moreover, the distinctions are neither shaped nor expressed solely in economic terms. We have seen that some households in the lower class do accumulate incomes which exceed those of the middle class and that their members occasionally acquire educational qualifications and even employments no less respectable than those attained by householders (especially women) of the middle class. Thus, by such criteria alone, the demarcations are not invariably clear cut. It is within the cultural domain that the boundaries between the classes become more apparent and immutable.

Although many anthropologists refer to culture in holistic terms, we are unable to comprehend it, either descriptively or analytically, as an integrated unity which embodies the collective representations of an otherwise differentiated society or community. Cultures (or, if you prefer, sub-cultures), like groups, are ranked, and in relationships of opposition and struggle. Cultural wholes evade us in a different sense as well. At best, we can highlight only some of the ideas and meanings which arise within a group or class, only certain of the 'lived traditions and practices through which [cultural] understandings are expressed and in which they are embodied' (Hall 1981*b*: 26). In the ensuing discussion I explore aspects of culture which are manifested in consumption behaviour. Following Douglas and Isherwood (1978) I find it useful to distinguish between small- and large-scale modes of consumption. The former concentrate, to a degree out of necessity, on expenditures close at hand—within the household, family, and neighbourhood. One effect of this concentration of resources is to intensify existing relationships. The latter, by contrast, direct income not only to strengthening such bonds, but in two other principal directions. The first concerns the purchase and display of luxury goods; the second, more importantly, involves expenditure on the development of extensive contacts and networks of information. The former constitute the visible messages of consumption, the latter its invisible messages. The differential patterns will be seen to assist in the establishment and reinforcement of class boundaries, situate distinctive values and attitudes within them, and communicate—to the participants themselves as well as to the observer—at least as much about social inequality as occupation and income distribution.

THE VISIBLE MESSAGES OF CONSUMPTION

While the growth of India's basic and capital goods industries has slowed considerably during the past two decades, the output of 'elite-oriented' commodities has risen 'astronomically'. This expansion, moreover, has occurred at the expense of investment in mass consumption goods (Shetty 1978: 197–201).[1]

The industries which produce such commodities, needless to say, apply considerable resources to the stimulation of a market for their wares. On any day, an English-language newspaper such as the *Hindu*, published in Madras, will contain numerous enticing advertisements for a host of expensive luxury commodities, each in its own way conveying the message that these products not only belong in a middle-class home, but actually help to define it as such.[2] Their customers, drawn from a small, affluent, and mainly urban segment of the population have, for their part, responded by establishing a high level of demand for these manufactures. Sau estimates that the top 10 per cent of the population consumes approximately 36 per cent of the total supply of industrial goods (1981: 49). Another way of expressing it, according to Kurien, is that 'industrial production is geared mainly for the sake of the top section in society . . . the scarce resources of the economy tend to gravitate towards areas of production which cater to the demands of the affluent few' (1974: 55). By contrast, a very large part of the urban population consumes little industrial output. If anything, the per capita consumption of the bottom 40 per cent of the population in Indian cities has been declining.

Protestant householders in the middle class are certainly among these privileged consumers. Their costly and generally spacious homes are comfortably, even (by European tastes) elegantly appointed. They have living, dining, and bedroom suites, telephones, television sets, video recorders, and, where there are teenage children in the house, a variety of other electronic goods (stereo or hi-fi equipment, radio-cassettes, etc.).[3]

Their kitchens are equally well-equipped, containing refrigerators, gas stoves,[4] pressure-cookers, and other gadgetry to assist in making meals. Even then, virtually every domestic unit employs at least one servant and at least a third have two or more. Most commonly, they come in on a daily basis to help with the preparation of food, washing-up, and general cleaning, but not with cooking. In the most well-to-do households, or in those where both husband and wife are busily engaged outside the home, additional servants—cook, driver, gardener, or *ayah* (nursemaid)—may be hired.[5]

Finally, the means of transport available to a household indicates, as much as the lavishness of the dwelling, its capacity for and level of consumption. The majority (60 per cent) of domestic units in the middle-class sample have cars, which involve considerable investments to purchase and substantial outlays to keep on the road. Householders who are provided with a car (and possibly a driver) by their employers are usually those in the most senior positions who can afford to own and run a second, private vehicle—and frequently do. The remaining domestic units tend to have motor scooters with which to get around, and these, too, are by no means inexpensive to purchase or maintain.[6]

The well-to-do thus convert income into consumer products which, not singly but in concert, make visible statements about their position in the urban hierarchy and the life-styles to which they subscribe: in short, about the kind of social space they see themselves in and wish others to see them inhabiting. These communications are directed primarily at others of like station who understand and interpret the messages. One important effect of this kind of consumption, therefore, quite apart from its distortion of national or regional resource allocation, is that it marks, by means of tangible symbols, the boundaries between the social classes.

The same messages are, if not intended for, certainly read by members of the lower class as signals of exclusion. Indeed, their perception of the distinctions between the strata are frequently articulated in terms of consumption rather than income. One informant summed up the contrast like this: 'They have cars and nice bungalows, with plenty of furniture, tv sets and electric grinders. We have none of these things. We grind with our own hands.' The latter reference is to the fact that several of the most common dishes in the diet of ordinary south Indians require the grain or pulses to be ground to a fine powder.

The housing conditions of lower class Protestants have already been referred to in Chapter 3. It was noted that the great majority inhabit small, cramped accommodation in squatter settlements, slum clearance tenements, multi-family houses or employer-provided, occupation-linked quarters. Because of overcrowding, every existing space must serve many purposes. 'In the morning and evening this is our dining room; during the day our drawing room; and at night our bedroom.' Concern is frequently expressed at the lack of privacy for families or individuals, and the difficulties which these conditions can create. I have been told of their potential health hazards, of how they restrict opportunities for children to study, and of the strains they encourage in inter-personal relationships, both within the household and among neighbours.

The inventory of consumer goods in these homes presents a striking contrast with that found among the middle class. Indeed, a few years ago, members of the élite CSI-Northern congregation were encouraged to think about these differences when the church magazine itemized what they would have to do if suddenly and dramatically reduced in circumstances. Among the consequences listed were (a) take away the house itself and move the family into a small room; (b) remove virtually all the furniture; (c) dismantle the bathroom; (d) get rid of most of the books and magazines and cancel subscriptions to newspapers. This was hardly an exaggeration, and it might have included the need to dispose of all luxury goods.

While very occasionally one comes across a conspicuously expensive product (such as a television set) in the midst of an otherwise sparsely furnished home—a point to which I will return later—the living areas of lower class dwellings tend rarely to contain more than a bed, a table, and a couple of straight-backed chairs. Small possessions and documents are stored in a metal trunk, and clothes hung from a line strung across the room. A few family photographs and religious mottoes on the walls,[7] a Bible and several tracts, a clock and, perhaps, a radio complete the household's meagre stock of possessions.

Kitchens usually contain only the traditional cooking and eating vessels which a woman brings to her marriage, and perhaps a single kerosene stove, but there are seldom any 'modern' labour-saving devices to facilitate the preparation of meals. Moreover, fewer than a quarter of the sample lower class households can afford to employ even a part-time servant. It is women, of course, who bear the brunt of this deficiency, rising early to prepare the day's meals (south Indian cooking is very time-consuming) and, as the majority are employed outside the home, returning after work to resume their domestic chores.

The consumption tendencies of members of this class are, not surprisingly, weighted in favour of food commodities. This is a common phenomenon among the less well-off. For India as a whole, Shetty quotes figures which suggest that the lowest 30 per cent of the urban population allocate between 77 and 80 per cent of their expenditures to food (1978: 212). My estimates for the households in the sample are between 60 and 70 per cent, which probably indicates, as I have already noted, that these Christians are not concentrated in the very lowest sectors of the class. The principal diet consists of a morning meal of steamed rice and lentil cakes (*iṭli*) or stuffed rice and lentil pancakes (*tōsai*) and coffee, and an evening meal of boiled rice and a curry dish. Hence, a substantial part of the budget is spent on unprocessed foods (sugar for coffee is one exception):

whole grains (mainly rice), lentils, fresh vegetables, fish, and, less regularly, meat.

Middle-class households, by contrast, spend a much lower proportion of income on food: the Protestant sample suggests between 40 and 45 per cent, which accords with the figures given by Shetty for the top 5 per cent of the urban population (1978: 212). However, although they allocate less as a proportion, it will be appreciated that they nevertheless have a great deal more to spend in money terms. Hence, they can afford to buy (a) better quality staples (those available under the ration scheme are commonly thought to be inferior); (b) more high protein foods, such as milk, eggs, and curds; (c) a greater range of edibles (e.g. fruit, poultry); and, increasingly, (d) the packaged products manufactured by large companies (e.g. baby food, tinned cheese, cereals, powdered milk, and vitamin tablets). Thus, even within the 'subsistence' sphere, the quality and type of food consumed announce distinctions of rank.

The most important way in which the consumption patterns of householders belonging to the middle class differ from those beneath them, however, is in their concern to extend relationships outside the immediate confines of family and neighbourhood. We saw, in Chapter 3, how access to jobs and promotions at senior-most levels of the occupational structure depend not only on possession of the relevant qualifications and experience, but equally if not more crucially on having a well-placed network of formal and informal contacts. Consequently, those who seek to preserve or extend their privileges must channel substantial resources to the cultivation of relationships within the élite. It is in this sphere that 'honour and preferment are to be had . . .' (Douglas and Isherwood 1978: 197) and within it lie the hidden messages of consumption.

THE JOYS OF TAMIL AND THE BENEFITS OF ENGLISH

Tamilnadu vigorously promotes knowledge and use of Tamil—it is the language of the state legislature, public ceremonials, and interactions with most officialdom.[8] Yet only mastery of English, as already noted, provides access to the professions and the top echelons of the occupational order. Executives, managers, and senior members of central bureaucratic organizations who have dealings in other parts of the country as well as abroad must, of course, be able to communicate in English. This much is recognized by all sections of the Protestant community. But, as one householder who speaks only Tamil pointed out, 'nowadays people like us who get ordinary jobs do not need to know any other language'. In any case, those in the lower class appreciate that the level of English competence which enables people to pursue the most favoured educational and career opportunities can really only be gained in private schools from which they are effectively excluded. In these exclusive institutions, the children of the Protestant middle class acquire not only fluency in the language (and an ability to pass public examinations). Just as importantly, they make acquaintances and sometimes close and lasting friendships with children from a variety of castes and religious backgrounds within the same class.

English also provides a passport to a comprehensive life-style which is most commonly glossed as 'Western'. The missionaries who sought converts in south India were anxious to stress the European face of Christianity, and, in the context of its association with the dominant power at the time, this had an obvious appeal (see Chapter 2). Converts, especially those who entered the faith outside the mass movements and left their villages to seek the safety and benefits of the mission compound took (or were given) Western names and imitated the missionaries' modes of 'food, dress and deportment' (Pathak 1967: 71).[9]

As Protestants entered the urban middle class they adopted certain of the interests and pursuits of the dominant European élite. Thus, many studied Western classical music and learned to play its instruments: it is still not uncommon to discover a piano as the centre-piece of a middle-class drawing-room, and children continue to receive instruction. These same Christians provide the main audiences today for musical recitals by both local and visiting artistes from Europe and North America, and are the driving force behind the still active Madras Musical Association, founded in 1893 by Europeans in the city to promote and perform Western classics. There are also choirs attached to most of the city's élite churches (see below) which keep alive the tradition of sacred choral music established by the expatriate colony. Among lower class Christians, however, interest focuses principally on Tamil 'lyrics', the devotional songs of popular fundamentalist preachers, (Negro) 'spirituals', and more modern forms of gospel music sung in and now imported from the West. There are numerous choirs in Madras performing such music.

At the same time, Protestants all but ignored the south Indian classical music tradition. Missionaries discouraged such an interest partly to promote their own hymns and sacred music, but mainly because they (rightly) saw in the Carnatic mode a direct expression of devotion to Hindu deities (see L'Armand and L'Armand 1978). Although there have, for many years, been sporadic attempts to fuse Christian liturgy with indigenous musical structures, for the most part, Prot= estants remain uninterested and unattracted to this art form. The same applies to Bharata Natyam, the south Indian dance tradition. Indeed, while I was in Madras the decision of a prominent family to sponsor the public dance début of their daughter raised a considerable number of eyebrows and led to correspondence in the parochial press. This is one of several instances that came to my notice of élite Protestants emulating their class counterparts within the Hindu community by adopting what are generally thought of as prestigious Hindu ways of behaviour. Those who defended the decision stressed that 'what is a religious experience for a Hindu can be enjoyed as a cultural experience by a Christian' (Devanesan 1980: 7).

But these are very recent and sporadic occurrences. On the whole, association with what were regarded as 'Western ways' became the preferred life-style of the better-situated members of the Christian community. Only such people, I have been told, 'were thought—or thought themselves—to be cultured'. With the rise of nationalism the generality of Indians came to associate these Christians with the British, and to revile them for what was seen as their contempt for their Indian heritage. Gandhi complained that 'aping' Europeans did 'violence to their country ... even to their new religion', and found it 'deplorable' that so many Indian Christians 'cut themselves adrift from the nation' (1964: 92).[10]

The image of Christians held by the society at large has changed considerably since independence. This is to some extent because many of them are known to have supported the nationalist struggle and subsequently the Dravidian movement, and are acknowledged to have played (and to be playing) an important role in the development of modern Tamil literature. But more importantly, the urban well-to-do, whatever their religious affiliation, have almost uniformly adopted many of the accoutrements of 'Westernization'—in their dress, occupations, speech, and leisure. Christians are, therefore, no longer seen as a cultural fifth-column. With the exodus of Europeans from independent India, moreover, it is the indigenous middle class which determines what is the *appropriate* life-style.

The acquisition of an English medium education in an exclusive private institution is virtually the only way of ensuring access to the limited number of places in the better medical and engineering colleges of the state for which Christians—as a 'Forward Community'—may compete. The increasing possibilities to work abroad for persons qualified in these fields has intensified the competition for these scarce facilities.[11] During the past decade, medical and, even more so, engineering graduates have virtually acquired preferred immigrant status in the USA, an acknowledgement not only of the high standards achieved in India's better educational centres, but of the considerable advantages to the West of importing personnel already trained at another country's expense. Zachariah reports that 20 per cent of graduates from Christian Medical College in Vellore—which is reputed to offer the best medical training in south India if not the entire country—go abroad to work (1981: 43). Further, according to a report in the *Hindu* (13 April 1982) 75 per cent of all the 1981 B.Tech. graduates in electronics (and half of those in the engineering branch) from the five Indian Institutes of Technology (IITs) in the country—there is one in Madras—left for the USA. While in 1965 a mere 500 'Asian Indians' were permitted to settle in that country, by 1980 the annual quota had reached 22,000.

Numerous articles in Indian newspapers and glossy magazines extol the considerable material advantages enjoyed by the Indian population in the United States, which is now estimated at 360,000 people. A former American ambassador to

India is reported to have remarked that 'no ethnic minority of recent entry is as affluent' (*Hindu*, 5 October 1981). The result is that, today, further studies, employment, and eventual settlement abroad is perhaps the most desirable prospect for suitably qualified members of the middle class. Half the households in the middle-class sample now have a parent, sibling, or child living in the West. And while the difficulties of maintaining close bonds at such a distance are acknowledged, the considerable advantages which accrue in terms of future prospects for the family are seen to make the drawbacks worth bearing. These Protestants, like the middle class as a whole, allocate finances not simply to enhance a child's career prospects, but in the not unrealistic expectation of establishing and building an extensive web of ties reaching to every (affluent) corner of the globe.

Other forms of consumption generate networks closer at hand, with persons of the same standing both within and outside the community. This brings us to the principal 'leisure' activities of middle-class Protestants.

LEISURE AND THE PURSUIT OF INFORMATION

Perhaps the most important contexts in which such links are forged are provided by the various select social or recreational clubs in the city. Many of these were established by Europeans during the latter part of the colonial period and, for a time, deliberately excluded Indians from their ranks.[12] There were Masonic lodges, associations focused on cricket, sailing, music, and drama, a Caledonian society (for the Scots), and a variety of other 'gentlemen's' clubs.[13] European women also created a number of welfare organizations to provide assistance for the European, Eurasian, and indigenous poor (see P. Caplan 1978).

The proliferation of European 'clubbism' in the late nineteenth century was at least partly related to the rise of an indigenous middle class resulting from the gradual Indianization of the upper reaches of the occupational and mercantile structures. As they assumed positions of greater responsibility, the traditional working relationships presupposing European superordination and Indian subordination underwent profound changes. Furthermore, with greater wealth, these modern élites

began moving into what had been exclusively expatriate neighbourhoods (see Lewandowski 1975: 355). One kind of European
response to this 'encroachment' on their traditional preserves involved a stringent emphasis on social distance in leisure contexts.
Segregation in exclusive associations reinforced the links among
Europeans, already tied by a common cultural background and
life-style in India.[14]

Middle-class Indians responded by creating their own Westernized associations at the end of the last century, although in
several instances they were open to expatriates and even intended to 'further social intercourse between Indian and European Gentlemen in Madras' (see Lewandowski 1980: 148). As
independence grew nearer, restrictions on joining most European sodalities were lifted, and just as indigenous élites began
to replace expatriates in the upper reaches of the occupational
order, so they assumed their places in a whole range of recreational organizations. Moreover, the variety of such associations grew considerably in the post-independence period.

Protestants are certainly active participants in this clubbism.
Within the middle-class sample, approximately one half of male
householders belong to such organizations. Nowadays, they are
found in a host of tennis, golf, and chess clubs, among the
Rotarians, Lions, Masons, and Round Tablers, and as members
of the Gymkhana, Royal Yacht, Cricket, Cosmopolitan, Presidency, Madras, and other exclusive clubs. Although Christians
do occasionally join secular women's organizations in the city,
these tend mainly to be run by and cater for Brahmin women
(P. Caplan 1985).

Some of these sodalities are local chapters of Western-based
international organizations, but even those without foreign ties
retain or cultivate a European structure and ethos. There are
regular meetings, as well as national and international conventions to attend, charitable projects in which to participate,
and a continuous round of activities making demands on members' time, energies, and finances—ladies' nights, guest nights,
film shows, sports competitions, and so forth. The atmosphere
in most such clubs is almost studiously foreign. Among the men,
especially, there is an exclusive use of English, an emphasis on
casual European dress, a preference for Western humour, even
a stress on drinking. All of these predilections create what is

thought of as a sophisticated milieu. The common understandings which emerge among persons belonging to such organizations are, therefore, not embodied in written codes and hardly, if at all, articulated explicitly. They involve, rather, a form of discourse which identifies its exponents as part of a select cultural group.

These Protestants thus invest heavily in extending their networks of friends and acquaintances within the dominant class, and acquire or reinforce an already acquired set of behaviours and outlooks shared with others at the same social level, whatever their religious affiliation. By so doing they gain access to certain vital forms of knowledge, the preserve of a privileged minority. They become, pre-eminently, as Douglas and Isherwood put it, consumers of 'information goods' (1978: 181). The benefits of the widespread connections so established may be direct, in the form of immediate preferment (as we have seen in Chapter 3), or diffuse and effective over the long term. Whichever, such benefits are refracted throughout the extent of their daily lives, both within and outside the work context. The overall implications of such informal relationships among élites have been demonstrated on more than one occasion by Cohen, most recently in his work on the Creoles of Sierra Leone (1971, 1981).

SERVING GOD AND ACQUIRING MERIT

Apart from involvement in this kind of cosmopolitan club life, these householders also occupy themselves in a variety of more specifically Christian activities. In addition to its formal ecclesiastical concerns, the church has responsibility for the operation of a variety of educational, medical, and other social service institutions. The proper care and functioning of these enterprises relies to a large extent on Protestant lay persons voluntarily contributing their time, knowledge, and experience. The Madras diocese, with its headquarters in the state capital, is not unnaturally one of the wealthiest and most active. It has an extensive and variegated network of organizations under its direct control, and requires a considerable number of volunteers to help run its numerous affairs. Because only the better-off can contribute their time in this way, and possess the special skills, qualifications, and contacts required, the lay leadership at the diocesan level tends to be drawn from those belonging mainly to the top social stratum.

A predominant role is taken by retired senior bureaucrats, executives, and professionals, who fill many of the key administrative posts in CSI establishments on a more or less honorary basis. The middle-class sample contains numerous individuals who are or were principals, managers, correspondents and governors of schools and colleges, administrators of hospitals, wardens of homes for the aged, and executive officers of the diocese itself.

Their Christian activities, moreover, are not confined only to the diocese. They are or were directors of the Christian Literature Society, managers of Bible institutes, leading participants in associations such as the YMCA, YWCA, Co-workers of Mother Teresa, and Toc H, and senior officials in numerous other organizations, including the World Council of Churches.

Individuals generally explain their readiness to offer this assistance in terms of 'serving God'. What is plain is that, having achieved some prominence and wealth in their lives, they acquire, by lending their abilities to the church and other Christian organizations in this way, what may be described as ritual 'merit'. This entitles them, in turn, to public recognition and the applause of the community. And it would be a rare individual who could or would expect to be held in high esteem by other Christians without this regard being earned, at least in part, by such 'social work'. But apart from the ritual reinforcement of their position within the community's dominant segment, the investment of time, effort, and, not infrequently, personal resources, in service to the Christian cause, enables these middle-class Protestants, whether intentionally or not, to enhance and reinforce their already extensive information networks.

By contrast, householders at a similar stage in life among the lower class do not possess the qualifications and previous work experience to be invited to assume positions of responsibility in these organizations. Nor do they possess the kinds of resources— contacts, English-language facility, finances, personal transport—which would enable them effectively to donate their services even if called upon to do so. Almost without exception, those in the sample who have reached retirement age are 'at home'. These Protestants, already refused the material advantages enjoyed by their middle-class co-religionists, seem thereby to be denied access to the community's moral rewards as well (see Sharma 1980: 5). It goes without saying that they are excluded from 'club life' on similar grounds. Some do become members of recreational associations at their places of work, and attend the occasional sports activities and picnic outings arranged by these organizations for the families of employees. A handful belong to political parties (usually the DMK or the ADMK)[15] or trade unions, and spend some of their spare time doing such work. But, for the most part, leisure hours are spent visiting or being visited by relatives and friends in the neighbourhood (or less frequently in other parts of the city) and reading at home (the Bible and religious books or magazines). An occasional evening out might involve a visit to the cinema, but is more likely to mean attending a gospel meeting to hear 'the word of God' from a popular fundamentalist preacher and listen to a choir sing religious songs. People also invest their spare time participating in local prayer groups which meet regularly in a nearby hall or private home to pray, 'witness', and perhaps engage in some form of collective healing. Leisure among most ordinary Protestants is, therefore, focused on a life-style which emphasizes religious piety. This is a theme to which I shall return in a later chapter. For the moment we need only note the contrast it provides with the more sophisticated, cosmopolitan, and social-work oriented activities of the middle class. The relationships which are valued by ordinary Protestants are those which crystallize existing kinship and neighbourhood bonds, in contrast to the extension of networks evident among the élite. This theme, as we will note in the next chapter, becomes even more pronounced in the context of marriage tendencies. In terms of consumption patterns, therefore, the access of most householders to information and hence to circles of influence and preferment is even more restricted than their access to industrial goods.

THE CULTURAL IMPLICATIONS OF CHURCH
AFFILIATION

The congregation is today an additional site for the cultural expression of stratification. While class did not constitute a basis for denominational affiliation among the first generations of rural Christians (see Chapter 2), it has emerged as significant for those who, in the course of becoming economically and socially mobile, have entered large cities, and attached themselves to the urban church. Within the CSI in Madras it is possible to distinguish congregations composed mainly of lower class members (the great majority) from those which attract predominantly the middle class. Indeed, it is worth recalling how the emergence of the CSI-Southern congregation underlined the concern of the well-to-do to separate themselves from those beneath them by establishing their own ritual enclaves (see Chapter 1, pp. 25-7).

The small number of élite churches in the city are of two principal kinds. There are those, like the CSI-Southern church, which were constructed mainly after independence under the auspices of the CSI, in well-to-do suburbs developed during the last few decades to house the city's middle class. Most worship in Tamil, although they may hold periodic services in another south Indian language or, even more commonly, in English. Thus, as I have noted, most evening services in the CSI-Southern church are in English for the benefit of Protestant students and staff of the nearby colleges and institutes who come from outside the state.

Others were originally established for the European community during the colonial period. Because of their role as major foci of public worship and/or their location in the more attractive garden suburbs, they retained their foreign membership throughout the period and established their reputations as the most prestigious churches in the city.[16] These reputations were reinforced in the post-colonial era as many Indian Protestants entering the middle class joined such congregations and, in a manner of speaking, assumed the pews being vacated by the departing Europeans. These congregations continue to worship in English. Those who attach themselves to such 'English' churches claim to do so for a variety of reasons.

CSI-Northern congregants cite the schedule of morning worship (9.00 a.m.) as an important motive, since it frees them early to enjoy the rest of the day as they please. Those with young children appreciate the fact that the timings of Sunday Services and Sunday School coincide. Not a few point out that they were encouraged to join because a spouse, close kin, or friend was already there. People from other parts of India who do not know Tamil, as well as Tamilians who attended or whose children attend English medium schools and read Tamil only with difficulty or not at all, welcome the chance to worship in English. Others mention a number of rights acquired by membership: specifically, to marry a child in the church, or be buried in its cemetery (very few CSI churches in Madras have their own burial grounds).

Other reasons provided by these Christians suggest more aesthetic considerations, but reveal status concerns as well. Members of the CSI-Northern congregation speak of affiliating in order to enjoy the 'calm and sober' services, the 'brief and pointed' sermons, or 'the glorious music'. Most 'English' churches have permanent choirs, some of them extremely good. I have several times heard the CSI-Northern congregation described as 'musically snobbish'. They join, moreover, in order to sit together as a family (in Tamil churches men and women sit apart), to relax in the midst of 'all this elegance', to be part of a 'sophisticated' atmosphere, or simply to savour the 'friendliness' and the 'absence of strife'. These latter kinds of rationale add up to a middle-class folk view of the distinction between English and Tamil churches. The qualities attributed to and favoured in the English church serve to articulate— either by implied or explicitly voiced contrast—their model of the other.

Tamil churches are said or assumed to be overcrowded and noisy; their services are characterized as lacking order and decorum: they 'go on and on'; the sermons are 'rambling' and excessively parochial; the singing (of Western hymns in translation) is 'uninspired'; and the atmosphere generally too charged to allow 'quiet reflection and prayer'. Educated people, I was told, 'don't feel at home in such a church'. These congregations are also represented as being narrowly centred on 'community' (i.e. caste), full of 'back-biting' and quar-

relling, and 'ridden with politics'. Even their pastors do not
escape censure. Far from standing above strife, they 'incite'
their members against one another, and 'show favouritism'.

Members of the CSI-Southern congregation subscribe to a
similar paradigm, but understandably, do not apply it to all
Tamil churches, only to those composed principally of non-
élites. CSI-Southern congregants praise the virtues of their own
(Tamil) church and denigrate those whose membership consists
principally of the 'uneducated' and 'unsophisticated'. Above
all, they appreciate the reticence of even their most eminent
members to appear ambitious by seeking office on the Pastorate
Committee. This is compared with the ordinary run of Tamil
churches, where 'everyone wants to be on the committee'. A
former minister, who spent several years in the CSI-Southern
congregation, looks back on his period there as 'a quiet time,
without politics'. This 'absence of politics' is, for many, the *sine
qua non* of a congregation worthy of élites.

There is a further distinction which aligns congregations of
the élite with the 'social gospel', and therefore involves them
in a variety of philanthropic and welfare projects. This is con-
trasted with the inward-looking Tamil congregations which,
because of both inadequate resources and particular theological
preferences, remain, for the most part, aloof from such activities. I will return to this theme in Chapter 7.

By contructing this model of Tamil churches to which the
generality of urban Protestants affiliate, members of the middle
class preserve the boundaries between their own and the ritual
bodies of the lower class from which many of them have originated. Devasundaram (1975) has suggested that, in the context of urban south India, removal to an English church is an
expression of upward mobility. The views reported here suggest
that any congregation—English or Tamil—which defines itself
in terms of an élitist, hegemonic life-style may provide an appropriate context for middle-class identification.

The 'reality' of Tamil congregations composed of ordinary
Christians looks quite different when viewed from below. Stark
contrasts with élite churches are readily apparent in the physical settings within which worship takes place: in architectural
styles, internal decor, and furnishings, amount of seating space,
and so on. There are also significant distinctions of theological

emphasis among devotees, as I have suggested. But services in such churches are not appreciably longer or less decorous, sermons no less interesting (though thematically different), hymns (and 'lyrics') no less enthusiastically sung than in their élite counterparts. While some congregations do appear actually to earn their reputations for being riven by caste quarrels, others, like the CSI-Western congregation, seem to conduct their pastorate affairs with minimal disagreements and a maximum of co-operative endeavour.

While some lower class Protestants have occasion to attend the odd service in an élite church, they seem not to come away with any strong impression of difference in the form or character of the ritual. Whereas middle-class congregants are concerned not only to note disparities, but to define them essentially in moral terms, those belonging to non-élite churches construct their image of the other primarily in material terms. From their viewpoint, people who belong to élite congregations are simply the rich who 'arrive for worship by car, wearing fine clothes and lots of jewellery'. Poor people 'will feel ashamed' to settle in this kind of church because 'we have only simple clothes and can give only *peysa* when everyone else offers rupees'. Such congregations are therefore 'not for ordinary people like us'. Both moral and material distinctions serve to explain, justify, and perpetuate this ritual hierarchy.

CONGREGATIONS AND THEIR MINISTERS

The views and experiences of clergy provide another perspective on certain aspects of the disparity between the two kinds of church. Since CSI pastors are transferred with some regularity around the diocese, over the years quite a number of them gain experience of working in both. Several aspects of the relationship between a pastor and his congregation are worth noting. The clergymen with whom I discussed this matter almost invariably mentioned and took delight in the deference shown the minister by members of lower-class churches. They respect his intellect, his learning, and vocation. His opinions on numerous matters, religious or secular, are assiduously sought, and his participation in the lives of parishioners sincerely canvassed and genuinely appreciated. One parson, de-

scribing his daily routine during an incumbency in one such
congregation, remarked with evident pleasure that he had
never had a moment's peace: 'I was on call 24 hours a day.'
And though several saw congregational politics as a difficult
problem to cope with, most thought it rarely got out of hand,
although everyone knows of instances where it obviously did.
One minister regarded vigorous contestation for places on the
Pastorate Committee as evidence of 'enthusiasm' for the life of
the church.

By contrast, pastors perceive their greatest challenges to
come from élite congregations. While they echo with approval
the sentiment about these groups being 'free of politics', and
welcome the comforts and perks which accompany such a posting,[17] it is seldom seen, at least in retrospect, as an unmixed
blessing. It takes a rare clergyman not to feel intimidated by a
highly educated and cosmopolitan group of parishioners, who
do not necessarily respect his office or his opinions, nor perhaps
even agree with his theology. Ministers indicate that in such a
setting the efforts they make to offer sermons which stir both
intellect and emotion often meet with indifference or criticism.
Even their command of language—English and/or Tamil—
does not escape notice, evaluation, or comment.

The situation is not helped by, indeed may have its roots in,
the kinds of background from which a considerable proportion
of the Madras clergy stems. A career in the church now constitutes an extremely low priority for the urban middle class,
although not a few of its members are in the position they
presently occupy precisely because a near forebear had entered
the ministry. The church was and for some remains an important avenue of social mobility. A majority of the city's clerics
are, therefore, drawn from quite humble families, and their
educational attainments reflect more those of the lower class
within the Protestant population than the middle class to whose
congregations they might be assigned. Over one half of Madras
clergymen have only attended high school, and not a few of
these have failed to matriculate (although all subsequently
completed theological training).[18] Given the impressive educational achievements of middle-class Protestants, assignment
to an élite church (however much desired) can lead to feelings
of inadequacy on the part of the pastor, who perhaps senses he

is more tolerated than respected. In light of this situation, it is no coincidence that for some time after independence many of the English churches insisted on being allocated European ministers who were presumably thought to be at least the intellectual equals of such highly sophisticated parishioners. Indeed, there are still several expatriate ministers seconded to the Madras diocese from their home churches in the West. As these expatriates are gradually withdrawn, however, the ecclesiastical hierarchy must take great care to find suitable and acceptable replacements. One pastor could not resist the observation that the committee responsible for ministerial placements prays harder for divine guidance than any other in the diocese.

This already difficult task is made more complex by the issue of caste. The problem is only partly that a minister belonging to one group represented in the congregation may be rejected by others on the assumption that he is bound to favour 'his own people' in a variety of church matters. Even more important is that the ease of intercourse which flows from the sharing of a common caste is denied a minister who is differently affiliated than his congregants. This is especially the case where the cleric of humble caste origin (as are the majority of the Madras clergy)[19] finds himself in an élite congregation whose members either belong mainly to higher castes, or, by virtue of their wealth, can claim to be casteless without risking the stigma of untouchability (see Chapter 6). In such a situation the minister may be kept at 'arm's length' by the majority of his parishioners. While he presides over both public worship and the numerous domestic rites which a pastor is called upon to perform, his role may end there. It is not unusual for him to be effectively excluded from the more informal aspects of these occasions, as more generally from the private lives of his parishioners. As one minister who had regularly experienced this situation put it: 'When I had done my official duties, they thanked me politely and sent me home.'

It would be inaccurate to suggest that such attitudes arise solely or even primarily from a concern on the part of parishioners to protect their caste status. Restrictions on interpersonal exchanges (including commensality) do not constitute an important part of the definition of caste among these urban

Protestants. The nature of the relationship between a minister from a poor and low caste background and an élite congregation has more to do with the importance of the church as a site for the cultural expression of inequality. As I have tried to show, the well-to-do take great pains, on the one hand, to extend and consolidate relationships within their own class and, on the other, to distance themselves from those whom they regard as beneath them. I have heard numerous comments from middle-class Christians which make this explicit. Several examples will suffice to give the flavour of these views: 'In our congregation we want to meet people of our own intellectual level'; 'This congregation is a refuge for the better educated with Western manners and outlook'; 'Our church is a place where people of like mind can gather and worship'; 'Here we can meet for at least an hour each week to get away from the poverty around us'.

They are no less aware of the role of an élite parish in knitting together disparate elements within the class. 'A congregation like this is important because it brings together people of so many different caste and regional backgrounds.' And so it does. They not only worship together, but co-operate in myriad ways in running the affairs of the church. These contacts, which become intensive and highly personalized over time, are further buttressed by informal visiting and entertaining, and lead to many close friendships among people who are otherwise unrelated. Indeed, they result occasionally in matrimonial alliances.

Through this constant interaction, élites communicate and reinforce a variety of behaviour patterns which are acknowledged as elements of a life-style appropriate to their standing within the community. These should be seen, therefore, in their ideological aspect as a 'cultural mechanism which integrates the dominant class . . .' (Abercrombie and Turner 1978: 165). Those who do not possess the financial, intellectual, or symbolic capital to invest in such relationships are effectively excluded from these privileged circles. A minister whose roots are in the lower class and/or a Harijan caste might be similarly disallowed a full part in the informal life of the parish.

CONCLUSION

Following Douglas and Isherwood (1978) we might identify two distinctive modes of consumption within the urban Protestant community. One, associated with householders in the lower class, is small in scale, characterized by a disproportionate amount of expenditure on (inferior and inadequate) accommodation, clothing, and food. Its scale is small, moreover, because the household's investment in other people tends to reinforce existing relationships among kin and neighbours within the same class.

Middle-class consumption profiles provide a clear contrast. These Protestants enjoy not only superior housing, a more varied diet, and more expensive dress with less financial strain, but purchase all manner of luxury goods, produced by and for the country's tiny élite. In this sense, the well-to-do are to be seen as active agents in the diversion of national resources to the manufacture of products which provide visible statements about their pre-eminent place in the social order. Their consumption patterns may be characterized as large scale because a relatively high proportion of expenditure is allocated to the acquisition of 'information goods'. Household resources are directed towards developing wide-ranging social contacts by means of which they obtain and secure their privileges and preferments. They invest heavily in exclusive education for their children and in forms of association which enable them to cultivate links throughout the extent of the 'power bloc'. Through 'social work' in diocesan and other Christian organizations, and the careful selection of congregational affiliation, their personal bonds cross the barriers of caste, region, and language; and in so far as Protestants participate actively in the city's 'club life', they transcend those of religion as well.

Cunningham has suggested that in Britain, following the industrial revolution, the dominant class 'gained at least part of its identity from its possession of leisure and the spending of that leisure in exclusive and status-enhancing settings . . .' (1982: 85). Similarly, in a variety of contexts, middle-class Protestants in Madras identify with, adopt, and communicate to others behaviours and values which in concert make up a distinctive way of life, the cultural expression of their superiority. These aspects of life-style are not simply beyond the reach of the lower class, but effectively outside their awareness. In so far as the luxury goods which are the hallmark of the middle class are observed and can occasionally be possessed, they are part of the everyday experience of ordinary people. They are the *visible* symbols of dominance, and, as we have seen, may be perceived by ordinary householders as the principal, perhaps the only expression of difference between themselves and those above them. In this respect, luxury goods, like a university degree, by appearing within the reach—if only just—of those members of the lower class who strive and save, become a form of ideology, hiding the processes at work to exclude them from the ranks of the dominant.

What they do not experience and cannot comprehend are the ways of thought and forms of discourse generated within certain institutions of the middle class to which they have no access. Because childhood is not spent in expensive, private English medium schools, youth in the best institutes of higher education, or adulthood in the exclusive leisure and spare time pursuits of the privileged, they cannot acquire the vital forms of knowledge which are the preserve of the latter. It is what Merquior implies when he refers to the limits imposed by 'life activities' upon ways of conceiving social reality (1979: 12). The élite's increasing monopoly of 'information goods', does not merely deprive those beneath them of the opportunities to acquire the resources with which they might alter their conditions, it effectively prevents the development of a consciousness about the nature of their disadvantages. Here, then, lie the *hidden* messages of consumption, out of sight of all save a tiny minority which experiences them. Ultimately, as Douglas and Isherwood point out, 'consumption is about power' (1978: 90).

I do not want to suggest that the life-style of lower class Protestants is entirely explicable in terms of insufficiency of means, or is an automatic response to exclusion from the pursuits of the dominant. Whatever its origin, it assumes—like that of the middle class—a momentum, a direction, even a logic of its own. This will become even more apparent in the following chapter, where we extend the discussion of class cultures into the domain of marriage.

MARRIAGE AND THE REPRODUCTION
OF CLASS

Restriction, Elaboration, and Matrimonial Sub-cultures

INTRODUCTION

THE matrimonial game, Bourdieu observes, is like a game of cards in which the outcome depends on the deal, the cards held, and the players' skill. It depends, in other words, on the 'material and symbolic capital' possessed by the parties concerned and on their 'competence' in making use of this capital (1977: 58). In a social system with rank inequalities, however, the marriage game does not favour the players equally. Participants in the matrimonial game to be discussed in this chapter occupy different levels within the class order.

I begin the chapter by examining the significance of family, household, and individual reputations in marital considerations. This is followed by an assessment of the comparative importance of denominational and caste (as well as 'casteless') affiliation. The discussion then turns to the rites and ceremonies surrounding a Protestant marriage, outlining the manner in which weddings are organized, celebrated, and financed. The last section explores the changing meaning of 'dowry' in Madras, and suggests how it might be understood in the context of both the urban class and caste orders.

What becomes apparent in the course of the discussion is the existence of quite distinct matrimonial sub-cultures within the Protestant community. Not only do domestic units in the middle and lower classes follow disparate marital practices, but they often perceive and approach in alternative ways the customary activities they do share. The emphasis on intensification of links among ordinary householders, and on the extension of bonds among élites, noted in the previous chapter's consideration of consumption behaviour, is seen to be replicated and reinforced in marital strategies. The effect of these different tendencies is to encourage closure of class boundaries and to deny entry into the dominant section of the Protestant community to those now outside it.

HOUSEHOLD AND FAMILY IN MATRIMONIAL ARRANGEMENTS

It is in relation to marriage arrangements, perhaps more so than any other area of activity, that the household's place in the wider family becomes evident. The concept of the 'family' here carries the connotation of kindred. Most typically, a potential bride's or bridegroom's 'family' would comprise not only her/his own siblings and parents, but parents' siblings and their spouses, as well as their children. But its limits are imprecise, and defined contextually: on the one hand, by 'insiders' through their concern with and participation in the marriage preparations of a constituent household, and, on the other, by 'outsiders' who consider themselves as belonging to other 'families', and thereby free to pass judgements.

Domestic groups, especially those within the middle class, acquire reputations not only as a consequence of their own actions and attributes, but of those of others within the wider family. The strengths of one household will add to the stature of all those associated with it by kindred ties. Alternatively, its 'defects'—which might include, for example, the excessive drinking, mental illness, or physical handicap of one of its members—may affect other households within the kin unit adversely. Not surprisingly, the greater the collective reputation of the family, the greater its ability to weather the failings of its component domestic groups. Alternatively, the higher the standing of a particular household, the less harshly its misdemeanors are likely to be judged both within and outside the family (see below).

Although Protestants generally prefer that the bridegroom's education and earning potential exceed those of his bride ('otherwise she will not respect her husband'), there is no systematic pattern of hypergamy in their alliances. This is belied by constant reversals in the direction of marriage and the frequent practice of 'direct exchange' of men and women between families and households. Moreover, the parents of a married

couple exchange visits and often develop close bonds of friend-
ship, all of which would not be possible in a hypergamous
system (see Vatuk 1975).[1] There is a widespread feeling, explicitly voiced within the middle class, and echoed, though
perhaps with less conviction, by those beneath them, that an
'alliance' (the English term is often used) should bring together
persons belonging to households of like standing.

Protestants, as we have seen, must rely for their economic
well-being on their earnings from employment. A household's
general standing within the family and wider community,
therefore, while a composite of more than one attribute, is
expressed primarily in terms of the occupations of its focal
members. Thus, wedding invitations will identify the fathers of
the bride and bridegroom by their current or pre-retirement
positions, and sometimes their mothers, as well, if they are
successful career women, well-known 'social workers', or otherwise prominent in the community, as some certainly are.

Increasingly, however, households are assessed not merely
on the basis of the positions held by their senior members, but
on the accomplishments (real or potential) of the individuals
being considered as prospective spouses. Thus, while family
and household status still count for much in determining the
suitability of potential spouses (especially among the better
off) increasing attention is paid nowadays to the attainments,
abilities, and future potential of the individuals themselves.
This is, of course, in addition to the personal qualities and
physical attributes (including skin colour) of the intending
spouses.

Regarding the appropriate marriage age, there is a near-
uniform pattern evident within the community. On average,
men tend to marry at around 28 years, and women at 22.
People suggest that these are the most suitable times for
wedlock, for at this juncture young men and women are ready
to assume the necessary responsibilities.

For men of the lower class, this point is usually reached some
considerable time after the end of formal schooling, since few,
as we saw in Chapter 3, go beyond matriculation and perhaps
a year or two of some form of vocational training. It often
comes at the end of an apprenticeship, or when a long span of
sporadic employment looks to become relatively permanent.

Up to this juncture, no family would willingly offer a daughter, since they would be reluctant to marry her to someone who is quite evidently unable to support her. Further, an extended period of bachelorhood may be required in order for the young man's household to accumulate sufficient resources for his wedding, since it must await the conclusion of his sisters' marriages. There is also the matter of a household's reluctance to do without a son's (or daughter's) income on which it may have come to depend.

A similar marriage age among the middle class must be understood somewhat differently. While here, too, young men must await their sisters' marriages, they are only considered ready for wedlock when they have acquired advanced qualifications and been launched on their careers. The marriage of one young man affiliated to the CSI-Northern congregation was delayed not only until his period of probation was completed, but until his management training period had been completed and it was known in which particular branch of the firm he was to build his career. At the same time, daughters must enhance their prospects by continuing their education up to at least graduate level. So, to retain their advantages in the urban hierarchy, children of the middle class must also remain single and dependent on parents for lengthy periods. However, there is a point beyond which it becomes too risky to delay the marriage of a daughter. In the words of one anxious parent: 'If she has not been found a husband by the time she reaches 25 years, people will suspect there is some problem with the girl or the family.'

While the notion of a 'good family' (*nalla kuṭumpam*) extends throughout the community, it too has somewhat distinctive resonances for those at differrent levels of the class order. Within the dominant sector, a family may be respected because of its links to a renowned forebear, perhaps a high caste convert who became a famous scholar, prominent clergyman, literary figure, or composer. A handful of Protestants who held positions of responsibility in the public services during the colonial period were awarded titles—e.g. Diwan Bahadur, Rao Bahadur, Rao Sahib—by the Viceroy on the recommendation of the Madras government. Such a title identifies its holder as a distinguished member of the community, and usually also the focus of a 'good family'. More commonly nowadays, however, families acquire a favourable reputation if they include persons of wealth and esteem who have earned considerable success in their careers, and 'serve' the wider society, or the Christian segment within it, in acknowledged and accepted ways. Following the death of a member of the CSI-Southern congregation, who had a considerable reputation in the field of higher education, a memorial booklet was produced by members of his family. It was full of effusive tributes from relatives, colleagues, former students, and the famous in the wider society (including the President and Prime Minister of India who sent messages of condolence). One of his nieces summed up the way in which such an individual becomes the pivot of a prominent 'family'. Writing in English, she notes: 'We are a very close-knit family: brothers, sisters, cousins, uncles, aunts. We keep up close contact by every means possible. We all loved uncle B. and respected him ... [his] New Year's Eve garden parties were traditional. About 50 family members from Madras alone met there . . .' Such prominent individuals provide a fund of esteem on which the kindred as a whole and its component households draw.

Because external assessments of a family's reputation are subjective and based on various and variously applied criteria, there is no agreed or objective system of ranking. The family of a senior diplomat, bishop, university vice-chancellor, successful industrialist, or important politician can be judged quite differently, depending on the personal predilections of those making the appraisal. Furthermore, as Bourdieu points out, such 'symbolic capital' is relatively precarious and can be diminished by the death or changing fortunes of an individual (1977: 67). Only where a family proliferates a number of such persons—as it often does, for success breeds success here as elsewhere—does a consensus form as to its general eminence.

A 'good family' within the lower class has quite different connotations. On the one hand, it tends to be more narrowly defined, in terms of a single domestic unit. The strengths or weaknesses of even a closely related domestic group, therefore, are unlikely to count for very much when considering the worth of a potential partner. On the other, in marking out the concept of a 'good family', these householders do not employ the language of prosperity and public acclaim, but of what may be described as 'Christian values'.

They characterize the sort of household they would seek out alliance with as one whose members are honest and hard-working, show concern for their kin and neighbours, attend religious services regularly, and give generously but within their means to the church. In such households, moreover, children honour their parents, and wives their husbands. For many, such a family is 'a living example of Christ's presence in the world'. Virtue is measured primarily in terms of piety. Of late, the idea of a 'good family' has come increasingly to reflect fundamentalist influences on the Protestant lower class. More and more it is construed in terms of a retreat from 'worldliness': from drink, tobacco, and cinema, from politics and frivolous leisure, from the wearing of ornaments, and so on. What is required is a commitment to 'God's work', i.e. evangelism or the support of those so engaged. I return to this theme in Chapters 7 and 8.

CASTE AND DENOMINATION IN MATRIMONIAL ARRANGEMENTS

Any discussion of Christian marriage in India must take ac-count of the fact that members of the community identify with a variety of castes, though a substantial minority have or claim no such affiliation. This is largely explicable in terms of the historical conditions of conversion. Whereas those who entered the new faith in large collective movements were able to re-produce themselves by endogamous marriages and so retain their caste pedigrees, individual converts usually did so in de-fiance of other members of their local caste units, and often at the cost of their most intimate social ties. Such individual acceptance of the new faith, therefore, entailed different con-sequences from 'mass conversion'. The most important to note for our purposes were the converts' isolation from caste and kin, from their resources, their status, and their connubial alliances.

When the time for marriage arrived, Protestants belonging to groups which converted in relatively small numbers were faced with problems of finding partners. Some did attempt to define their matrimonial boundaries in caste terms. But it seems that wherever such tendencies appeared they were defeated by harsh demographic realities. Even the Vellalars, who provided a not inconsiderable number of converts, were unable to maintain strict endogamous practices and by the end of the nineteenth century had begun marrying with members of other castes. Ponniah was evidently surprised to find 'many cases of intermarriage on the part of educated Christian Vellalars' (1938: 43). Oddie similarly notes how the few Protestants of Brahmin origin in the Kaveri delta of Tamilnadu 'married women of a different caste' (1981: 59). One retired professor of pharmacology whose father had been a Brahmin convert told me that, since there was no woman from within the same caste to marry, his father had wed a Chettiar—'the next best thing'. Thus the special conditions of individual conversion ultimately imposed a more or less uniform marriage pattern: namely, alliances across the boundaries of caste.

A substantial number of individual converts were married to products of the orphanages and boarding schools run by the missionaries. The greatest volume of accessions to these institutions took place during periods of plague and famine. The government also entrusted to their care many young girls 'rescued by British civil servants from low and immoral surroundings' (Pathak 1967: 67). Children raised in these institutions developed no sense of attachment to caste groups, for the missionaries did not encourage them to do so. Gehani suggests that orphan girls provided spouses for a 'large army' of Indian mission workers (1966: 134). They were also recognized as a potential source of wives for Christian men who were not necessarily products of these institutions, nor employees of the missions. Indeed, for many years these girls were virtually the only educated females in the Madras Presidency since, as one missionary wrote, 'families refuse to have [girls] educated'.[2] They were, therefore, considered suitable partners for well-educated (especially high caste) male converts. The girls were apparently taught the English language and 'English habits' for that very purpose (see Mullens 1848). Needless to say, all such unions took no account of the caste affiliations of the young men and women involved.

Thus, the Protestant community in Madras today consists of a not insignificant minority of persons who, as a result of the marriages of the original converts and/or their offspring, are of hybrid ancestry. Moreover, the category of persons who cannot claim a pure caste pedigree is not limited to the natural increase provided by their descendants. It also contains the offspring of later inter-caste marriages entered into by persons belonging to mass movement groups, voluntarily and without the compulsion of demographic circumstances. The rate of increase of such 'love marriages', as they are sometimes called, is rising, at least in large cities, although they still represent a tiny proportion of Christian unions in Madras.

For many Protestants, however, caste is an important if not overriding consideration when contemplating an alliance, and a good caste pedigree becomes part of the definition of a good family. Certain groups within the community, such as the Nadars and Syrian Christians, have a reputation for insisting on the strictest qualifications. 'We make elaborate investigations to see if the other family has got mixed up with any other caste', I was told by one prominent Nadar at the time of his daughter's marriage. While some will admit privately that such an attitude is unbecoming in a Christian, if not actually un-Christian, those responsible for arranging matrimonial unions scarcely consider any alternative possibilities. Nor is such behaviour confined to the wealthy: members whose circumstances are more modest take equally stringent precautions. Referring to the strength of caste boundaries among Christian Nadars, Hardgrave remarks that marital links with Hindu Nadars are preferred to unions with Christians belonging to other groups (1969: 90–1).

Nevertheless, prominent families within a caste are able to overlook (or escape the negative consequences) of a misalliance, provided it is not considered too outrageous. Thus, the marriage of a highly respected Nadar man to a woman of another 'clean' caste raised eyebrows in its time, but did not affect the household or family so adversely as to prevent the marriage of their 'hybrid' daughters to Nadar men, which effectively meant their reincorporation into the caste. The fact that the husbands of these women were themselves from reputable households and families ensured that the offspring of these mixed unions would carry no permanent stigma.

In another case, the highly educated and well-employed son of distinguished parents (the father a Vellalar, the mother a

Nadar) received numerous offers of marriage from families who would normally define themselves as unequivocally belonging to one group or the other. 'They were ready to regard me as either Nadar or Vellalar if I agreed to marry their daughter', he remarked. In the end, he wed a young woman of differently mixed parentage, and their own children, in his opinion, 'will probably be too "contaminated" to be seriously considered marriageable by members of either caste'. While such re-incorporation is possible where important families and significant interests are involved, there are limits which cannot be exceeded. At several removes from the original outmarrying forebear, the 'purity' of the succeeding generations is seriously at risk.

Protestants within the dominant class are also able to effect a redefinition of endogamous boundaries by creating alliances with similarly named and homologously placed families previously outside the reach of their own marriage circles. Such unions are increasingly common in large cities where the traditional endogamous units are expanding and being altered to satisfy new demographic and socio-economic conditions. In Madras, Nadars originating from Tinnevelly now create alliances with others from Kanya Kumari, Madurai, etc. Lewandowski (1980: 109) reports an identical trend among Kerala migrants in the city, who now marry across the traditional geographical divisions of Malabar, Travancore, and Cochin. I will return to this point later in the chapter.

An important concern of householders who belong to 'respectable' castes, or assert no caste affiliation whatsoever, is to maintain a distance between themselves and others of known 'untouchable' status. The latter generally do not refer to themselves by specific caste labels, but by more widely employed official designations ('Scheduled Castes', 'Adi-Dravidas', or 'Harijan Christians'). Since a tiny proportion within the middle class—hardly three per cent of my sample—are identifiable as Harijans, the matter of guarding against their matrimonial encroachments hardly occurs within these circles. In any event, the few households of such castes who make their way into the middle class are able, in time (if they have not already done so), to shed their caste label altogether and, with sufficient wealth and influence, attract alliances with respectable families.

Within the lower class, a high proportion of whom are Adi-Dravidas (50 per cent of my sample can be so categorized)[3] the problem of distancing is more complex. Among these Protestants, the whole question of affiliation is fluid. The boundary between Harijan and clean caste can be crossed or, more accurately, dissolved, by assuming a 'casteless' designation. This requires the acquiescence of others who carry such a stigma, as well as of those who belong to non-Harijan groups, or who have successfully shed similar origins. But such acts are not always possible or desirable (see Chapter 6), and the fact remains that a significant proportion of lower-class Protestants identify themselves and are labelled as Harijans. While these are extremely sensitive issues to probe in any depth, I have a very strong impression, and certainly no evidence to suggest otherwise, that householders claiming affiliation to non-Harijan castes or to no caste, rarely entertain the prospect of matrimonial unions with persons of known Harijan status. According to one Vellalar woman in the CSI-Western congregation: 'As Christians we should have no objections to such unions, but if we agreed to a proposal of this kind, our relatives would object and there would be endless trouble'.

While caste is a focus of concern during marriage negotiations, the question of denomination attracts comparatively little attention. As one church historian, and a prominent Indian Christian, has pointed out: 'Old social [i.e. caste] ties have everywhere proved to be much stronger than the newly accepted denominational convictions' (Paul 1958: 16). But it would be an exaggeration to suggest that no account whatsoever is taken of the religious preferences of potential affines. Fewer than half of the marital unions in my samples crossed denominational barriers, and hardly one in five marriages of parents of these householders had done so. This is because, as I indicated in Chapter 2, persons of the same caste in a particular region tended to be converted by the same mission, and thus to belong to the same denomination. In time, with greater mobility, and movement into urban centres, the convergence of caste and denomination ended. To the extent that members of the same caste came under the influence of different mission Societies, marital unions increasingly took place across denominational boundaries, with obvious consequences for the strength and significance of these boundaries.

Nevertheless, there are important differences in attitudes about such affiliation as between members of each class. As a rule, among élites, alliances are created only within the body of orthodox Protestants, (i.e. those affiliated to the CSI, Lutherans, Baptists, etc.). Marriages with Hindus (provided they first convert) are tolerated, but occur very rarely, simply because few Hindus at this class level do become Christians. Then, there is active opposition to marriages with Roman Catholics. Even Syrian Christians attached to Protestant congregations in Madras—who freely marry with other Syrians belonging to the Orthodox Jacobite and Mar Thoma churches (the woman assuming her husband's affiliation)—refrain from creating ties with Romo-Syrians (i.e. Syrian Catholics).[4] The avoidance of these unions tends to be explained in terms of fear for the children·of such alliances, who might be brought up as Catholics. This, of course, is also the basis for official CSI opposition to such marriages (see Synod of the CSI 1959).

Matrimonial links with persons belonging to or associated with fundamentalist sects are also avoided by households within the middle class. This is to do with the fact that such religious groupings have, for some time, been disdained by the 're-spectable' churches. Such an attitude might also have been encouraged by the fact that the generality of their members are not found among Christian élites. Of equal importance, however, is that such marriages are eschewed because the kind of commitment, in terms of religious practice and belief implied in a fundamentalist stance, is totally at odds with the life-style prevalent among the Protestant middle class today (see Chapter 4).

No such constraints operate among lower class Christians. There are few householders in the sample who are not in one way or another associated with fundamentalist activities themselves, or linked by kinship and affinity to persons who are. The relevance and significance of this fact will be explored in some detail in later chapters.

Within the neighbourhoods of the lower class, there is also regular interaction among adherents of all religious faiths, who, after all, live cheek by jowl, and greater likelihood of marriages across these borders. Lynch, in a discussion of Adi-Dravida migrants in Bombay, notes that Hindu–Christian marriages occur 'without difficulty' (1974: 1658). While there are strong pressures for the non-Protestant partner to convert, there is also 'slippage' the other way, although the extent to which this occurs is impossible to gauge. Approximately one in three of the focal householders in the lower class sample were born Hindus, and a significant proportion became Christian primarily in order to marry persons known locally to them. As a result of such unions, many more people in this than the middle class have close relatives who belong to other religious communities, and with whom relations of kinship are maintained. Regular visiting takes place, but they generally refuse to take an active part in Hindu family rites (and vice versa).

RESTRICTED AND ELABORATED MARRIAGES

Matrimonial unions within the lower class, by and large, fortify existing relationships of kinship and locality. One third of focal householders in the sample were already related at the time of marriage. Most commonly, a man wed his (real) cross-cousin (patri- or matrilateral), although other traditionally south Indian marriages—for example, with an elder sister's daughter (see Good 1980)—also took place.[5] I was told on several occasions that in the past there was a greater tendency for close kin marriage to occur, and genealogies seem to bear out this claim. In recent times, it is suggested, people have learned about the (genetic) 'dangers' of such unions, and that they are frowned upon in many parts of India, as in other Christian countries. Hence people are now slightly 'embarrassed' and reluctant to encourage them.

Within such social environs, therefore, we find ample evidence of 'multiplex ties', which are reinforced by fresh marriages. When taking genealogies from members of the CSI-Western congregation I was struck by the extent of relatedness among them. As one member remarked, with only some exaggeration—making allowance for the separation between Harijans and non-Harijans—'in this church we are all related'.

The intensification of relationships within the lower class is, in a sense, the obverse of the restrictive connubial strategies pursued by households in the dominant sector of the community. Reflecting on the possibilities for inter-class unions, one householder of modest means and position put it this way:

Suppose I go and ask a rich family, even one in my own caste, if they would allow their daughter to marry my son. They would give an evasive reply, but they would be thinking: 'This fellow is not of our status. Our daughter will feel out of place in his house. What will we gain by such an alliance?' And if I offer my daughter to their son, they would not accept that either, because I have nothing to send with her. So these rich people will never mix with us.

Those who have made their way into the upper reaches of the class order follow a careful, not to say exclusive, marriage policy. They examine prospective marital allies with a view to union of young people from families of equivalent standing and financially commensurate households. Frequently, the rhetoric focuses, as the above comment attests, on the importance of daughters enjoying after marriage similar comforts and facilities—in short, a life-style—at least equal to that they have become accustomed to in their natal groups.

Kin marriage among the affluent ensures that persons who already occupy a similar standing reinforce their existing links. However, the reduction in the frequency of such marriages over the years (only one quarter of focal householders in the middle-class sample were related before wedlock), while also explicable in terms of assumed genetic disadvantages, may have much to do with the dispersal and fragmentation of many successful urban families. Equally, it may reflect the importance attached to extending networks of influence and thereby increasing what Bourdieu calls their 'capital of alliances' (1977: 70). These householders, therefore, seek out unions with those from previously separate marriage circles. Thus, as I noted above, persons belonging to what were non-intermarrying subsections of the same caste category have begun to create affinal links in the metropolis. This distinction between the kin- and locality-focused matrimonial concentration of lower class Prot-

estant families and the more expansive tendency of the middle
class is recognized linguistically in notions of 'small (alliance)
circle' (*siṟiya iṭam*) applied to the former and 'big circle' (*periya
iṭam*) which refers to the latter.

Strategies of extension preclude the formation of in-marrying
occupational categories. Rather, they bring together householders engaged in a wide range of employments—professionals, bank officials, top bureaucrats, company executives,
businessmen, and so forth.[6] This results, as I pointed out in
Chapter 3, in a blurring of distinctions between the owners of
capital and those who serve it, and between persons engaged in
public and private enterprises. Marriages also create conjugal
bonds between men in these senior cadres and women engaged
in occupations earning considerably fewer financial or status
rewards. This underlines both the difficulty of attributing a
class label on the basis of occupation alone, and the need to
consider the household rather than the individual as a primary
unit of categorization.

Extension also occurs as a result of the increasing participation in marital arrangements by the prospective spouses
themselves, especially those who marry without regard to caste.
Denied access to a corporate group defined by 'common blood',
they seek partners from a more heterogeneous pool of potential
affines, the extent of which may not be known to their family
elders, nor accessible to the latters' networks. Thus, the initial
proposal for a union within such 'casteless' households, especially within the middle class, not infrequently originates
with the young people themselves. They meet at college, at
church, at social clubs, or other select associations. Usually,
the persons concerned describe these as 'love marriages', even
though in most cases they are condoned by parents who subsequently negotiate the precise arrangements surrounding the
wedding.[7]

It would be wrong to interpret the greater freedom enjoyed
by these young people in the selection of a mate as a 'rebellion'
against the wishes of parents in these matters. There is enough
evidence from this and other urban studies to indicate that
middle-class marriages are both ideally and in practice either
initiated or vetted and ultimately controlled by senior householders and family members. This accession to parental

authority is sustained by a widely shared and frequently articulated set of values assigning clearly delineated rights and duties within the household, as well as by readily acknowledged material 'realities'. Children in these 'casteless' domestic units—no less than those in caste households—are reliant on parents for maintenance over a long period, and with the time spent in educational institutions by members of this class increasing, the need for support shows no signs of diminishing. Furthermore, since parents continue to bear responsibility for the arrangement of suitable employment for their children (especially sons), the dependence of these young people on their elders remains, if anything, greater now than in the past.

The risk of such 'love marriages' traversing class barriers and thereby undermining class endogamy is small. These Christians live in similar (salubrious) neighbourhoods, join the same clubs, and send their offspring to the best English medium schools and colleges. As already noted, they also concentrate in a few élite congregations (usually those worshipping in English) like the CSI-Northern church. As I indicated when first introducing the unit of study in Chapter 1, a substantial proportion of these congregants are 'casteless', or are themselves partners in hybrid unions. They are, therefore, understandably much less concerned about caste than are the members of élite Tamil congregations, like the CSI-Southern, which counts virtually no members without a caste identity or who have married across caste lines.

Because of the kinds of everyday social contexts in which they circulate, young people from such casteless households are unlikely to have much opportunity of associating on a more than casual basis with others from a different class background. This selectivity, as much as any deliberate parental policy, ensures that these unions occur only between persons in households occupying similar positions in the social order. Hence, they are condoned if not encouraged. While one hears of odd cases of 'love marriages' between Christians and Hindus of the same class, or between Christians of different class levels, the intensive socialization of the young to marry only within their own community and status level, results in precious few unions across the religious or class divide.

The somewhat different emphases in matrimonial arrangements as between householders in the lower and middle classes extend to the way the wedding rites and ceremonies are celebrated, and to the nature and direction of marriage payments.

THE RITES AND CEREMONIES OF MARRIAGE

After preliminary discussions have taken place and the prospects for an alliance look promising, a meeting is arranged at which the young man, in the company of close relatives, 'views' the prospective bride at her home. Following an initial exchange of pleasantries, the young woman appears briefly to be introduced—sometimes she serves tea or coffee. No householder in the lower class sample, male or female, recalls having spoken a word or even been invited to do so on this occasion, and the women, especially, remember it as one of the most frightening experiences of their lives.

Middle-class 'viewings', however, do allow the couple—usually at their own insistence—to exchange a few words out of earshot of senior relatives. Moreover, if the discussions towards a union are to proceed further, they may meet again privately on one or more occasions at the girl's home or that of a mutually approved relative, and the more 'sophisticated' families might even permit them to 'date' openly. At these meetings they exchange information about themselves, their hobbies, interests, aspirations, and so forth. It is certainly the antithesis of lower class Christian usage, which denies the prospective spouses any opportunity for private conversation. They generally address one another for the first time—and even there only briefly and publicly—at their 'betrothal' (*niccayatārttam* or *parisam*).[8]

This ceremony, which may take place any time prior to the wedding (*kalyāṇam*) but most often follows soon after the match has been agreed, consists in members of the bridegroom's family visiting the bride's home with trays containing flowers, sweets, coconuts, fruits, and other items which are auspicious within south Indian society generally. If the wedding is imminent, they will also bring the bridal *sari* and the wedding necklace (*tāli*) at this time. Among the middle class, this has now become the occasion for the young man to present his impending bride with an 'engagement' ring, or even for rings to be exchanged by the couple. The event is sacralized by the participation of a minister, who blesses the couple. The wedding usually follows a few months after the betrothal, and it is customary for banns to be read in church for three consecutive weeks prior to the date. Among the middle class, it is increasingly common for a young man settled abroad to return home on leave for a brief period with the intention of marrying. Not only are arrangements hurriedly made, but the normal procedures somewhat foreshortened. The 'betrothal' and wedding take place within a few days of one another, and special permission is obtained from the church authorities for the banns to be read only once instead of three times.

It is widely accepted—much to the displeasure of the ecclesiastical hierarchy—that ordinary Christians avoid celebrating marriages during inauspicious months of the year or days of the month. One wedding I attended had been quickly arranged, I was told, so as to complete the festivities before the onset of an inauspicious Tamil month. While there is no suggestion that these Christians seek guidance—as do Hindus—on the most favourable moment for the rite, people do consult astrological calendars which are widely available.

In the church, the bridegroom (*māppiḷḷai*) is accompanied by a male relative (at the wedding referred to above it was his elder sister's husband)—called the *tōlaṉ*—and the bride (*peṇ*) by her *tōḷi* (in this case her mother's elder brother's wife). The latter carries the tray containing the wedding necklace, a coconut, betel nut and leaves, bananas, and a cash gift for the pastor. The essential elements of the CSI wedding service are a declaration by the parties that they know of no impediment to the union; an attestation of their 'will to live together in Christian marriage'; and a promise to live in lawful wedlock 'according to God's holy ordinance'. After the bridegroom has placed the necklace around his bride's neck the officiating clergyman declares that they are husband and wife, and offers a prayer and blessing (see Synod of the CSI 1959: 10).

Although there is a degree of flexibility regarding the venue for the ritual, among lower class Protestants in Madras it tends to take place in the bridegroom's church—mainly because most are from castes or regional backgrounds where this was or is the practice. Other, more pragmatic considerations, such as the seating capacity of the church, its reception facilities or nearness to them, or its location in relation to the main body of guests may influence the decision of where to hold the wedding rite. Not infrequently, of course, both bride and groom worship in the same church. The bridegroom's household also usually hosts the reception which follows, and this is attended by quite substantial numbers of relatives on both sides, as well as friends and neighbours. Receptions following weddings in the CSI-Western church are generally held in the community hall of a nearby government housing colony. The couple, seated on a dais, receive well-wishers who bring mainly cash gifts, which are recorded in a book. People then sit under a large awning (*pantal*), constructed for the occasion, facing the newly-weds, where they chat and listen to records of religious songs by popular evangelists (see Chapter 8). Guests are summoned in turn to the dining hall for the obligatory feast which, by custom, includes as its principal dish a *biriyani*[9]—among the less well off it is vegetable-based, since mutton (the most favoured meat) at Rs 20 per kilo (1981) is prohibitively costly. The cheapest meat available is beef (Rs 8 per kilo) but while a few householders admit to eating it at home, no one would consider serving it at a public feast. At an appropriate point, the minister offers a prayer for the couple, and the guests, after eating, gradually drift away.

The groom's household also meets the travel and subsistence expenses of its invitees from out of town, the costs of the mandatory gifts of clothing to particular relatives on the occasion of a marriage, and of the bride's wedding dress and gold necklace. The bride's side must provide, in addition to the groom's wedding clothes (nowadays a western-style suit), a 'dowry' (*sītanam* or, in more popular usage, *sīr varisai*). This consists mainly of cooking vessels and household furniture, as well as the jewels she brings to her conjugal home. Households, of course, spend differing amounts on gold ornaments for the bride, but the majority provide between one-quarter and three sovereigns—the common measure of gold in this part of India. In 1981–2 one sovereign cost approximately Rs 1,400. The amount spent on cooking vessels and furniture by households in the lower class sample ranged between Rs 150 and Rs 3,000.

In law, as in Indian tradition (see Tambiah 1973), these items—the ornaments especially—are acknowledged to be the bride's property, and therefore the groom's side should express no more than a passing interest in the extent of the settlement. Male householders in the middle class would certainly make a point of affecting disinterest in and ignorance of the amount of jewellery their own wives had brought with them to the marriage. But among the less privileged, not only is the amount of dowry to be provided often a subject of contention between the parties considering a marriage, but once these goods leave her natal home, she can no longer assume that they will remain in her possession. Her husband or (though less frequently in an urban neolocal context) his parents can appropriate, even dispose of them, though to do so is considered somewhat disreputable. Yet it appears to occur regularly enough within lower class households for such a practice not to be regarded as unusual.[10]

The most likely time for a woman's jewels to be pawned or sold is, indeed, when the household must meet the costs of a marriage. Even ordinary workers, living in conditions of relative hardship, insist that weddings—and especially the first child's—must be grand affairs. They regard Rs 10,000 as a minimum requirement nowadays for a modest wedding, and report expenditures of up to three times that amount. It will be recalled that gross average annual household earnings in the lower class sample are approximately Rs 11,000, although some 70 per cent of domestic groups earn less than this figure (see Chapter 3). The greatest part goes to meet the costs of entertaining and providing for the wedding guests, who, in my own experience of these occasions, seldom number fewer than 300 and sometimes exceed 500.

Apart from some savings and the sale of a few assets (usually a woman's ornaments) these expenses can only be met by borrowing. The fortunate ones who are employed in the public sector can take a limited interest-free wedding advance, but, for the most part, family members, friends, and neighbours, as well as local money-lenders, are relied on to provide the assistance necessary. While a portion of the outgoings is recouped from gifts in the form of cash donations from wedding guests, most domestic groups go into severe debt at the time of a marriage.

A few householders seek or are compelled by the most dire circumstances to avoid incurring this level of expenditure by marrying in civil ceremonies. ('If you marry in church you have to invite people.') Still, the overwhelming majority, despite the financial implications, prefer a church wedding, not simply because it is the 'proper form of service for a Christian', but the only appropriate and acceptable way in which a household can marry its children in 'full view of our own people'. The tendency to allocate a disproportionately high level of resources to marriage was already noted (and criticized) by European missionaries at the beginning of the century, when all but a handful of Protestants were materially very far from well off (see Houghton 1981: 242, 352).

Such 'extravagance' must be understood as an investment in maintaining a household's name (*peyar*)—its 'symbolic capital'—however limited its material capital may be. This becomes evident in the reported response of an impoverished widow to the suggestion of her prospective son-in-law that she refrain from providing furniture or cooking vessels for her daughter. Since she had several children to marry off he intended merely to ease her financial burden. But, he explained, 'she insisted that this is the custom; the bride must bring a cot and all. "No one should refuse this *sīr varisai*"', she scolded me. What would her neighbours think?' Here we have the Maussian dictum that the obligation to receive is as sacred as the obligation to give.

Equally, the heavy expenditure on a wedding by those least able to afford it may be read as a means of confirming the household's place in an existing network of kin, neighbours, and friends, a reaffirmation of ongoing obligations to those around them who matter, in what is otherwise seen as an inhospitable, even hostile, urban environment.

Some householders (though by no means all) take part in a ceremony held three months after the wedding, at which the bride's parents give gifts of clothing to the couple. (If they can afford it, they should also provide her with additional ornaments at this time.) It was interpreted by several individuals who had participated in such an event as a symbolic recognition of the fact that the marriage has survived its initial stages, and the young people are now joined together like the ball/clasp and cylinder (*kuṇtu kuḻāy*) of the wedding necklace, after which the ceremony is called.

Post-marital gifts culminate in those which parents are obliged to give their daughter and her husband on the first Christmas following the wedding, and then to her and her first child. Since she is expected to join them for the latter stages of her confinement, they also defray any expenses connected with the birth. However, Protestant women in Madras are less likely nowadays to join their natal households if these are outside the city. They tend increasingly to have their children in hospitals: lower class women in free or nearly free municipal, state, or other public institutions; middle-class women in expensive private clinics. Thereafter, all obligations on the part of parents cease, although some, needless to say, voluntarily continue to make gifts to their daughter and other members of her household. But there is no notion here, as exists in some parts of India, of a permanent obligation to provide gifts for affines (see Vatuk 1975).

The weddings of middle-class Protestants include the same basic elements, in terms of ritual and ceremonial, although there are, as we might expect, differences of scale and emphasis. Thus, their weddings take place in the bride's church, invariably an 'English' or other élite place of worship. There are usually two receptions on the day of the wedding. The first directly follows the service and may be held in the (generally spacious) grounds of the church or, as is common nowadays, in an exclusive hotel nearby. The guests are greeted by the bride's parents as well as the couple, hear a few words of blessing and congratulation by the minister, present their gifts to the newly-weds, and are served a light snack. It is seen by those in the middle class as a gesture of appreciation to the large numbers of casual friends, business associates, and other acquaintances (many of them status inferiors) in addition to the relatives who have attended the nuptials and so honoured the girl and her family.

The comment of one householder in the lower class sample who was present at such a reception is worth quoting for an alternative way of perceiving the occasion. As a junior em-

ployee in the same firm as the bride's father—who is a senior
executive—he was invited to attend the service in church and
the reception held afterward at a large and expensive hotel.

When I reached the hotel I was shown a place at a long table, which
was covered with a white cloth. The waiter soon brought everyone a
piece of cake and a cup of coffee. When I finished that I thought
there would be something else, but nothing came, and I got a shock.
I'm a poor man, but if I gave my guests what this man gave his,
everyone would rebuke me and go. You must give people food, *biriyani*, and only then will they be happy and praise you!

Among the lower class, as we have seen, there is only one
reception, where all guests are feasted equally, in the approved
manner.

An elaborate dinner, at which (mutton-based) *biriyani* is
served, is held later in the evening for close relatives on both
sides, and special guests, who often include a few celebrities. It
is not unusual for invitations to be sent to ministers of the
state and even central legislatures. Other invitees might include
High Court judges, directors of large corporations, or other
public figures, both within and outside the Protestant community, who are known to the family. It is a measure of the
latter's eminence if several such noteworthies are seen to attend
its weddings. In the speeches they are called upon to make they
pay respects to the hosts and offer good wishes to the couple.
These are occasions, therefore, when Christian élites not only
celebrate the union of two young people, their households,
and families, but demonstrate the range of their networks and
influence.

The costs of these receptions, as well as those of the bride's
dowry goods—which are substantial at this class level—are met
entirely by her domestic group. Parents of marriageable girls
would be demeaned by having to ask for financial help from
friends or relatives outside the household (a common and accepted practice within the lower class).

The expenses of the bridegroom's household comprise the
traditional items of clothing due to special kin and the bride's
sari and necklace. If his relatives must travel to Madras for the
wedding, their expenses are met by his household, in addition
to the costs of a separate dinner for them. But, on the whole, it
has a comparatively light burden to shoulder. In this regard,

there seems to have been a definite shift of responsiblity for meeting wedding expenses during the past several decades, which coincides with the emergence of an urban middle class within the community. While there are a variety of regional and caste customs in south India (see Miller 1980), many of them represented within the heterogeneous Protestant population of the city, there is emerging among the privileged families what they refer to as a 'proper Madras wedding', which places the major part of the financial obligations on the bride's household. Indeed, it has become, for all intents and purposes, a rough and ready means of distinguishing these élites from the generality of co-religionists where the burden lies with the bridegroom's side or is, at any rate, more equally shared. They are not entirely clear as to how this consensus came about. It may have arisen through emulation of Brahmanic practices in the city, or widened and crystallized a tendency found among those castes—like the Syrian Christians and the Nadars—who contribute disproportionately to the Protestant middle class in Madras.

Few households at this level of the urban hierarchy reckon to spend less than Rs 50,000 on the wedding festivities (and this may not necessarily include the costs of furniture, cooking vessels, and jewels settled on a daughter). The majority, moreover, assume an additional obligation to offer a large (usually cash) payment to the bridegroom or to his parents—figures for this vary between Rs 10,000 and Rs 100,000.[11] The remainder of the chapter examines such transfers of wealth among middle-class Protestants in Madras.

CASTE, CLASS, AND 'DOWRY'

The employment in an Indian context of a Western concept like 'dowry', with its particular European meanings and implications, presents certain difficulties which are by now familiar enough to anthropologists. However, in India, 'dowry' has become an indigenous term in its own right, and is applied to two analytically distinct sets of transactions. As we have seen, it connotes the traditional goods which accompany a bride to her conjugal home. But, as Beck writes, *dowry* implies more than the bride's jewels and household effects. 'It refers to

an actual lump sum of money demanded by the groom from
the bride's family' (1972: 237). Srinivas (1942) and Gough
(1956) distinguished the two kinds of transaction, and indicated
the latter by the term 'bridegroom wealth' or 'bridegroom
price'. I have elsewhere explored the analytical differences between the two aspects of dowry (Caplan 1984). Here I want to
relate the circulation of wealth among certain middle-class
households, on the one hand, to the extension of marriage networks, and, on the other, to the identification within the dominant sector of the community of exclusive marriage circles
defined by caste. The use of *dowry* will indicate that I am
employing or underlining others' employment of the indigenous
term (which conflates both kinds of wealth transfer); without
italics, it will connote only the 'bride's portion', i.e. *sīr varisai*.

The consensus in the literature is that the practice of paying
bridegroom price is spreading, that the amounts concerned are
increasing, and that its significance seems to be greatest among
the well-to-do in urban areas (see Rajaraman 1983). Within
the lower class, those affiliated to certain castes, like the Nadars,
which guard their boundaries carefully by endogamous marriages, do recognize the obligation to transfer resources in this
way, but, for the most part, economic circumstances either
render such payments an impossibility or limit them to token
amounts. Most Protestant householders in Madras who are not
part of the dominant class usually display little interest in such
a transaction. The main thrust of wealth transfers in those rural
castes and regions from which the majority of them stem were
in the opposite direction. As Miller notes, among the lowest,
unpropertied groups, payments were (and in the rural areas
still are) in the form of bridewealth (1980). In the urban setting,
as we have seen, this practice no longer obtains, but its contemporary expression takes the form of an acceptance by the
bridegroom's side that it must bear the brunt of wedding expenses. On the whole, then, outside the dominant class, people
do not transact bridegroom price.

What seems to be occurring is that alongside the notion of
dowry as a 'familial fund'—to use Goody's (1973) familiar
term—whereby a middle-class household confers on a daughter
a portion of its estate which, by tradition, remains in her possession, there is an increasing tendency for resources, in the

form of bridegroom price, to be alienated from both the daughter and her natal unit. Among these Christians, by and large, the bridegroom price is paid not to the young man but to his parents. According to Ross (1961: 261), this seems to be the tendency throughout urban India. And while these assets may be dispersed to meet a number of specific domestic needs— including assisting the young couple to set up a separate household—they are conceived by the recipients as being primarily intended to secure husbands for their daughters, or alternatively, to replenish resources already spent on the latters' marriages. Miller notes how this payment 'does not remain under the daughter's control, but frequently goes to the groom's family ... to provide a *dowry* for their daughter' (1980: 103). In other words, these payments become part of a 'societal fund'— again, Goody's term—circulating among households within particular marriage circles, as wealth received for sons is used to marry daughters.

At all levels of official India this transaction is ceaselessly condemned. Such universal censure of the practice has led to a number of legislative measures to ban it, the most comprehensive of which was the Dowry Prohibition Act of 1961. Certain legal 'loopholes', however, have enabled the custom to persist (see Devadason 1974). Within the Protestant fold, countless sermons and church publications reinforce a hostile attitude to what is widely termed '*dowry* evil'. Most Christians with whom I discussed the question know and share in the rhetoric.

Middle-class householders, if asked why they participate in such prestations if they are so widely disapproved, reply in several ways. The first is to plead no alternative: that unless they do so, their children will remain unmarried, and such a prospect is as unthinkable for them as for the generality of Indians. The second is to bewail the fact that there are simply not enough 'suitable boys' to marry. They refer, of course, not to any objective demographic condition, but to a cultural notion of scarcity, defined in the context of the intense competition among families and households to secure the most attractive alliances and so retain if not improve their place within the dominant class.

The third mode of response is to justify involvement as a means to 'recoup [the] investment'—to use Tambiah's phrase (1973: 63)—in sons' education. The latter rationale appears less than convincing in a community which, as we have seen, emphasizes the need to educate daughters as well as sons, and has done so for some time. Despite the asserted link between bridegroom price and the costs of education it is never suggested that the latter amount is actually calculated and a demand made accordingly. The criteria for setting the levels paid lie elsewhere. People constantly refer to a notional hierarchy of degrees and occupations to which bridegroom price is supposed to be related. To quote one man who had taken part in many such negotiations: 'If the boy is merely a BA, the price is a certain amount; if an IAS [Indian Administrative Service] officer, it is much more; if he is an engineer, even more still; if a doctor, the highest of all. Then we have to see if he is employed and where. So the price varies according to education, profession, achievement, and employment.' The recent emigration of professionally trained men (and, to a lesser extent, women) to the West has added a new dimension to the profile of attractive marriage partners. A permit to work and settle in the USA, for example, now constitutes what many regard as the most desirable qualification of all.

The amounts actually negotiated, however, vary considerably, even within a single occupational category, which suggests that the prospective husband's career prospects, like his educational attainments, are not the only determinants of bridegroom price levels. Other factors bear upon the amounts negotiated. One is the bride's personal qualities and accomplishments, although these affect the figure only marginally.[12] A more important—though unvoiced—influence is the notion, current within the marriage circles to which people belong, regarding the appropriate financial limits beyond which they are not expected to go. There are, in other words, accepted bounds to the demands for and willingness to offer bridegroom price, although these limits obviously do not remain static over time, nor are they the same for each of the various intra-marrying circles.

Because a substantial proportion of Christian marriages are confined to a unit defined by caste, it is entirely possible for differential bridegroom price exchanges to occur as between persons of separate castes performing similar occupations or placed contiguously in the urban class order. The amounts transacted by Syrian Christians are known to be higher than those of other Protestant groups in the city. These were described, with a mixture of awe and disapproval, as 'ridiculous' by one Nadar, a caste whose own demands are often decried by members of other groups as excessive. Because, in marriage terms, each caste operates like a closed 'sphere of exchange', there is little risk of spouses or payments to bridegrooms moving between, and thereby dissolving, the separate spheres. In the sense that more or less autonomous scales exist as between different caste units, these transactions fall somewhere between the highly variable and individual status-based dowry conferments and the considerably more standardized payments of a bridewealth system (see Goody 1973: 18).

Alternatively, there is some differentiation of bridegroom price scales within any particular caste, which reflects subtle distinctions of wealth and standing. One informant explained it like this: 'My wealth and status are fairly well known in the community. As my daughter approaches marriageable age I let it be known what kind of *dowry* is to be offered, so excessive demands are not going to be made.' These distinctions, as we might expect, provide opportunities for a certain amount of movement between separate in-marrying circles, as household and family circumstances improve or decline. But, as I have suggested, competition for limited economic resources during the past two decades has led to intense pressures on and within the middle class, and precluded any widespread intrusions, through the strategic use of bridegroom price, by those from outside the dominant group. An interesting case in point is the small but quite well-to-do population of Nadar merchants. Through careful cultivation of a distinctive life-style and closed connubium, the professional/bureaucratic/industrial élite within the caste has managed to prevent the utilization by these merchants of what Douglas and Isherwood (1978: 85) call 'consumption finesse' to infiltrate their ranks. (It must be acknowledged, on the other hand, that for reasons of their own, the majority of merchants may prefer to remain in their own social niche and outside the circles of the former.)

There are circumstances where wealth transfers of this kind are either unnecessary or unthinkable. Some individuals detect in bridegroom price a violation of their religious or moral scruples, and refuse on these grounds to consider partaking of such exchanges. Then, the most prominent households may desist from asking for or accepting these payments, and are equally reluctant to offer them. This is because, at a certain level, to give or receive bridegroom price can adversely affect a household's reputation. It may also be connected with the fact that such families are in a stronger position to insist on marriage settlements which maintain a daughter's rights to the property originating from her natal group. In other words, she is the primary recipient of its largess (in the form of *sīr varisai*), and not her husband's household (in the form of bridegroom price).[13]

Finally, we have to note that, within the middle class, households without an affiliation to a particular caste group eschew the transfer of resources to the bridegroom's family. Though no less concerned to demonstrate and maintain their position as élites by careful marriages, they refuse to play the bridegroom price game. Since domestic units without such a caste affiliation cannot and/or do not seek to marry within a tightly bounded circle defined in terms of common 'blood', they must, as I indicated earlier, find their matrimonial allies from within a more heterogeneous field. Hence, they are unwilling to tolerate the alienation of property outside the domestic group. They complain, like caste Christians do, of a dearth of acceptable bridegrooms for their daughters; but their efforts to secure 'suitable boys' does not lead to competitive bidding in the shape of bridegroom price. They continue, however, to devolve upon daughters the traditional dowry of jewellery and household effects.

The transfer of wealth from one household to another which the practice of offering bridegroom price (like bridewealth) entails, and its use as a 'circulating pool of resources' (Goody 1973: 17), is only feasible if it is conveyed within a more or less closed group—a caste or caste section. Therefore, while such transactions demonstrate the superior resources at the disposal of middle-class households, and serve thereby to restrict matrimonial unions to members of this class, they cannot be explained in these terms alone. In the changing urban milieu of a large city like Madras, which contains members of previously separate marriage circles within the same or closely related caste categories, who now regard one another as suitable partners, the movement of bridegroom price becomes a means of redefining endogamous boundaries. At the same time, a willingness to transfer wealth in this way reaffirms the caste credentials of the households linked by connubium, and so assists in gaining entitlement to its status and privileges in the increasingly competitive metropolis.

CONCLUSION

I have tried to look beyond the collective representations and symbolic meanings underlying marriage in an urban context, to focus on differences in the way rites and ceremonies within the Christian community are prosecuted and understood. Thus, common structural features can mask significant contrasts of perception and organization as between members of each class. A near-uniform (and comparatively late) age at marriage, for instance, reflects on the one side the realities of poverty and, on the other, a need for young people to remain single and dependent on parents for long periods in order to acquire the accomplishments necessary to preserve a position within the dominant class.

A 'good family', too, is a phrase in general currency, and its pursuit an important consideration in all marriage arrangements. Yet there are clear disparities in how householders on opposite sides of the class divide understand the term: in one view it connotes secular success and public acclaim, while in another it is a gauge of the perseverance with which Christian values are courted. Parkin's (1978) argument about the usefulness of regarding word, idea, and action as separate (though related) realms may be relevant here. We could say that, in spite of sharing a common set of terms, there are significant disparities in how they are thought about; this affects the manner in which matrimonial alliances are sought, and has various behavioural implications for persons at each level of the urban hierarchy.

As we have seen, there are also contrasts in several other customs connected with Christian marriage: in the denominational and other religious preferences of potential partners; the part played by the young couple themselves in the arrangements; the siting of rites and ceremonies; the flavour of festivities (even of the food served at receptions); the dimensions of marriage prestations, their direction, the focus of responsibility for their payment, and the sources available to those who must pay them. All these divergent practices and ideas amount, in effect, to distinctive matrimonial sub-cultures within each class.

Perhaps the most basic divergence is to be found in the wider social implications of the numerous individual marriage decisions. Those in the upper reaches of the urban hierarchy endeavour, above all, to preserve their favourable position and, in pursuit of this goal, effect the closure of boundaries by excluding from connubium others whose material circumstances and life-styles do not at least match their own. The increasing competition for limited space within the dominant class, moreover, encourages an extension of the household's matrimonial networks to include persons from other regional marriage circles with which they did not previously intermarry. Those who prefer to retain a caste identity and to marry within a unit defined by 'common blood', must be prepared to transfer wealth in the form of bridegroom price—the circulation of which reinforces and where appropriate redefines endogamous boundaries. The effect, overall, is to ensure the in-marrying of wealth and privilege.

By contrast, lower class Protestants adopt the converse policy of marrying close at hand, with those to whom they are already related by kinship and locality.[14] Intensification of links ensures some measure of security and solidarity in what is otherwise seen as an alien and alienating environment. Thus, excluded by those above them, as well as by the logic of their own circumstances, these householders are denied any possibility of approaching, through the creation of affinity, the citadels of power and privilege. Every marriage, to conclude the chapter as we began it, by quoting Bourdieu, 'tends to reproduce the conditions which have made it possible. Matrimonial strategies ... belong to the system of reproduction strategies ...' (1977: 70).

6

IDEOLOGY AND CONSCIOUSNESS
Caste, Class, and Church Discourse

INTRODUCTION

IT would be surprising if those divided so starkly by material circumstances and cultural proclivities should not—in appropriate situations—place a class construction upon their condition. Protestants in Madras certainly perceive themselves as relatively advantaged or disadvantaged, privileged or disprivileged, superordinate or subordinate, and so on. This is what Lloyd (1982: 40) calls the 'lowest level' of class consciousness. They utilize a range of expressions to differentiate themselves by income, employment, status, education, and consumption. There exists a comprehensive vocabulary of interpersonal and inter-class antipathy. Hopkins's insistence on the importance for a class to have the appropriate verbal idioms for the expression of its consciousness would appear to be satisfied (1977: 455).

Nevertheless, dominance does not necessarily imply resistance to dominance. The rapid growth of urban migration and poverty in the Third World has not resulted in a widespread rise of revolutionary movements, or even of a radical class consciousness among the urban poor, as predicted by many scholars (see Nelson 1970). Events in south India have certainly not borne out such forecasts. This should encourage a reassessment of that tendency in political science and political philosophy—and its vestiges in political anthropology—which seeks insights not so much by investigating what occurs but in speculating on what *ought* to occur (Therborn 1980: 104). What does seem necessary is to examine particular ethnographic contexts for clues which might help us to understand the ways in which human subjectivity is shaped and transformed. How can we deal theoretically with such a problem?

Anthropological writings on 'the self' provide a useful opening. These stress both its social and historically specific character, as well as its dynamic and multiple aspects. Epstein views identity as a 'concept of synthesis', by means of which the individual's various statuses, roles, and experiences are integrated into a 'coherent image of self' (1978: 101). Selfhood, moreover, is not a static notion, but is 'continuously created and recreated', a process generated by the attempts of 'interest groups' to 'manipulate and structure' the selves of their members (Cohen 1977: 117-18). Following Mauss (1979: 88) we may regard the self as the 'primordial category' of consciousness. We are thus encouraged to think of a person's consciousness as a constantly changing 'repertory' (Hannerz 1980: 291), a 'complex configuration of elements, inherited and acquired' (Turton 1984: 43). Consciousness, moreover, is vitally related to ideology. For Therborn, 'ideologies differ, compete, and clash not only in what they say about the world we inhabit, but also in telling us who we are, in the kind of subject they interpellate . . . It is a struggle over the assertion of a particular subjectivity' (1980: 78). Such interpellations, moreover, are 'consciously and unconsciously received, interpreted, accepted, rejected, maintained, or transformed by individuals, groups and classes' (ibid.: 103).

The instruments of these ideological interpellations are, on the one hand, various 'apparatuses' of the state (Althusser 1971)—the education system, the media, the religious establishment, etc. On the other hand, people are addressed regularly—and, in the context of a less industrially developed country, more effectively—by a variety of non-official or informal agencies and institutions (neighbours, families, workmates, congregations, rituals, and so forth). 'Ideological interpellations are made all the time, everywhere and by everybody' (Therborn 1980: 84). So that 'the production of forms of social consciousness . . . may occur in any or every sphere of existence' (Turton 1984: 38).

Earlier chapters examined some of the everyday contexts within which this ideological process occurs, though their thematic foci lay elsewhere. This chapter brings the issue of consciousness to the forefront. It looks first at the circumstances which define the significance and meanings of caste for members of the Protestant community in Madras, then turns to those ideological discourses and practices which promote or, alternatively, inhibit consciousness of class.

CASTE IDENTITIES

Whatever significance urban Protestants themselves (or ourselves as observers) attach to class as an indigenous concept, subjectivities constituted in terms of other, traditional, cultural categories remain significant. Caste, as I have indicated at various points in the narrative, is another form of consciousness which is important, and situationally paramount in its 'affective appeal' and/or as an 'ideological rallying-point', as Parkin remarks of the tribal group in Kenya (1978: 7).[1] The great majority of Protestants belonging to castes which converted in mass movements (see Chapter 2) continue to classify themselves in terms of these traditional status entities. A strong and exclusive caste attachment is most frequently explained by individuals themselves in terms of near-primordial feelings of belonging. Those who claim Nadar affiliation, for example, regularly point to their common origins (in the far south of the peninsula), traditions, history, and peculiar life-ways. Even members of this group who are most vociferous in denouncing the 'evils' of caste, are persuaded not only that they belong to a distinctive collectivity with a unique character, but that it is virtually impossible for outsiders to be successfully absorbed, or for Nadars themselves to 'fit in' anywhere else. Such identity, as Epstein observes, 'touches the core of the self', and is 'fed by taproots from the unconsciousness' (1978: 101). The rest of the Protestant community in Madras, for its part, chides the Nadars and other such exclusive groups for being 'clannish' and 'inward-looking'.

Purity and pollution

Self-ascription in terms of caste can be partly understood by reference to concepts of purity and pollution. There is plenty of evidence to suggest that the earliest converts sought to protect their ritual status by retaining commensal and other forms of restrictive practice *vis-à-vis* members of other groups. Hudson remarks that Vellalar converts in the nineteenth century thought lower caste Christians to be 'unclean' and 'polluting'

(1970: 438). Over a century ago one LMS missionary noted how Sudras would not 'in common life' eat with lower castes or drink the water they touched (Mullens 1854: 87). Adherence to traditional symbols of hierarchy and separation was not the prerogative only of members of the more highly placed castes. Luke and Carman point out how Christians belonging to different untouchable groups in rural Andhra Pradesh refused to draw water from the same well. As recently as twenty years ago, they report, 'the caste barrier is ... rigidly maintained ... on matters of food and drink . . .' (1968: 78). High ecclesiastical rank apparently counted for little where such barriers operated. Grant reports that one Indian bishop is never invited to dinner by certain members of his diocese 'because he is of the wrong caste' (1959: 25).

Inter-dining restrictions, however, are rarely invoked publicly in the urban setting to signify status differences. Thus, communion is no longer an occasion, as it once was, for the demonstration of caste hierarchy.[2] In Madras, nowadays, it is quite common for Protestants of high caste to take the cup from ministers of Harijan background. Nevertheless, distance, inequality, even hostility, may continue to be expressed verbally in commensal terms. One hears people say 'I wouldn't accept a cup/glass of coffee/tea/water from him/her'. I have also heard remarks—usually made in a combination of jest and derision—to the effect that members of certain groups consider that their 'blood is superior', but such observations are metaphorical rather than statements about 'bio-substance' (see also Stirrat 1982: 16).

While the onset of puberty continues to be marked ritually by rural Christian women this is rarely observed by urban dwellers, especially within the middle class. Moreover, urban women are no longer segregated within the home, nor compelled to refrain from cooking during menstruation (see Eichinger 1974: 127-8). Even so, some women (especially within the lower class) are hesitant about entering a church, or, more especially, receiving communion during their menses.

Protestants do not attribute these observances to Hindu doctrine—although if pressed they might acknowledge the link—but relate them to a more general, all-India code of practice.[3] The more educated members of the community sometimes explain adherence to certain practices in terms of modern notions about hygiene and public health (see also Good 1978: 492).

Dietary habits are thought of in a similar way. While Christian doctrine does not forbid it, the majority of Protestants do not eat beef or pork. To most Protestants the reasons are self-evident: such items of diet are regarded by the society at large as 'dirty' and 'polluting', and they would be reluctant to eat them, and ashamed even to be seen purchasing them.

Observances related to death also point to an unstated belief that the relatives left behind are not merely bereaved but somehow polluted by their loss.[4] In the urban context, the emphasis is on proper Christian burial rites (cremation is regarded as a throw-back to Hindu practices). The burial usually takes place some 24 hours after the death. After a prayer led by the minister, the body is taken from the house, by male relatives, to the hearse and again from the hearse into the church for the standard CSI ritual for the dead. The body is placed with its feet towards the altar and mourners circumambulate the open coffin for a last sight of the deceased. After the service, the body is taken to the gravesite for the brief rite of interment, presided over by the pastor, and the mourners, after bathing and changing clothes, return to the house of the deceased for a meal. The room in which the corpse had lain meanwhile has been thoroughly cleaned and washed (purified?), and a candle is left to burn overnight.

The situation among these Protestants contrasts with that described for the Syrian Christians of Kerala by Fuller. He notes that they 'have no concept of bodily pollution consequent on birth, death, menstruation or other bodily conditions, nor do they observe pollution for them' (1976: 64).[5] Clearly, within the Tamil Protestant community, there is ample evidence of such notions, although they are not to be seen as part of a system of ritual exchanges which express or establish differential caste ranking. Among Protestants, moreover, it would be inappropriate to overemphasize the uniformity of commitment to these observances and, by implication, the values they embody. For one thing, most people, as I have noted, see certain of these customs as part of an Indian—as distinct from a specifically Hindu—cultural context. For another, there are significant differences in the degree to which certain menstrual,

dietary, or funerary practices are followed, as between rural
and urban residents, and within the urban setting, as between
those divided by wealth, education, or religious commitment.

The contemporary descendants of those who came to Protestantism in mass movements are certainly more concerned
about pollution and the consequences of breaking its taboos
than are the offspring of individual converts, most of whom
were of high caste. The Anglican bishop Sargent is reported to
have observed, in the latter part of the nineteenth century, that
'Vellalars have more decidedly given up caste than the Shanars
(Nadars) or any other of our people. This is due no doubt to
the fact that they came over largely as individuals isolated from
home and ties, whereas the Shanars came in bodies' (Hudson
1970: 423). A not dissimilar observation was made half a century ago by bishops Azariah and Whitehead: '. . . it is noticeable
that the higher the caste from which the converts come the
more completely they abandon ... caste prejudices. It often
seems easier for a Brahmin convert to eat with an outcaste than
for different sections of the outcastes to eat together' (1930: 61).

Self-identity

Within the urban Protestant community, as I have shown,
there are households containing only members of the same
named caste group and others comprising persons who are
descended from previous inter-caste matrimonial unions, or
who have themselves made such marriages. An unwillingness
to identify oneself or one's domestic unit in caste terms may,
therefore, be related to the circumstances which encouraged
or compelled forebears or living individuals to abandon such
concerns, and to marry without regard for them. Many of the
contemporary progeny of earlier non-endogamous marriages
profess neither knowledge of nor interest in their own caste
backgrounds.

However, refusal to acknowledge or claim a definitive caste
identity is found not only among the genealogically hybrid.
Some members of mass movement groups also disclaim any
caste affiliation and refuse to employ these categories when
identifying themselves. To raise the matter of caste membership
with all such persons is to risk being met with incredulity or
bemusement, and occasionally with annoyance. 'These things

belong to the past', they might say, 'nowadays there is no caste; we are all Indian Christians'. Indeed, it would be a rare discussion of caste (and there are many) which is not punctuated by several statements of this kind, for such an assertion, which echoes a much proclaimed theological position, is accepted as morally proper within the community.

Opposition to what was regarded as any manifestation of caste within the Protestant fold was a recurring theme in missionary rhetoric for well over a century before India's independence (see Forrester 1980). Although it took some time for a consensus to be reached,[6] the missionaries finally assumed a fairly consistent position on caste, inveighing against what one of them called the 'citadel of Hinduism inside the Christian Church' (Sharrock 1910: 194). Caste was placed in direct opposition to, indeed, was regarded as the very antithesis of, basic Christian values. Along with such a position went the contention that, through the act of conversion, a person ceased to be part of the caste system. Thus, the American Arcot Mission Jubilee brochure of 1903 proclaims that 'Christianity frees these outcastes from their thraldom, educates and uplifts them'. By opposing totally two religious world-views in this way the missionaries argued that adherence to one must involve rejection of the other. Since 1947 the ecclesiastical leadership of the CSI has also taken a firm and consistent stand against all forms of casteism within the ritual body and community. Caste is regularly denounced from pulpits, attacked in the parochial press and on public occasions, and widely regarded as a blemish on—even a sin within—Protestantism.

Negation of caste assumes special conviction among many householders in the lower class who have fundamentalist leanings, for it is widely believed and much admired that this form of Christianity, in particular, has no place for such 'satanic influences'. People at this level of the urban class order are also more likely to be from Harijan backgrounds, as I have noted. Like all Protestants, they have a positive religious sanction to renounce such affiliations. However, for one thing, the process does take time, perhaps generations, and is certainly not available as an option to recent converts. For another, the abandonment of this status is not without difficulties. The concern of the church to press the central government to grant Harijan

Christians the same rights as their Hindu counterparts—there have been numerous conferences, demonstrations, and petitions over the past quarter century[7]—while undertaken with the best of intentions, has had the effect of singling out these Protestants as the one category within the community to be labelled officially by a caste designation. Then again, while Harijan Christians are not entitled to these constitutional concessions, they do have an opportunity to benefit from certain state programmes for the 'depressed' and 'backward' castes. Thus, like the 'Koli dilemma' discussed by Parry (1970), Harijans, to the extent that they have any choice in the matter, must assess the advantages of each course of action. The assumption of a 'casteless' identity, however, can be represented as a form of status mobility. In Kerala, Fuller tells us, those who claim to have 'forgotten' caste are usually untouchables or 'New Christians' (1976: 57).

We have to note the propensity for some Protestants who are the products of non-endogamous unions to define themselves, none the less, in terms of caste. Despite genealogical 'realities' which would make nonsense of any notions of 'blood purity' through descent, claims to particular caste statuses are presented and, on the whole, accepted. Persons making such an assertion may do so in terms of a link (through either males or females or both) to a distinguished Protestant of known high caste. Most commonly this is an original convert, who subsequently earned a reputation as a scholar, literary figure, respected clergyman, etc. These ties are not difficult to trace since they seldom extend back more than a few generations. Most middle-class Protestants descended from high caste converts can, if they choose to do so, find such a distinguished forebear on whom to focus.

With the establishment of such an ancestral link, a household or family acquires its caste by association, so to speak, and does not have continually to demonstrate and reaffirm its claim. Because of this, the particular unions which individual members enter into do not affect such an identity and so are of no special concern, provided these unions do not knowingly and blatantly involve partners of Harijan status.

The products of mixed unions within the lower class who cannot find such eminent forebears may also profess a respectable caste identity, though do so without reference to the past. Such claims are facilitated by the existence of a caste category (Vellalar) found throughout Tamilnadu which, in any local hierarchy, is generally ranked next to the Brahmins. Those seeking to enhance their status often take Vellalar titles (Barnett 1970: 44). The process is apparently a long-standing one, and may indeed have been encouraged by the very process of colonial census-taking. The 1871 edition included as 'Vellalar' a variety of separate, named groups (Oddie 1981: 51). By 1901, the census-takers themselves noted the confusion, identifying a plethora of groups which had assumed Vellalar titles, including some (untouchable) Paraiyans (see Baker 1975: 231 n. 69). Thus, like the Patidars of Gujerat (Pocock 1972) and the Shresthas of the Kathmandu Valley (Rosser 1966), the Vellalars became subject to a great deal of 'infiltration' from below. They were, in the words of one proverb, 'like an aubergine pickle mixing palatably with anything'. In the heterogeneous milieu of a metropolis like Madras the tendency remains fairly widespread, and is certainly found within the Protestant community. Generally, there is no attempt to embarrass others by reference to their hybrid character, nor, on the part of the household itself, to manipulate or otherwise disguise its genealogical record. Nor, again, is there concern to adjust behaviour to conform with more widely accepted notions of high caste standards.

The absence of collective action of this kind reflects the fact that assertions of caste status are not made in an interactional context and, therefore, do not have to be supported by genealogical or behavioural 'evidence'. There is no formal or informal group either to impose controls or offer corporate judgements on caste claims. Even persons who might regard themselves as of 'pure' caste are reluctant to question the bonafides of the 'pretenders', since the line between them is sometimes very thin indeed. The former, for demographic or, more commonly, status reasons, occasionally draw partners from the ranks of the latter, as we saw in Chapter 5.

The tacit acceptance of these assertions is also to be understood in the same spirit as the claims themselves. Simply stated, they underline the fact that the Protestant community in south India originated not only as the consequence of mass conversions by depressed low castes, but as the result of profound religious experiences undergone by individual converts belonging to higher Hindu groups. To refuse the claims of these individuals and households to high caste status would be effectively to deny the historical links of the community to the most respectable sections of the wider society.

At this juncture, several observations might be made. Firstly, caste identity in the urban Protestant milieu is a complex matter and cannot be understood by reference to a single, all-embracing cultural model, whether informed by notions of ritual attribution and interaction, substance and code, purity and pollution, or even the 'official' Christian position negating caste. All of these ideologies speak to individuals and influence their consciousness in varying degrees. Moreover, such subjectivities are seldom, if ever, totally constituted by a single mode of discourse. Thus, it is possible for the same person to claim one kind of identity in a particular situation and another in a quite different one. An individual may refuse publicly to assert a caste attachment, but at the same time subscribe to and proclaim, utilizing the appropriate euphemisms, the benefits of marriage between households who have similar 'ways', which comes of sharing a common origin, 'tradition', and life-style. Then, the union of someone from a hybrid family which eschews any caste affiliation, with another which takes an opposite stance, can lead the individual to emphasize a different aspect of his or her 'self' from that which was previously stressed. Just as commonly, various members or closely related branches of a family might identify themselves in different ways. Two people recognizing kinship may yet claim quite distinct relationships to caste.

Finally, for these Protestants, as for most Indians—as Béteille (1964) and others remind us—the notion of caste has a variety of referents and meanings. Indeed, it is frequently rendered in English, and so has become an indigenous term in its own right. On the one side, as we have seen, it is applied to different levels of the formal hierarchy—in one context to *jati*, in another to *varna*, in still another to a vague category of similarly placed castes or even an informal alliance of quite disparately labelled individuals or groups. On the other, it has clear political connotations. When Protestants rail against its 'evils', they have in mind not so much the existence within the church and community of a Hindu counter-theology of hierarchy, pollution, and the like, but the intense rivalries generated by and/or expressed in terms of caste hostilities. For the most part, then, it is the ethnic dimension of caste which attracts most attention and comment.

THE POLITICS OF CASTE IN THE CHURCH

For some time now, caste distinctions have ceased to be reflected in the formal rituals of Protestantism. Seating arrangements in church no longer symbolize separation and differences of rank; congregations now accept (if somewhat grudgingly) ministers without regard for their caste backgrounds; and, as already noted, communion is no longer an occasion for the demonstration of inequality within the ritual body. However, in spite of an official ideology of intense hostility to casteism, it does manifest itself in a political form inside the church and its related institutions. Within the CSI, caste frequently serves as a reference point for the creation of informal political associations through which people compete for pre-eminence in church affairs. At the same time, it may be employed as a device by means of which one's own failure or success, as well as that of others, can be explained and evaluated.

It would be inaccurate to suggest that pre-1947 denominational structures were free from caste-based politics. Nadar-Vellalar rivalry within the former Tinnevelly diocese of the Anglican church is legendary. Relations between the two during the latter part of the nineteenth century were reportedly 'very hostile' (Hudson 1970: 431).[8] Parenthetically, I have on numerous occasions been told that the main obstacle to the entry of Lutherans into the church unions of the first half of this century were not due to theological or liturgical considerations, or even the highly fragmented character of the Lutheran structure in south India (see p. 45). It was and remains the fear on the part of the Vellalars, said to be the dominant voice in the Lutheran fold, of being absorbed into a larger religious organization which would be controlled by the more numerous and 'aggressive' Nadars. There is both evidence and compelling reason to suggest that political struggles have generally been intensified and expanded since the creation of the ecumenical CSI (see Hollis 1962: 30). This is not altogether surprising for, with the amalgamation of many disparate denominations into a single organization, the united church became the repository of considerable and varied resources. The former adherents of diverse persuasions—some of them dominated by members of a single caste[9]—were brought, for the first time, face-to-face within the new corporate body and, in effect, compelled to struggle for control of its structures.

Furthermore, since the union occurred at the moment of national independence, it symbolized the newly won freedom from the constraints of European domination within the missions and Indian church. Senior ecclesiastical as well as lay positions, previously all but monopolized by foreigners, became available, many for the first time, to Indian Christians.[10] The CSI has become, therefore, not surprisingly, an arena within which many persons from many backgrounds struggle for a share of these benefits: they contest with one another to control the allocation of finances; to gain office and access to various perks of office; to exercise spiritual as well as temporal power, and generally to achieve positions, lay or clerical, which will bring them influence, respect, and esteem.

Some of this competition occurs within the congregation, especially in the context of elections for the Pastorate Committee which, along with the minister, is responsible for most decisions taken on behalf of the membership. The 'democratization' of the Indian church has, somewhat paradoxically, created new opportunites for caste rivalries to be vigorously expressed.

Since most congregations, at least in the urban areas, are composed of persons belonging to different castes, elections to and, thereafter, the conduct of business within the Pastorate Committees are frequently conceived and explained in terms of caste affiliation. Antagonistic relations among members of the Pastorate Committee and the congregation at large, or between the latter and the minister may be similarly interpreted.

There must be few congregations which at some time or other have not experienced difficulties due to what is perceived as caste conflicts, while some have reputations for being permanently riven by them, as I noted in Chapter 4. Diocesan officials admit to spending an inordinate amount of time investigating and mediating quarrels of this kind, while not a few clergymen suggest that their present assignments were motivated by an urgent need to bring order out of the chaos of casteism into which their predecessors had allowed the pastorate to sink. One minister, expressing a fairly widespread sentiment, offered the opinion that 'the main problem in any congregation boils down to caste'.

A handful of congregations are acknowledged to be 'peaceful', and they are almost invariably those to which the Protestant élites are attached. It is widely believed, with some justification, that persons belonging to such congregations are already successful and respected members of the community and do not require or seek positions on Pastorate Committees to earn or enhance their reputations, although they accept honorary office in various organizations associated with the church (see Chapter 4).

Casteism exists—perhaps in its most intense form—at supra-congregational levels of the church as well. It is believed to affect the Śynod itself (see below). Composed of all CSI bishops, as well as lay delegates from each diocese, this body is the ultimate authority in the CSI, although to most ordinary members it is very remote indeed. The forum within which the latter perceive the most effective decisions to be taken is the diocese. Diocesan Councils, composed of ministers and lay representatives from each pastorate in the unit, are responsible for a range of policies which closely affect all church members and their clergy. Not uncommonly, persons belonging to a particular caste, or association of castes, or *varna*, succeed in gaining a predominant influence on the important committees within the Council, to the virtual exclusion of other groups. The existence of such alignments can lead to extreme bitterness on the part of those excluded from office and influence, and to accusations against the entrenched groups of caste arrogance, preferment, and the like.

An instance of this kind of situation is reported in one study of factionalism in a CSI diocese in Kerala in the 1960s. The study reveals how Syrian Christians and a few other high caste groups, though comprising somewhat less than half the population of the diocese, provided nearly four-fifths of the Diocesan Council's membership. Harijan groups complained of inadequate representation on the Council and on its various policy committees, and of the failure of the diocese to help them improve their position. The eventual outcome of the agitation, which at times took a violent turn, was the formation of a separatist church by some 20,000 Harijans from the diocese (see Thampan 1968).

Baskaran (1970) records a similar mass exodus from the CSI in a Tamil-speaking diocese. There, the chief protagonists were two Harijan castes, 'bitter rivals' from 'time immemorial'. When one group felt itself excluded by the other from playing its full part in the affairs of the diocese, it left to form an independent church.

While these cases are probably exceptional for the manner of their eventual resolution, they are by no means unusual in the pattern of diocesan politics which they reveal. Within the Madras diocese, the principal opposition of late (as it was represented to me) is between Harijans and a miscellaneous category of persons who are labelled simply as non-Harijans (although it is common to hear the Nadars identified as the most influential voice within this 'alliance'). As it happens, the division is not only caste-based, but has (acknowledged) geographical and denominational overtones, and a (generally unacknowledged) class dimension as well. Because of their wealth and prominence in the wider society, middle-class members of the CSI's Madras diocese—who predominantly belong to or stem from various higher 'clean' castes—exercise a dominant influence in church affairs. Their denominational backgrounds are mainly in the Anglican (CMS and SPG) and Congregational (LMS and American Madura) missions. Geographically, their origins are in the southern parts of the state.

Their antagonists within the diocese are Harijans whose native places are in the northern districts of Tamilnadu. They are, by and large, from poor rural origins, and in Madras are found predominantly within the lower class. In denominational terms they are the products mainly of the American Arcot mission (of the Reformed Church), the Church of Scotland, and Methodist missions. The church has been an important avenue of mobility for them, and indeed they provide a disproportionate number of the diocese's ministers, comprising well over half the clergy in Madras city's CSI congregations.

Despite their by no means insignificant presence within the diocese, Harijans, and especially those from the North Arcot region, frequently complain that they are not allowed to play as full a part as they would want to in its affairs. Their grievances are expressed in terms of two principal and situationally appropriate modes of ideological discourse: denomination and caste. As I have discussed elsewhere the contemporary implications of previous denominational attachments (Caplan 1980), here I want to focus on the significance of caste, and to do so in relation to events surrounding the election of a diocesan bishop in 1974.

With the resignation of the former Bishop in Madras (a European) in the spring of that year, a special session of the Madras Diocesan Council was held to choose three names for submission to the Synod, a sub-committee of which was to make the final selection. The vote in the Council suggested that there was overwhelming support for the incumbent Assistant Bishop, who, though near retirement himself, was a widely respected cleric from the North Arcot region and, like most clergymen in the district, probably of Harijan background. (Even the few who denied that he had untouchable origins agreed that he was the 'Harijan candidate'.)[11] But, since the rules insisted on a panel of three names, the Council also chose a second Arcot minister and, as its third candidate, a younger man whose origins were in a different part of the state, a Vellalar (married, as it happens, to a Nadar woman). To the surprise of most and the consternation of many people, the Synod's selection sub-committee chose the last, apparently by a narrow majority, to be the new Bishop in Madras.

Although it is impossible to know the precise details surrounding the selection, virtually all the people with whom I discussed the matter—including a senior Synod official— unequivocally identified caste as the principal motive behind the decision. The *Christian Focus*, a leading independent monthly published in Madras, asked rhetorically, with reference to a pamphlet circulating in the city at the time which made such an allegation, 'Does caste enter into the Election of Bishops, also?' (15 September 1974). Supporters of the favoured

but defeated candidate were convinced that what they described as the Nadar-led, non-Harijan, 'faction' had succeeded
in influencing the Synod to appoint its own favourite against
the expressed wishes of the Diocesan Council (in which the
Harijan 'faction', led by the North Arcot delegates, had a
strong voice). These claims were supported by widespread al-
legations that a letter had been sent to the Synod by an unnamed but apparently influential person declaring that because
the Madras diocese was the most important in the CSI it would
not do to have a Harijan bishop. That the existence of such a
letter was confirmed by several 'disinterested' informants is
neither here nor there. The universal belief in its existence
among these Protestants served to reinforce their conviction
that, in the words of one of their ministers, 'Harijans have no
chance in the church'.

The bitterness generated by this election—and other incidents which followed soon after (see below)—undoubtedly
contributed to the decision a few months later to bifurcate the
Madras diocese. The new diocese was formed mainly from
pastorates in the North Arcot area. Indeed, in the view of some
observers of and participants in these events, bifurcation was a
convenient administrative solution allowing the Harijans in
this and adjacent regions to escape from non-Harijan control
of diocesan affairs.[12]

During the course of these conflicts, caste identities are cla-
rified, confirmed, or even adopted. Those whose genealogical
credentials deny them ready access to a particular caste status
may yet reinforce their claims by alignment with a faction
which carries a caste designation. Alternatively, others who
would abjure any such affiliation, yet take an active part in
church affairs, find that in supporting one contending party or
another, they are allotted, willy-nilly, a particular caste label.
Certainly, to seek office or rally support without benefit of a
caste following (even if not actively canvassed) can lead
nowhere, so the ambitious individual without a clear attachment to caste may have to assume one or agree to be tagged
in this way.

The caste encounters which take place within the church and
its related structures do not follow a classic segmentary pattern.
On some occasions, structurally equivalent units are deemed

to be the protagonists: Nadars are engaged by Vellalars, or (Harijan) Malas by Madigas. On other occasions, the adversaries may be structurally unequal: Harijans (a *varna*) rival Nadars (a *jati*, or, in the Madras setting, a caste category). On yet different occasions, the rivalry might involve an identifiable unit and its alter, defined simply as not-the-unit. Thus, as I indicated above, the principal opposition within the diocese is reported as being between the Harijans and non-Harijans, or occasionally as between Nadars and non-Nadars.

Clearly, there is no pattern here of lesser units dissolving their conflicts to unite against a greater antagonist. It is each situation which determines the contours of the specific confrontation, and within which individuals assume and/or are assigned particular caste identities, although these are not necessarily permanently construed (a person might be a Nadar in one context and a 'non-Harijan' in another). Moreover, these various aspects of identity are equally part of the indigenous lexicon of caste, no less so than those underpinned by notions of purity/pollution, or the like.

Whatever the status of these caste mentalities, they cannot be regarded as a form of miscognition. Far from being misrepresentations of 'reality', they are the affirmations of specific social categories and ways of thought. Nevertheless, it would be wrong to stress the 'primordial' nature of such subjectivities, for they are continually being reconstituted. Caste, as we have seen, is not an immutable identity, fixed in an indeterminate past (though it is sometimes represented as such), but a variable and varying category whose contours and meanings undergo periodic redefinition. As an ideology, therefore, caste is far from being an integrated or consistent discourse; rather, it emerges as something of an ill-blended mixture of disparate, discordant, and often jarring messages.

Ethnic loyalties, in as much as they constitute an important aspect of 'the self', may be seen to compete with those of class, or, as Giddens puts it, foster 'types of structuration which deviate from that established by the "class principle" . . .' (1982: 162).[13] There are, moreover, other kinds of ideology which would inhibit and suppress the emergence of class consciousness among the dominated groups. It is to these discourses and the manner of their address that I now turn.

THE INHIBITION OF CLASS CONSCIOUSNESS

Within the neighbourhoods, kindreds, and households of the lower class, trust in the possibility of individual improvement has a vitiating effect on the development of a common awareness of deprivation and subordination. Bujra (1978–9) shows how 'penny capitalist entrepreneurs' in a Nairobi slum, despite sharing the life-styles of the poor, provide models of success for those amongst whom they live. Similarly, Protestants in Madras can point to numerous 'success stories' near at hand. Indeed, they are frequently held up as an example of a community which has, through education and hard work, 'come up' in the world (though only a tiny proportion have in fact done so). More immediately, as I showed in Chapter 3, persons employed in the relatively secure formal sector are frequently found in the same tenement blocks, slum settlements, and even households, as those either without employment altogether or struggling within the informal sector. Such local and domestic amalgams not only help to keep at bay the severest consequences of poverty and insecurity, but in a literal sense, bring home the possibilities for alleviating and overcoming these conditions. Even the striving for and occasional acquisition of expensive luxury goods plays a similar ideological role in appearing to render economic and social improvement a matter of personal competence and effort. The hopes of the underprivileged are, therefore, more readily focused on individual achievement than on solidarity for collective action. Alternatively, the blame for failure is placed not on the structures of inequality, but on the individual.

This emphasis also emerges clearly in the views held by members of the middle class about those beneath them in the social order. The latter are generally represented as intrinsically deserving of their inferior position in society. Their association with low levels of education, absence of skills, inadequate housing, poverty, and lack of sophistication is frequently explained in terms of personal failing. Such people are considered intemperate, lacking discipline, ill-suited to responsibility, and so on. I have on numerous occasions heard expressions of middle-class horror at the thought that such people even possess a vote. The rhetoric of class, as Michaelson suggests, 'closely follows the ideological justification for the caste hierarchy', with its emphasis on natural distinctions (Michaelson 1973: 162–3).

At the same time, the middle class fosters a subjective aware-ness of its own identity, seeking constantly to establish the primacy of its privileges and the legitimacy of its dominant position. In numerous conversations and writings, some of them reproduced in the Christian parochial press, the middle class is presented as 'the backbone of the social and economic structure of the nation', the principal 'stabilising influence' and agency of well-being. It is said to play a 'pivotal role' in planning, production, research, marketing, administration, and defence, and in the 'orderly development' of the State. It is, in short, the 'core of society' (Nambiar 1982: 6–8).

Such a class, it is then argued, merits better than it gets. Its members are under-paid and over-taxed, and their incomes and savings eroded by inflation. For example, to illustrate the 'difficulties' of middle-class life, the glossy *Illustrated Weekly* magazine printed a feature article containing the household budget of an executive earning Rs 4,000 per month (Rs 2,680 after tax). After noting the amounts spent on school fees, hous-ing, parental support, transport, insurance, newspapers, and club memberships (a total of Rs 937), the executive concerned is quoted as remarking that 'the money left for household and other expenses [i.e. Rs 1,743] is so meagre that it very difficult to maintain even a reasonably good standard of living'. The article (Nambiar 1982) was reproduced without comment in the Madras Diocesan monthly magazine *News and Notes*.

So, the middle class is 'angry' and 'disaffected' and requires greater consideration and more favourable treatment from the State—higher tax and estate duty thresholds, enhanced urban land ceilings, increased and improved high income housing, even special hospitals designed for middle-class patients.[14] An almost continuous rhetoric of self-aggrandizement, coupled with demands for an even greater share of the nation's resources, maintains a heightened sense of awareness among members of this class of their unity, common cause, and what is seen as their richly deserved place of pre-eminence in the social hierarchy.

They support mainly the Congress (which is regarded as the party of the well-to-do in the state) and oppose the populist

DMK and ADMK. They have no sympathy for unions (especially if these are independent or affiliated to the two main Dravidian parties), nor indeed for any reforms designed to improve the condition of labour (Misra 1961: 356).[15] Both directly and indirectly, therefore, they bolster and encourage represssive measures against those organized sectors of the lower class which might serve to articulate a more radical oppositional consciousness. In pursuit of their own privileges, they tend to uphold the aims of capital, even if they are not themselves its principal owners. Their discourse thus incorporates what Therborn would call an 'ego-ideology', serving to form the subjects of the middle class itself, as well as an 'alter-ideology'—i.e. ideological elements through which the latter strive to shape the formation of other, lower class subjects (1980: 27–8).

Middle-class Protestants, who have a dominant voice in the church, share these viewpoints. According to one indigenous critic, 'they are supportive of the status quo and uncritical of the inequalities in the social order . . . their preoccupation with rules and regulations, order, control, management, possessions, security . . . savings, professional education, respectable careers, and so on, describe their situation'. Church policies, he suggests, 'despite the profession of solidarity with the poor, reflect middle class bias and expediency' (Prabhakar 1981: 9). Attempts to organize primary and middle school teachers in the diocese's educational establishments have been strongly resisted, as have endeavours to bring the conditions of employees in Christian health centres and hospitals in Tamilnadu into line with those of similarly placed public servants (see below). In light of such attitudes, we can understand the enthusiasm of the middle class for the Emergency of 1975–7. Strikes were banned, trade union rights denied, wage cuts imposed on various sectors, and so on (see Selbourne 1982: 76). Most middle-class Christians saw the Emergency in terms of greater efficiency. 'Clerks and low level employees, peons and all, were at work when they were supposed to be. Everything ran on time. From that point of view, it was a golden period.' The response of most ordinary people among the lower class was, as one man phrased it, 'to keep silent and do our work. We were simply afraid to say or do anything to offend our superiors.'

Official Christian support (both Catholic and Protestant) for these measures has subsequently been described by critics as expressing identification of the church and community leaders with the existing central government and its programmes. The Secretary of the CSI Synod at the time declared that the church saw the Emergency as a 'short-term necessity', so that 'people have to be willing to sacrifice a little of their freedom to let law and order prevail'. It was thus welcomed 'as a means of putting an end to the chaotic conditions in the country' (see Pro Mundi Vita: Dossiers 1980).[16]

Although partly attributable, no doubt, to a 'minority complex' and the fear of jeopardizing its special status, the church's attitude must be primarily understood in the context of its historical association with the dominant class. During the colonial period, most orthodox churches, as distinct from the missions, were heavily subsidized by the government, and were unequivocal in their support of the authorities. After the 'mutiny' of 1857, for example, services were held in European churches each year on a day appointed by the Governor-General to give 'public Thanksgiving to Almighty God for the quelling of the late mutiny and the restoration of peace to Her Majesty's Indian Empire'.[17] Since independence, the CSI has tended to follow a similar line, behaving 'in such a way as not to question fundamentally the prevailing Indian social ensemble but on the contrary to contribute to its maintenance and reinforcement' (Prabhakar 1981: 9). We have already noted how senior lay personnel, within both the CSI and its associated organizations, are drawn from the middle class. It is, therefore, no surprise that as the prevalent voice within the ritual body, they should espouse the values of that class.

In the process of reproducing its superordinate position within a social order, the dominant class seeks, among other things, to limit consciousness of its domination on the part of the subjugated. In the south Indian Protestant context, the church contributes to the containment of a class-related consciousness by prosecuting an ideology which effectively denies the reality of class. While it readily acknowledges (and protests) the existence and implications of caste differentiation within the community, it 'lives with its problems of class divisions without admitting them' (Kurien 1981: 47). For one thing, they are frequently identified as caste problems. The conditions of the lower class are perceived and dealt with, essentially, as manifestations of Harijan status (and, of course, there is a great deal of overlap between them). The efforts of the church to alleviate these conditions are directed towards gaining for Christian Harijans the same constitutional rights enjoyed by similarly placed groups within the Hindu community. In like vein, the efforts of some Christian activists to secure improvements in conditions of service for low paid employees of the diocese are often phrased in the vocabulary of caste. Though one would not wish to deny the desirability of such projects, nor the sincerity of their promulgators, the discursive mode in which they are conceived and promoted serves to hide and thus deny the common experience of subordination by all those occupying a similar position at the bottom of the class order.

Class divisions are denied in other ways as well. The church's industrial mission, for example, seeks to produce 'better workers, loyal citizens and responsible family members' (according to the Madras Diocesan's *News and Notes*, 15 December 1981). Essentially, it deals with the symptoms of disprivilege, and not its underlying causes; the 'problem', moreover, is diagnosed as lying with and to be overcome by the individual. Thus, workers in debt are urged to attend courses on better budgeting, while guidance is provided on the avoidance of absenteeism and on overcoming alcoholism. (Those without employment in the formal sector are less well catered for, although advice is available on the uses of leisure.)

A constant theme is that labour and capital, worker and manager, need each other, and are related organically in a grand and harmonious divine plan. On the occasion of the annual Industrial Sunday—designed to coincide with the *Ayodhaya puja*, when Hindus worship the tools of their trade—CSI Protestants are encouraged, as one member of the CSI-Southern church wryly put it, 'to do our jobs, executives and peons alike, because God loves us all equally'. This kind of ideology has a considerable history. Moisa (1983: 171) cites a fourteenth-century church encyclical which denies the existence of conflict, emphasizing instead the mutually beneficial links between worker and employer, and the role of the church in bringing them together.

For the most part, such a view of Christian solidarity and integrity is accepted as received truth. There are moments, however, when this consensus is challenged, and the possibility of a contrary truth offered in its place. The final section of this chapter will consider one such moment: the circumstances of a dispute in a Christian hospital.

AN INDUSTRIAL DISPUTE

The strike at Christian Medical College Hospital (CMCH), situated in the North Arcot district's capital of Vellore, began on 5 January 1975 and went on for 10 weeks.[18] The two unions which called the strike represented the majority of lower clerical and menial grade employees, i.e. grades 3 and 4 in the hospital's own employee categories. The larger of the two had formal links with Tamilnadu's ruling DMK party, while the other, with a politically more heterogeneous membership, was not so tied, although it acted in close co-operation with the former.

When it began, the management terminated the services of fifteen workers who were alleged to have engaged in acts of violence. At the beginning of February, the Chief Minister of Tamilnadu's DMK government suggested they be reinstated in return for 'letters of regret' and guarantees of good behaviour in future. Management offered only to set up a review panel, provided the strike was first called off, a proposal which was (rightly) interpreted as a rebuff to the Chief Minister. After several weeks of apparent stalemate—during which time the wrath of the state government was turned against the hospital management[19]—the central government (at the time led by Mrs Gandhi) threatened to intervene actively in the dispute. At this point the Chief Minister urged the unions to call off the strike with the assurance that the state would provide alternative employment in its own hospitals for the fifteen dismissed workers. The strike ended on 17 March. The reported cost to the hospital was Rs 2.5 millions.

In the context of Tamilnadu, the DMK represents itself and is (or was until the 1977 state elections when it was defeated by the ADMK) widely regarded as the party of the poor and the oppressed. By contrast, the Congress (even if it prefers not to see itself in this light) is the party of Tamilnadu's urban rich, its professionals, managers, and capitalists. Thus, it was to the DMK that the striking employees, and to the Congress that the management of CMCH turned for their principal support during the dispute.[20]

Whatever the original 'causes' of the strike action,[21] or the subsequent involvement of state and central powers, the dispute may be seen (and was certainly presented this way by the striking workers) as a fairly straight-forward industrial confrontation. For their part, the unions were able to identify several areas of employee grievance. Firstly, hospital workers do not have the protection of the Industrial Act or the Shops and Establishments Act, and therefore have no formal recourse to the machinery of labour relations available to many other workers. In consequence, although unions at CMCH are registered with state authorities, they have no legal standing, cannot therefore engage in a legal strike, and are not (and cannot be) officially recognized by the hospital management, although the latter does have informal procedures for dealing with them. One of the demands of the striking workers was, thus, the reform of the law to enable hospital workers to be covered by one or other of these Acts.

Secondly, and to an extent following from the absence of a legal standing, employees of the hospital have little security. They are liable to dismissal without recourse to impartial mediation or adjudication. Thus, there was no formal enquiry held before the fifteen employees were dismissed. Apparently, no grounds need be given for termination of employment, although normally one month's salary is granted. Indeed, following the ending of the strike, it was reported that some eighty 'casual' workers—many of whom had been employed for a number of years—were dismissed without explanation.

Finally, workers claimed that management had failed to implement pay scales and cost-of-living allowances already agreed. The strike action was, therefore, explained by the unions as an attempt to press their demands, and was decided upon, they insisted, only after all channels of negotiation had been exhausted.

The strikers received considerable encouragement and expressions of support from other unions in the town and district. A committee was formed to collect money and food, and many workers contributed a day's earnings. The solidarity of large sections of the working class in Vellore also expressed itself in a continuous programme of demonstrations, fasts, and marches—the most dramatic of which was a procession by members of twenty-two unions attached to the Federation of Trade Unions.[22]

The management, for their part, received support from the better-off sections of the local community. Within a week of the commencement of the strike the Vellore Traders Association passed a resolution urging its abandonment, while merchants, tourist-taxi owners, and hoteliers belonging to the neighbourhood in which the hospital is situated sponsored appeals for a return to work, and took part in processions and demonstrations to emphasize their solidarity with the management. The Vellore branches of associations such as Rotary, Lions, Round Table, and Jaycees also called on striking employees to resume work, pointing out that 'in an establishment such as [CMCH] devoted to the service of mankind, there is no room for trade union activities'.

Management's position was fully endorsed by the vast majority of medical staff and the higher grades of non-medical personnel at the hospital, who did not participate in the stoppage. On the whole, management did not reply to union grievances over wages and conditions, but rather stressed time and again their determination to take a stand against 'corruption' and 'indiscipline' in the hospital. I was told by a senior member of the hospital's directorate that 'this is a strike in favour of corruption'. It is no coincidence that the 'need to stamp out indiscipline and corruption' was also very much the rallying cry of the Congress-led central government in this period, and was later presented as a principal justification for imposing the Emergency. Moreover, it was a slogan echoed constantly by the urban middle class, especially in relation to the periodic labour strife occasioned by India's rapid industrialization and the growing demands of the unions.

Since the hospital is wholly funded and run by Protestant organizations, including the CSI, and was at the time of the strike within the latter's Madras diocese, the church's leaders not unnaturally played an important role in these events. They continually stressed the hospital's status as a Christian institution, and the Christian basis of its values, and maintained all along that the strike should be settled internally (i.e. within the church and community). By emphasizing the Christian character of the hospital, the ecclesiastical leadership sought to prevent the DMK government from interfering in the strike, since only as a minority institution could it be assured of remaining constitutionally outside the jurisdiction of the state government. At the same time, such statements were intended to alert Christians to what was portrayed as a threat to the community from the 'outside'. The successful creation of this kind of consciousness would have isolated the strikers and compelled them to accept the settlement terms of the Protestant leadership which was unequivocally against (and seen to be against) the strike. Seven bishops of the CSI wrote a 'strong letter' to the Chief Minister in support of the management's position, while the Synod's Secretary spoke of taking 'a stand for discipline'. The newly elected Bishop in Madras (see above) observed that the attitude of management was 'in the best interests of the institution'. And in keeping with what was generally regarded as the 'even-handed' approach of the ecclesiastical establishment, added that 'I am interested in labour. But at the same time I also have a responsibility for management.'

The local clergy were more equivocal about their alignments. Ecclesiastics in the North Arcot district originate mainly in the same villages as the strikers, and are related by kinship to many of them. As already noted, they also share a common denominational background in the American Arcot Mission. The largest CSI Tamil congregation in Vellore, built originally by the mission, to which many of those on strike (including the union leaders) belong, is referred to as the 'Class 4 church', in contrast to the prestigious (formerly Anglican) English congregation—the 'management church' as it is labelled. Attempts by representatives of the region's clergy to intervene in the dispute were rebuffed by management, and they had to remain content to preach on 'forgiveness' and 'reconciliation' from their pulpits. Indeed, a variety of biblical themes were invoked at congregational level (and in the hospital chapel) to support different positions on the strike.

Numerous meetings and informal gatherings throughout the diocese were preceded by appeals to the Almighty for deliverance from what were portrayed as threats from the state authorities. To meet this challenge, the CSI hierarchy called for unity, and the full force of Protestant ritual and symbolism were invoked to underline this theme. Days of prayer and fasting were held both at the hospital and the CSI Cathedral in Madras city. When several 'dissident' doctors who objected to the management's handling of the strike chose to underline their opposition by fasting and praying at the hospital gates, they were attacked as 'hypocrites' making a 'travesty of Christianity'. All this was interpreted by union leaders, I think correctly, as a refusal on the part of the church hierarchy to accept the reality of class schisms within the community.

The unions resisted these attempts by both management and the top ecclesiastical echelons to restrict and mould their discourse. Calls for a closing of ranks in defence of minority interests, an acknowledgement of ecclesiastical authority in all matters, and a return to the organic harmony of church and community were ignored. They elected instead to focus their own discourse on grievances over pay and conditions, in an attempt to demonstrate that the strike was over 'bread and butter' issues. Unions employed the national and international idioms of class struggle, which not only linked them to other unions in the town, but stressed their identification with the 'working class' in general. They also concentrated their rhetorical efforts on regional issues, i.e. against the predominance of Syrian Christians ('Malayalees') in the hospital's medical and skilled personnel (see Caplan 1981).[23]

It is interesting to note that neither side made any public reference to caste, although informally it may have played some part in the dispute. Thus, several of the 'dissident' senior medical personnel who sided with the unions were Vellalars and so bound, it was said, to oppose the hospital's director, a Nadar. Indeed, the decision of some workers not to support the action was sometimes attributed to the fact that they were Nadars, although a number of those on strike and at least one union leader were members of this caste.[24] Publicly, it was the DMK government which reminded people that many of the strikers, and most of the fifteen employees dismissed were

Harijans. While, as we have seen, in other situations, such as the election of a bishop, caste may well emerge as the single most significant form of discourse, the ideological address which won overriding acceptance among low grade employees at Vellore was that which appealed to class (and to a lesser extent linguistic/regional) identity. In the context of this dispute, any call for caste solidarity would have narrowed the support of the unions. It would, moreover, have fragmented the heterogenous management, which preferred to direct its rhetoric to appeals for religious unity.

CONCLUSION

As a basic ingredient of consciousness, 'the self' is not constituted primordially and permanently, but may be understood as an aggregation of 'potentialities'. In assessing the relative significance of particular forms of consciousness, the material and ideological 'surroundings' must be exposed. Therborn's metaphor of street sounds and signs is apt. The ideological environment is conceived as a 'cacophony' of voices, constantly addressing subjects. In the process, these voices compete against, struggle with, drown out, and reinforce one another (1980: viii). Individual consciousness comes to be seen as an important sphere of ideological struggle, with varied and many outcomes, and not as something determined once and for all by fundamental material conditions.

In the south Indian urban context, the ideology of dominant international and national capital is transmitted mainly by the middle class. In various ways and situations they proclaim the virtues of the social order it has established, and seek to justify, preserve, and enhance their privileged place within it. The church's voice, as we have seen, is prominent and authoritative in the Protestant context. Though some lower clergy or those with a particular regional interest occasionally provide an alternative view of the world, on the whole the ecclesiastical and lay establishment defines the nature and parameters of the dominant discourse. This is not to suggest that the church in India should be seen as an ideological 'apparatus' of the State, as Althusser (1971) suggests. As a minority voice, the Protestant church is not infrequently called upon to defend what it perceives as the interests of all Christians against the Hindu majority view. Nor is it meant to imply that the discourse of the church, or even that of the middle class within its lay ranks, is unified and consistent. We have seen how the dominant ideology in respect of caste at once opposes and condemns its every manifestation among Protestants, yet pleads for the special needs of Harijans, and acknowledges, though with some regret, the existence of rampant casteism at all levels of the ecclesiastical structure, including its highest councils.

Where class is concerned, the ideology is similarly discordant. At times, the interpellations of the church are unequivocally and blatantly those of the dominant middle class, which presents its 'particularistic' views as the authentic, 'universalistic' voice of the community (see Cohen 1981). At other times the realities of class and class conflict are either submerged or denied altogether. Thus, discourse may focus on caste ('Christian Harijans must obtain their rightful privileges'), on social welfare ('we must help the poor'), or on community harmony ('God loves employer and employee equally'). These kinds of interpellation which would deny lower class Protestants consciousness of their condition 'impugn their right to speak and act on it' (Parkin 1984: 361).

In a complex and heterogeneous social environment, however, the church does not provide the only discourse impinging on the lives of urban Protestants. Nor, for that matter, can those who constitute the 'power bloc'—both within and outside the community—invariably and unfailingly control the formation of lower class subjects. The former could not and do not monopolize all sources of ideological communication, nor drown out every address which they do not themselves originate. There are, as Turton (1984) proposes, limits to ideological domination. The experience of poverty, disprivilege, and domination, and of disjunctions between promise and fulfilment, expectation and actuality, inevitably create a fund of self-knowledge and awareness among those at the bottom of the social order.

These reserves are drawn upon when, as in the case of the hospital action, in response to a strike call, there is assertion of a particular subjectivity, that of a member of the 'working class'. This kind of consciousness is further buttressed by mes-

sages of support (and material) from others who make similar
assertions. Such solidarity encourages resistance to certain ideological propositions emanating outside the working class. Thus,
striking workers at Vellore dismissed and ridiculed the idea that
the church was competent to settle the dispute in an impartial
manner. Moreover, the intensity with which a 'working class'
identity can be felt and expressed throws some doubt on the
suggestion that ethnicity is generally more acute than class
because the former, but not the latter, is bound by 'powerful
affect' (see Epstein 1978: 95).

In the context of an economy characterized by a severe
dearth of job opportunities, alongside an over-abundance of
potential workers, fear of unemployment itself becomes a major
ideological mechanism discouraging the emergence of class
solidarity (see Therborn 1980: 98; Turton 1984: 60). Furthermore, where organized labour must struggle to survive in
a climate of intense hostility, such individual and collective
expressions of 'trade union consciousness'—in Lenin's famous
phrase of derision—must be understood as having an importance far in excess of similar manifestations in the West.

It is, of course, significant that activities—such as the strike
described in this chapter—designed to improve workers' conditions or promote their perceived interests are not invariably
spontaneous manifestations of solidarity, but may be at least
partly encouraged, financed, and manipulated by political
parties for their own purposes. They are certainly far from
expressions of revolutionary class consciousness.

In another respect, however, they are indications of opposition to the existing order of things; they connote resistance—however meagre—to the dominant discourse of the
middle class. In the cacophony of ideological sounds and signs
which continuously instruct, cajole, threaten, constrain, and
mystify the great mass of people, these moments speak of other
possibilities, and provide glimpses of how things are or how
they might be. Such challenges to the dominant class have of
late also assumed an overtly religious form, with the growth of
a strong fundamentalist movement among lower class Protestants. The last section of the book considers this development.

7

THE NEGOTIATION OF CULTURES
Piety, Social Gospel, and Popular Theodicies

INTRODUCTION

IN the remainder of the book, I consider the religious changes which have occurred within the Protestant fold in south India over the past 200-odd years, and particularly since the turn of this century. The present chapter examines, first of all, the importation by the missionaries of a theology of 'piety' and its communication to and adoption by an economically un-differentiated population of new Christians. It goes on to note the subsequent attraction of the 'social gospel' to a minority of intellectuals within the missions and, notwithstanding the rejection of this theology by the great mass of ordinary Prot-estants, its establishment as the preferred discourse of the eccle-siastical hierarchy and the new middle class. The discussion then turns to the 'traditional' beliefs of the majority concerning the nature of affliction, which are shared with Hindus of the same class level, and the hostile attitudes towards these views of first the missionaries and, latterly, the dominant segment within the church and community. The next chapter will relate these themes to the growing influence of fundamentalism on Protestant Madras.

MISSIONARY ATTITUDES TO HINDUISM

The history of nineteenth-century missions in south India must be understood in the light of the 'Evangelical Awakening' in Europe, which gathered strength from about 1780. Like the Pietism movement a century earlier, it concentrated on the salvation of the individual, effected through the substitutionary atonement of Jesus Christ, and on a personal relationship with the Lord. Its authoritative source was the Bible, regarded as inerrant, and interpreted literally (Neill 1964: 227; Sharpe 1965: 25). To both the pietists and evangelicals Hinduism was not only 'idolatry', but a 'false religion', the 'work of the devil', and the encounter between Christianity and Hinduism was seen as a simple conflict between good and evil.

By the turn of the nineteenth century, moreover, Protestant attitudes towards 'idolatrous' religions in India had hardened. Evangelicals, pressing in the House of Commons for the inclusion of a clause in the 1813 Charter Act of the East India Company allowing more open missionary access to the subcontinent, stepped up their attacks on Hinduism in order to prove that India was in dire and ever greater need of Christianity. Whereas, during much of the eighteenth century, there had been numerous sympathetic accounts of Hinduism, and the beginnings of an 'Orientalist' tradition,[1] by the century's end the tone had become much more one of disdain and devaluation. At this juncture, Gombrich remarks, Europeans abandoned 'an interest in what [they] might learn from Indians for a determination to teach them' (1978: 8). In concert with evangelicals at home, missionaries in India were increasingly successful in challenging the Company's patronage of Hindu religious institutions. Some eventually argued that the 'mutiny' of 1857–8 was a divine judgement for earlier official tolerance of 'heathenism' (see Sharpe 1965: 28).

In south India, despite considerable differences of theology and ritual among the many denominations, there was a common basis of evangelicalism, and a sharing of the view that there could be no meeting point with non-Christian religions. The gospel, suggests one modern church historian, 'was presented against the background of errors, weaknesses and abominations of Hinduism' (Estborn 1961: 26). One British missionary wrote contemptuously of 'the opposition to truth, the love of idolatry in the Hindu', attributing this failing to 'dense ignorance of the first principles of religion' (Mullens 1854: 39). Another warned his colleagues that 'it is to consciences thus cramped, into lives thus enervated and depressed [by Hindu philosophy, religion, and caste] that the message of the Gospel must be brought' (Mylne 1908: 39). Even so eminent a figure as Bishop Heber, whose attitudes were later considered to have been more enlightened than those of most missionaries of his time (i.e. the first quarter of the nineteenth century), is reported to have regarded the study of Sanskrit and the ancient literature as 'useless and worse than useless' (see Shiri 1969: 10).

American missionaries of this period were no less prone to depict Hinduism in an unfavourable light. They portrayed the Hindu deities as 'exemplars of every vice and crime' (Pathak 1967: 80-2). One medical evangelist, a member of the legendary missionary family which established the world famous hospital and medical college at Vellore in North Arcot (see Chapter 6), is quoted by Houghton as stating that all the works in which Hindus believe, 'are nothing else than lying fables, wickedly concocted by false and designing men' (1981: 111-12). Their 'homiletic' methodology, as Houghton terms it, involved the denigration of all things Hindu in order to demonstrate the superiority of Christianity. Most recent mission histories contain numerous examples of the derogatory formulations employed by the missionaries—American and European—to describe and condemn Hinduism (see, for example, David 1983: 57-9).

What had become the accepted missionary outlook was given further encouragement at the end of the nineteenth century by what some have termed the Second Evangelical Awakening, associated with the name of Dwight Moody in America, so that even by the turn of this century such attitudes had not disappeared. Gandhi records, how when he was a young man, Christian missionaries 'used to stand in a corner near the high school and hold forth, pouring abuse on Hindus and their gods. I could not endure this' (1964: 33).

But, by this time, there was a perceptible change in outlook among at least some within the mission fold. Several factors encouraged a revival and expansion of eighteenth-century tolerance. For one thing, the serious study of Hinduism by missionary and 'secular' scholars like Monier Williams and Max Müller (who were also committed Christians) led to greater understanding of and respect for the cosmic themes revealed in the sacred literature, as this was translated and examined. Müller's interest in a 'science of religion' necessitated a comparative approach, a search for truth in every faith, if only to demonstrate ultimately the superiority of the Christian message (see Forrester 1980: 136-7).[2]

For another, the growth of liberal theology, which took account of Darwinian ideas, countenanced biblical criticism, and sought to 'socialize' religion, to make it more responsive to social concerns, could not fail to influence the tone and style of Indian missionary judgements of Hinduism. While among Western thinkers, Hinduism was still regarded as a lower stage in the evolution of human religious forms, it ceased to be universally portrayed as the road to perdition (see Farquhar 1913).

Finally, the growth of Indian nationalism challenged not only the established political order, but a whole range of European pre-conceptions about Hinduism. This new self-awareness among Indians served to inhibit at least some of the more excessive and provocative missionary declarations. Moreover, not a few Indian Christian intellectuals identified with the nationalist movement, and found themselves out of sympathy with much of the missionary rhetoric concerning Hinduism. Many of them, in associating themselves with nationalist aspirations, acknowledged Hinduism to be an integral part of India's cultural traditions and, though they could not subscribe to its beliefs and practices, found no difficulty in accepting it as part of their own heritage (Baago 1966: 324). Indian Christian theologians also increasingly sought to establish bridges between the two faiths (see Boyd 1969).

The extent of this transformation in attitudes to Hinduism is difficult to gauge. Some mission historians seem to suggest that it was very nearly universal. Farquhar observed that 'missionary books using denunciatory language and hard judgements are now a thing of the past' (1913: 35). This was probably a fair assessment, since missionary writing was largely confined to a relatively tiny circle of scholars and intellectuals. They were, by and large, persuaded by the liberal views flowing in from theological centres in the West, indeed, were themselves contributors to the development and dissemination of these ideas in India. In the decades immediately prior to independence the ecclesiastical establishment as a whole grew increasingly estranged from the pietistic tradition, and from the aggressive and insensitive evangelism which went with it. The leadership of the Indian church inherited and continued these liberal and ecumenical tendencies after independence.

It is much less certain, however, that this new accommodative mood was shared by the great majority of missionaries 'in the field'. Sharpe notes that sympathy for
Hinduism was 'slow to make an impact on the rank and file of
Protestant missionaries' (1965: 54). David, for another, writes
that 'we do not have any evidence to show that the missionaries
[of the Reformed Church in America] were influenced in any
way by the ideas of liberal theology . . . they reacted negatively
to those ideas' (1983: 87). This was due partly to the fact that
some missionaries (like those of the Reformed Church) came
from a strongly conservative tradition. But it was also that
most missionaries were, after all, removed from the intellectual
circles within the universities, colleges, and seminaries where
the Hindu scriptures were studied and discussed. Of importance, too, was that they came in daily contact with ordinary
Hindu beliefs and practices, many of which, Sharpe tells us,
'disgusted them' (1965: 26). For centuries, Europeans distinguished between what they saw as philosophical and popular
Hinduism, reserving for the latter their utmost contempt. Even
for those operating in the more liberal climate of the twentieth
century, the religion of the majority was still 'a jungle of magic,
myth, taboo and propitiation, normally classified as "anim-
ism", or "primitive religion" . . .' (ibid.: 32). Missionaries who
laboured among the poor and uneducated lower castes, and so
came into continuous contact with folk religion, were not much
persuaded by Farquhar's thesis. They considered that his views
only confirmed how out of touch he and other liberal thinkers
were with 'the level to which popular Hinduism had sunk', as
one critic put it. Such missionaries regarded as 'little short of
blasphemy' the postulate that there is a direct organic con-
nection between Hinduism and Christianity, implied in the
notion that the later supersedes and fulfils the former (ibid.:
317).

THE CULTURE OF PIETY

Missionaries sought to establish, both institutionally and sym-
bolically, clear boundaries between their Christian followers
and Hindu society. Raised in a mission environment, almost
totally dependent on their European patrons, and discouraged

from participating in social life outside their own community,[3] the converts came inevitably to acquire the missionaries' judgements on Hinduism.

While their public pronouncements about Hinduism are nowadays more circumspect than in the past, most ordinary Protestants still perceive the religion of the majority in terms inherited from the dominant pietistic tendency within the mission fold. There continues to exist the widespread feeling that people who have failed or refused to accept Christ are doomed to an eternity without salvation. The communication of Christian doctrine to non-believers is, therefore, of prime importance to ensure that as many as possible are spared eternal torment. Numerous congregations of the lower class have well-supported (and well-financed) programmes of public preaching and the distribution of Christian literature. Many of their members also belong as individuals to a variety of organizations outside the orthodox church which engage actively in evangelism. Several such groups whose activities I am familiar with organize visits to hospitals, prisons, and institutions of the poor, principally 'to show them the love of God', and to 'help them by leading them to a better spiritual life', to summarize the general tone of their rhetoric. The distribution of charity is distinctly secondary and incidental.

More informally, Hindu neighbours and acquaintances are encouraged to take part in Christian household rituals (especially at Christmas and other important religious festivals), and in local prayer meetings. But such invitations are not intended to dismantle barriers between those on opposite sides of the religious divide, or establish inter-faith links and greater understanding. On the contrary, the general view is that the very proximity of Hindu doctrines and practices can adversely affect the well-being of devout Christians. Various steps are therefore taken to avoid or minimize such contaminating influences. These Protestants, by and large, take immense care to avoid participation in Hindu rituals, an abstinence originally imposed on converts by their missionaries (David 1983: 167). They refuse to set foot inside the precincts of a temple, some even claiming never to glance in the direction of one—no small feat in certain parts of Madras. The few who admit to having entered such a place (usually inadvertently) do so only to re-count a terrible misfortune which followed the transgression.

Since the majority of Protestants work alongside Hindus, they are unable completely to avoid being present at acts of worship which occur from time to time at the factory or office. This is particularly so in the case of the *Ayodhaya puja* when the tools and implements of work are blessed. On these occasions food is offered to the deities, and the sacred left-overs (*prasad*) are distributed among the participants. Protestants are ad-amant in refusing to take *prasad* because, as they frequently remark, 'it has been offered to idols'. Few of them, however, have senior enough status at work to emulate a foreman at the Campa Cola factory in Madras who refuses to subscribe to the annual *puja* fund organized by the workers, or even to be pres-ent during the worship.

The avoidance of 'defilement' is particularly acute for recent converts who still have close relationships with their Hindu kinsfolk. For the most part, a kind of *modus vivendi* is reached, whereby visits are exchanged, and their presence on most social occasions is continued. What converts seek to avoid is par-ticipation in what they themselves assess to be undesirable Hindu practices. Hindu relatives, of course, have their own views on what should be the appropriate role for Christian kin in these ceremonies. Together, this makes for a certain amount of interpretive creativity, and some variation in what is tol-erated and what is not. One man whose Hindu father had died took what he described as a full part in the cremation rites (though he did not observe a period of pollution), on the grounds, firstly, that a Christian son is compelled to honour his father, and secondly, that by fervent prayer a devout Christian remains unaffected by the otherwise harmful effects of being in the presence of Hindu supernatural beings. Another, in a very similar situation, attended as an 'observer', but refrained from participation in the rituals, which he claimed no longer had meaning or efficacy for him.

Certain other practices are designated as symbolic of Hin-duism, and consequently shunned. The ritual mark worn by Hindu women on their foreheads (*poṭṭu*), for example, is so regarded, and most lower class Protestants refrain from wearing it. This also distinguishes them—a fact of which they are well (and proudly) aware—from most middle-class Christians, who regard the mark as an innocent female 'embellishment', and furthermore as part of a 'glorious Indian tradition in which Christians must share', as one writer in the CSI-Northern congregation's magazine argued. The distinction is explicitly made, by ordinary Protestants, between, on the one hand, the liberal, accommodative, and ecumenical attitudes towards Hinduism of the middle class and the higher clergy (see below) and, on the other, their own preferences which one informant described as a 'refusal to compromise with error or evil'.

Quite apart from these 'external' views of the non-Christian world, for the most part contemporary descendants of the converts also inherited a rigidly pietistic set of 'internal' doctrines and practices from their Western Protestant benefactors. In any number of conversations I had with elderly members of the three focal congregations, and in private letters and papers referring to the early part of this century, mention was often made of the 'simple' Christianity to which families subscribed a generation or two back. 'My parents', writes one diarist, 'like their contemporaries in general, had a strong religious faith with an implicit confidence in the inspiration of the Bible ... The only book apart from the Bible that I recollect was the *Pilgrim's Progress*, which was a hot favourite in every household.' Recollections also attest to the centrality of prayer in Protestant life. Family prayers were held daily in the morning and evening. Indeed, prayer seems to have been the pre-eminent means of communicating with the divine—to ask for guidance and assistance, to give thanks, and so on. In his childhood village, one acquaintance remembers, there were 'prayer women' to whom people went when special prayers were needed 'for or against' something. Sundays, in the majority of Protestant homes, I was frequently told, were—at least in retrospect— 'dull and cheerless'.

Today, the prevalent religious orientation among ordinary Protestants is still much closer to the conservative evangelicalism of the nineteenth-century missionaries and their converts than to the later liberalism of the clerical and missionary élites. Their lives outside of the work-place continue to be circumscribed by activities centred on the enhancement of individual piety. A popular aphorism found prominently displayed on plaques in many Christian homes—'Jesus is the head of this household'—sums up the general ethos. One still frequently hears (and occasionally reads) comments like this one by a woman disturbed by the views of the ecclesiastical hierarchy: 'Modernist leaders of the churches are well-known for their disbelief . . . Many do not believe in the infallibility of the Bible. I can name some who preached from the pulpit that the Old Testament is a collection of myths, fables and fairy stories . . .' (letter to the *Madras Guardian*, 19 March 1964).

While not a few of the lower clergy within the CSI sympathize with and encourage these opinions, they are also exposed to more liberal influences emanating from the theological colleges they attend,[4] the diocesan committees and conferences in which they participate, and the disciplines and expectations of the ecclesiastical hierarchy. The persons who most regularly articulate the conservative evangelical view favoured by the great preponderance of Madras Protestants are the lay preachers.[5] They may be seen as the successors to the indigenous catechists and Bible women on whom the European missionaries relied so heavily to preach the message of Christianity. Emerging from, indeed, selected for training by the congregations to which they belong, sharing the neighbourhoods and social backgrounds of the membership, they share too its religious predilections. I have heard lay preachers derided by senior ecclesiastics and diocesan officials for their lack of originality and anti-intellectualism. But most ordinary churchgoers find relevant and welcome the Bible-based sermons they preach that call for simple devotion, warn of the dangers of sin (smoking, drinking, cinema, etc.), and promise individual salvation; the lay preachers are still very firmly planted in the church, which after all provides their training and licenses them to preach. It is the ubiquitous 'prayer cells' which offer a consistent challenge to the preferred theology and authority of the church. For they not only provide a context for the full expression and reinforcement of pietism, but link people within the orthodox church with others outside it who share a similar outlook.

PIETISM AND PRAYER CELLS

A few prayer cells, like the Madras All Night Prayer Fellowship or the Madras Intercessory Prayer Fellowship, which provide a constant 'chain' of volunteers to pray for those who feel themselves to be in need, are independent, bureaucratic, city-wide associations.[6] But, for the most part, prayer cells are small, informally organized groups. Some are based on a single congregation, although they would be unlikely to involve the entire membership; more commonly, there would be several such cells—with some overlapping personnel—within a congregation. Other prayer groups, and these seem to be the most common, comprise persons of diverse Protestant affiliations living in a neighbourhood, who are equally committed to a conservative evangelicalism.

The individuals who join such cells usually feel that Sunday worship alone is insufficient, and so meet regularly in each other's homes to fast and pray, sing hymns and gospel songs, read the scriptures and give 'witness' to their faith. A guest evangelist may be invited to address the meeting, and to deliver a 'strong message', as the Bible-based, heavily didactic, and exhortative sermon is termed. There is also ample scope for individual expression and enthusiasm, what Wilson (1973: 66) calls a 'heart experience'. In such settings, prayer is often accompanied by tears, indicative, I was told, of the depth of participants' feeling for Christ. Tears are an important symbol in the Tamil *bhakti* tradition as well (see Egnor 1980: 20).

While men can and do attend, the majority who take part are women. On the basis of figures I have from the CSI-Western congregation, I estimate that 40–60 per cent of women in the congregations of the lower class attend such gatherings on a more or less regular basis. The preponderance of women is sometimes explained in terms of the men having insufficient time to attend, since many (but by no means all) meetings are held during working hours. There is probably some truth in this, since working women are also less active than those who are not employed. But it would suggest that retired males should then play a fuller role, which does not seem to be the case. Other kinds of reasons are proffered, as well. It is often claimed that pastors seem to have no time to listen to congregants' problems, an assessment concurred in by a good many clergymen themselves. Women imply that, in any case, they might be reluctant to share some of these problems with a (male) minister. By contrast, they would have no hesitation in revealing confidences to the mainly female members of a prayer cell, and especially to the 'godly woman' who generally helps to lead such a group.[7]

Considerable time is given to the detailed submission by participants of their personal difficulties. But while women are preponderant among those volunteering problems for the cell's attention and concern, it is not only their own anxieties which are presented, but their spouses' and children's as well. They seek divine assistance for the successful conclusion of a daughter's marriage arrangements, the recovery of a sibling's stolen jewels, a favourable response to a son's job application, or a satisfactory outcome to a husband's impending surgery. Again, there is a striking resemblance between these submissions and those made by Hindu women to, for example, mediums of the Goddess (see p. 205). Thus, in a very real sense, women assume the burden of their family's health and well-being. Generally, these problems are dealt with by a patient and sympathetic hearing, collective prayer, and, recently, through access to the power of the Holy Spirit, a development to which I shall return in the next chapter.

Historically, Indian women were a vital component of the missionary enterprise. They were the 'Bible women' and mission 'sisters' who sought out and preached—in the vernacular—to members of their own sex in the villages. Yet their part in the church structure which arose alongside and eventually superseded the mission organizations was comparatively minor. They were not accepted into the clergy or even the lay ministry, and were found hardly at all in congregational or higher ecclesiastical offices. Despite the educational and occupational advantages which accrued to them from conversion, women were excluded from playing a formal role in the indigenous church. Even today, in the CSI, the position has changed little. At the highest level, the Synod Executive, consisting of sixty members, there is only one woman (though at the time of field-work she held the crucial post of Honorary General Secretary). At congregational and other levels beneath the Synod their numbers are slightly higher, but it is clear that here, too, men completely dominate church administration, to say nothing of ecclesiastical offices (see Paul 1973). In many of the CSI congregations with which I am familiar, only the mandatory minimum of three women serve on the eleven-member Pastorate Committee.

Because women are largely excluded from playing a direct part in the formal structures of the church, it is tempting and not unreasonable to argue, *pace* Lewis (1971), that they have become associated with, even relegated to 'marginal' religious observances. The women themselves, however, do not conceive of such informal rites as peripheral, nor as merely supplementary to the prescribed worship and organized practices of the congregations. On the contrary, they see these prayer groups as the most important means by which what *they* regard as the 'central morality cult' (to recall Lewis's term) is affirmed and preserved. The men, though they play a lesser role in these cells, would not disagree. Notwithstanding the efforts of the lay preachers, and even the more sympathetic among the lower clergy, to give voice to and perpetuate the dominant conservative sentiments of the majority within the Protestant community, the church, it is often claimed, has grown 'cold' with liberalism. The 'traditional' piety of ordinary people, it is believed, can only be nurtured and survive through engagement in informal rites such as those provided by prayer cells.

The ecclesiastical hierarchy views their existence with mixed feelings. It acknowledges that the church has 'neglected its evangelism' and 'failed to excite the people', so must allow its members to 'find their own level'—as one senior CSI administrator put it. But the church seeks to retain some influence over these groups by encouraging them to operate under its general sponsorship. The establishment of the Women's Fellowship [*sic*] by the CSI, some twenty-five years ago, was partly aimed at bringing some of this activity within its purview. Hence the clergy attempts to ensure that prayer groups meet openly, at fixed times, in church or other trusted premises, preferably under the leadership of the pastor. The women of many congregations, therefore, participate in weekly prayer sessions organized by their own Fellowship, and meet elsewhere, independently, on other occasions.

It is interesting to note that the Women's Fellowship of the élite CSI-Northern congregation does not hold prayer meetings in the accepted sense of the term, though of course its deliberations begin and end with a brief prayer. Weekly gatherings are, rather, devoted primarily to discussions on topical issues, both sacred and secular, of interest to the members. In one year they considered issues such as the indigenization of ritual, caring for the aged, women's place in church and society, the Book of Hosea, Christian marriage, and so on. The women themselves are dismissive of the kind of cells I have been discussing. I heard one woman refer to the people who take part in them as 'tambourine' Christians. The frequent plea by a member of the Fellowship to devote at least one meeting in four entirely to collective prayer is regularly refused. In her words: 'the women in this pastorate are not interested in spiritual things; they think people like me are cranks.' Members of the CSI-Southern church are less hostile to such religiosity. There are a comparatively small number of members who meet both under the auspices of the pastorate, and privately, to engage in prayer activities of the sort found more widely among Protestants of the lower class.

These cells are sometimes regarded by the ecclesiastical leadership as a threat to both the unity of the church and to its spiritual authority. The clerical hierarchy feels most menaced when these *ad hoc* bands threaten either to separate from or operate as semi-autonomous pressure groups within the church. A circular notice from the bishop's office to all congregations of the Madras diocese, some years ago, warned explicitly of how such units form 'splinter groups' and that 'even those who do not break away are often not a source of strength to the Church, but self-righteous cliques ... virtually independent of and even hostile to the Church'. The history of any CSI diocese would reveal a number of confrontations between the clerical establishment and such prayer groups.

In one well-known case within the Madras area, some women of a congregation had been meeting over a period of years in each other's homes before a split within the church— occasioned, it is alleged, by elections for the Pastorate Committee—led one faction to create out of these *ad hoc* gatherings a formal prayer association. It chose its own executive, sought recruits from outside the congregation, collected subscriptions, and organized activities without reference to the minister or the elected Pastorate Committee. In its first (printed) report to members, the association's secretary (a man) paid homage to the women of the congregation, who had, for many years prior to the establishment of the association, met and 'prayed most earnestly ... in order to inspire a spirit of revivalism among the male members of the congregation ...'.[8] In the end the bishop had formally to advise members of the congregation to avoid participation in the activities of the group.[9] Though this is by no means typical of the developmental cycle of prayer groups, the possibility of similar kinds of schism occurring cannot be very far from the minds of ecclesiastical authorities. Collective prayer, fellowship, and mutual support within what can be an emotional atmosphere, create a sense of unity and purpose within the collective, and such ties may be tapped by an ambitious individual or clique with designs on office or influence within the church's lay leadership.

But these cells challenge the ecclesiastical establishment in another, more profound way as well, by offering a critique of ministerial piety and liberal theology. The prayer association referred to above, in its annual report, explicitly gave as the reason for its establishment, 'to create the right atmosphere of piety in the churches, and to lead the people to a life of spiritual fellowship ...'. The social gospel, as the discourse favoured by the CSI hierarchy and the congregations of the Protestant élites, challenges and is in turn challenged by this popular pietism.

THE CHURCH AND THE SOCIAL GOSPEL

The social gospel, which emerged in the United States towards the end of the nineteenth century, is regarded by some church historians as America's special contribution to the ongoing stream of Christianity. It has been defined as 'the application of the teachings of Jesus and the total message of Christian salvation to society, the economic life and social institutions ... as well as to individuals' (Pathak 1967: 93). In one respect, the importance placed by the Indian missions on offering educational, medical, and other forms of welfare services had already anticipated the kinds of concerns called for in such a theology. In another respect, however, it profoundly challenged both the dominant motive for these missionary schemes, i.e. personal conversion, and their primary emphasis on providing for particular individual needs. All such missionary activities were evangelical in purpose. The south Indian missionary conference of 1858 stressed, for example, that educational operations 'must be conducted with a special view to the salvation of the souls of pupils, not merely their intellectual and moral improvement' (see David 1983: 170). Similarly, healing the sick was regarded as a means of gaining access to the 'heathen' and winning them to Christianity. David reports how 'in the medical establishments of the American Arcot Mission no medicines were given out until the Gospel was first preached' (ibid.: 186–7).

The social gospel called on the church to be concerned not only for the healing of individual souls (and bodies), but for the regeneration of society as a whole. This kind of Christianity did not separate God from the 'world', the religious from the social (Thomas 1977: 21).

After 1947, the CSI assumed the welfare responsibilities of the Western denominational groups it had succeeded. It now operates, either alone or in concert with other Protestant churches in south India, the missionary schools, colleges, and hospitals it inherited. It has also become involved in a variety of major development schemes. A few are indigenously generated and financed. Most, however, are run in collaboration with or through the funding of national or internationl agencies, both secular and religious. The CSI originates and/or participates in, among other things, programmes for the relief of drought-stricken regions, the improvement of water resources in rural areas, the provision of agricultural extension services, industrial and craft training, the betterment of urban slum sanitation, and the building of low-cost housing in the city. Kurien remarks that 'they are the *avant-gardes* of the modern age and of the social gospel of the church', and have won for the latter 'a certain respectability in this land' (1981: 4).

The Madras diocese, through a special co-ordinating Board of Socio-Economic Concerns, takes an active part in these projects and, in addition, organizes a number of more local initiatives of its own, such as a Leprosy Rehabilitation Centre, a Home for the Aged, and a Community Development scheme. Similarly, congregations composed mainly of the well-to-do are drawn into 'social work' of this kind. The CSI-Northern church, for example, in its 1981 report to the membership, notes how the congregation has gone 'far beyond the normal boundaries of church concern ... sharing what [resources] we generate ... involving ourselves with [poor] people around'. The indigent of both the congregation itself and the neighbourhood engage its attention. The least well-off members— the majority of whom, as in the past, are Eurasians (or 'Anglo-Indians', as they are now called)—receive regular financial assistance. Poor residents of the locality are also recipients of aid, though they need not necessarily be (and are not usually) Christians at all. Thus, a day-care centre feeds some forty children from the hut dwellings near the church compound, while a number of adults from these same slums have been helped to become self-sustaining by the provision of such capital goods as cycle rickshaws and handcarts.

The congregation's energies and resources are not confined to helping those near at hand. Increasingly, funds are being directed to a host of welfare enterprises which, though run by Christian organizations of various kinds, benefit the indigent in the society at large. In one year, financial grants were provided for, among other things, a hospital, a home for the aged, a training centre for the deaf, polio and leprosy rehabilitation centres, Mother Teresa's Leprosy fund, and the Madras Christian Council of Social Service.[10] One of the projects organized in collaboration with various municipal and state agencies involves participation—mainly by provision and administration of funds—in a development project to aid a group of villages about thirty miles from the city.

Members of the congregation are involved personally in feeding children in the day-care centre, in visits to hospital patients and elderly people, in running adult literacy classes, providing vocational training, working with the deaf and mentally retarded, and spending time in the villages to whose development the church has committed financial resources. The church's magazine records the pride taken in its 'concern and compassion for others', and hopes that people will think of it as 'The Church That Cared For Others'.

In various capacities, the well-to-do also take part in a host of welfare, philanthropic, and development activities run by the diocese, synod, and inter-church agencies.[11] Because of the complex organizational problems attached to such projects, and because most of them rely on unpaid volunteers for assistance, expert advice, and influential contacts, those responsible for their administration tend to be drawn from a relatively small circle of successful (sometimes retired) professionals, managers, businessmen, and bureaucrats, most of whom are, as already noted, affiliated to élite congregations— such as the CSI-Northern and CSI-Southern churches[12]—in large cities like Madras.

One obvious corollary of this kind of intense engagement with the 'world' is that relationships to persons of other faiths are conceived in a more positive light. The ecumenical tendency finds expression in a greater readiness to acknowledge a common Dravidian culture with Tamils and other south Indians irrespective of religious affiliation, the increasing participation of non-Christians in Christian activities and ceremonies (see below), and, above all, the church's readiness to acknowledge the need for co-existence with other faiths. In April 1980, Protestant leaders in Madras met with representatives of the Tamilnadu branch of the RSS, a militant Hindu organization, to hear and examine 'the impressions and grievances [of] influential Hindus concerning the work and life of the Christian Church in India' (*Christian Focus*, 15 July 1980). The CSI's bishop in Madras writes of 'spirituality in other religions', and the need to learn from them, even to incorporate certain of their qualities (e.g. *bhakti*), and to find Christ 'in the lives of men and women of other Faiths'. He calls for dialogue which will 'lead . . . to knowledge of other religions which is so lacking in the Indian Christian community' (Clarke 1980: 95–8). Such views are frequently heard from the pulpits of élite congregations, and are widely shared by those, mainly within the middle class, who are regularly engaged in welfare and development activities as part of their commitment to the social gospel.

While there is recognition of the obligation of Christians to spread the message of the gospel, it is regarded as most effectively communicated by the example of 'social work', and therefore implicit rather than explicit. People in the CSI-Northern church, I was told by a leading member of the Pastorate Committee, 'are not very much in favour of standing on the pave-

ment and preaching to people'. A CSI-Southern congregant
related how, during a hospital visit, he and several other members of the delegation from the church were appalled and embarrassed when one of their number refused to distribute the
light magazines they had collected and brought along. 'He felt
that these sick people should be given evangelical literature, so
that they would see the error of their ways before it was too
late'. This kind of 'vulgar evangelism' is thought suitable for
those in the lower but not the middle class.

CRITICISMS OF THE SOCIAL GOSPEL

Criticisms of the social gospel come from various directions.
Proponents of a more radical theology take the churches (including the CSI) to task for their endorsement of the traditional
Western liberal approach to development as 'something good
and necessary exported from the richer western world ... to
the poorer "Third World"' (Kurien 1974: 200). This view,
which sees progress and change for the better as inevitable,
provided only that appropriate technology and adequate resources are available, still dominates the global discourse of
development. It is little wonder, then, that the progressive
churches should endorse such an approach. Wider debates on
'underdevelopment', the world capitalist system, North–South
relations, and so forth, which strike at the root of this liberal
model, have not yet seriously impinged on attitudes to development within the churches of India (although many individuals are certainly aware of them). In the south Indian
setting, moreover, the church is sometimes censured for its
concentration on welfare activities which, though acknowledged as well-meaning, are seen to foster an 'ethos of
dependence' among the beneficiaries (Prabhakar 1981: 18).
Such philanthropic activities, it is suggested, draw attention to
and emphasize existing inequalities between donors and recipients. The anniversary ceremony of a CSI Home for the
Aged which took place in 1981 illustrates the point.

The Home's 'inmates' (as they are referred to) were seated
on the floor, flanked on either side by invited guests (on chairs),
facing the platform dignitaries, who were senior churchmen
and important non-Christian political figures. The speeches

were all in English, which the elderly residents did not understand. None of them was invited to address the gathering. Indeed, throughout they were rendered invisible. The rhetoric was mainly to do with helping those in need, who in this case were old people without anyone to care for them, a result, as one speaker put it, of 'family breakdown' among the poor.[13]

In the wider sense, the proponents of a more radical theology argue that a concentration on welfare is, at best, palliative. It does not 'change or challenge', nor does it put the church 'decisively on the side of the poor and their oppression ... Our programmes have been instruments of charity, but not of justice ... They have stopped short at the point where they could challenge the existing order ... ' (Zachariah 1981: 33). Such voices urge the church to stand with the poor, and join them in their 'battles'. What is required, in the opinion of one Madras clergymen with whom I spoke, is to present Jesus as a 'fiery revolutionary', deeply concerned for the disinherited and the oppressed. But these are very much the views of a tiny minority of intellectuals who sympathize with the 'liberation theologies' of many Third World Christian thinkers. They find no echo within either the congregations of the middle class or the ecclesiastical establishment.

So far as I can gauge, such radical attitudes, by and large, remain outside the consciousness of the majority within the lower class. There are occasional attempts by members of the clergy to bring them to the attention of their parishes, but these are invariably met with indifference. I recall one young minister remarking that when he tried out his new-found radical ideas—learned at theological college—during a sermon to the CSI-Western congregation, he was as much as told by his audience to confine himself to expounding the 'word of God', by which they meant the familiar, Bible-based themes to which they are accustomed. 'As soon as I took charge of a pastorate I had to forget everything I had been taught', he concluded.[14] But, for the most part, these ideas are not aired from the pulpits occupied by the lower clergy or the lay ministry, nor propounded, in their diverse media, by leaders of the church.

What is surprising is that while most members of the CSI are very much aware of the hierarchy's commitment to the social gospel, this theology, too, receives little popular support.

Congregations whose adherents belong mainly to the lower class are hardly involved at all in welfare or development projects, nor do their members, as individuals, concern themselves with 'social work'. Protestant leaders have frequently commented on the apathy to social welfare within the community (see Thangasamy 1969: 69). The social gospel, though widely disseminated through the written and spoken word, hardly engages the great majority of Protestants. In terms of their social commitments, there is a striking contrast between the higher ecclesiastical echelons and 'the church of the parishes' (Kurien 1981: 4); or, to put it another way, between the dominant middle class and the overwhelming mass of ordinary Protestants.

It is, of course, partly a question of limited finances. For example, the CSI-Western congregation has an annual income from members' contributions approximately one-quarter that of either the CSI-Northern or CSI-Southern pastorates. It simply does not have anything like the same level of funds to devote to assisting others. As for individual lack of involvement in welfare programmes, this is undoubtedly related, as I have already noted, to the fact that, from the viewpoint of the project organizers, Protestants in the lower class have little to offer in the way of occupational experience, contacts, or personal means. It might be thought somewhat inappropriate, therefore, to accuse those who themselves possess relatively few resources of failing in their concern for the poor and needy. Nor, it should be noted again, do they benefit themselves from these welfare programmes, as many once did from the educational facilities offered by the missionaries.

But it would not be accurate to relate a weak commitment to the social gospel among ordinary Protestants entirely to their material circumstances. Liberal doctrines, now, as in the past, are seen to threaten the pietism which, for the better part of two centuries, has formed the core of popular south Indian Protestantism. It is frequently suggested that the price of the social gospel is the neglect of people's 'spiritual needs', that it replaces 'salvation through faith' by 'salvation through social work', as one lay preacher phrased it. 'The poor, after all, have always been with us', I was told on more than one occasion, 'so perhaps God intended it to be that way. Who are we to try and alter His will?' The social ministry is misguided, others say, because 'people will only agree to follow Christ if they get something in return'.

Even those who are not totally opposed to welfare efforts on behalf of the less fortunate are convinced, nevertheless, that these should be accompanied by intense evangelism. The missionaries are thought to have arrived at a perfect balance between their social concerns and their promulgation of the Christian message. But the social gospel, it is protested, has come to mean 'giving without preaching the word of God'. One man, who had been involved for a short time in a development project sponsored by an inter-denominational organization linked to the World Council of Churches, complained bitterly that 'agencies do not allow us to proclaim that these programmes come from a spirit of Christian charity; so they are bereft of the love of Christ. Social welfare is divorced from evangelism ... if we insist on tying our giving to preaching our religious views, these agencies refuse to have anything to do with us'. The reference is to a policy meant, in part, to take account of the Indian government's extreme suspicions of the motives underlying Christian aid, but one which also reflects liberal Protestant regard for the sensitivities of people of other faiths, and, as already noted, a less aggressive and overt approach to evangelism.

To this point I have presented the Protestantism of the masses as characterized mainly in terms of a pietistic legacy from the missionaries. It consists, I have suggested, of an attachment to the notion of individual salvation and, as a corollary, an anguished and, at times, aggressive disdain for those still unable to see the 'light of Christian truth'. Yet the very persons who are so concerned to define the boundaries between themselves and Hindus share with the latter a considerable corpus of beliefs about the nature of affliction, and the means of coping with it. It is to these ideas, and the practices to which they give rise, that I turn next.

POPULAR NOTIONS OF AFFLICTION

While acknowledging, among other things, the possibility of natural phenomena, divine retribution, personal sin, the 'evil

eye', or even astrologically related 'bad days' as causative
agents, ordinary Protestants, like the Hindus among whom
they live and work, tend to attribute many if not most kinds of
everyday misfortune either to sorcery (*sūṉiyam*)[15] or the capricious acts of evil spirits (*pēy*).[16]

Sorcery

The human instruments responsible for sorcery are the *sūṉiyak-*
āraṉ, who are thought to have access to secret knowledge and
sources of mystical power which they employ on behalf of
paying clients. The persons who engage their services bear
personal grudges against the intended victims or against their
close kin. Thus, rejected suitors, clerks who fail to obtain promotion against less experienced colleagues, dissatisfied co-heirs,
business or political rivals may turn their anger and frustration
against those whom they feel are responsible for their failures
and suffering.

Even close kin are not immune from suspicion. One of the
numerous instances I heard about concerned a dependent aunt
who did not want her niece to get married, for she feared losing
her sole means of support. The aunt is said to have obtained a
magical substance which she surreptitiously applied to the girl's
head; the result was that whenever prospective suitors saw the
young woman she appeared to them as a horrible demon, and
they fled in haste. Other cases were brought to my attention as
illustrations of how sorcery causes illness, drink problems, lost
pregnancies, marriage breakdown, disobedience in children,
examination failure, and all manner of accidents. A car crash
which involved a prominent lay official of a CSI diocese outside
Madras was attributed by several informants to the sorcery of
his own bishop. The two men were reported to have long-
standing disagreements over a number of diocesan matters.
Since I did not meet him, I have no way of knowing if the
'victim' himself concurred in the popular diagnosis.

The opinion is widespread that the most powerful sorcery
originates in Kerala, and that Malayalees are the sorcerers
most to be feared. Muslims are also said to engage widely in
these rites. Practitioners of magic never refer to themselves as
sūṉiyakāraṉ, for this carries the implication of evil and de-
structive activity. They prefer the terms *mantiravāti* or *mantirīkar*,

which connote the recital of spells (*mantra*) and performance of protective rites to 'serve people in need' (Diehl 1956: 267–8). Their potential clients do not make such a careful distinction, however, often using the terms interchangeably. Such magicians generally acknowledge and encourage belief in their power, but publicly insist that their role is to defend their clients from others who would injure them. One *mantiravāti* described the possibility of a transition from defence to offence like this:

I use a spell (*mantra*) to nullify the sorcery against my client. When the *sūnyakāran* learns that the effects of his sorcery have gone, he does something else and my client suffers again. So the client comes here a second time for help and I ask if he wants me to attack the one responsible. If he refuses, then I do what I can, but perhaps the *sūniyam* will come again. If he gives me permission, I act quickly, and the matter is finished.

People therefore retain a healthy respect for all those engaged in these practices, acknowledging that as innocent clients they can easily get caught in the 'crossfire' between rival sorcerers. Believing that there are significant power differentials among magicians, they are particularly anxious about the dangers of being 'represented' by a local and probably lesser practitioner. Only the rich, they say, can afford the most powerful sorcerers. Some people, therefore, stay well clear of involvement in these activities, not through absence of a belief in their efficacy, but out of fear for the possible consequences to themselves.

Sorcerers are known in their neighbourhoods, and their practices are open to the public, some even displaying quite enticing signboards in prominent places to publicize their services. Diehl (1956: 267–8) was told that the police in Madras keep files on them, although a lawyer friend assures me that no court today would entertain a case involving a claim that sorcery had led to injury or death.

Sorcery in its 'aggressive' aspect implies a variety of ritual techniques to inflict harm, including the utterance of spells or their inscription on copper plates which are then buried in the victim's house or place of work. Sorcerers also perform contagious or associative magic. The latter may include the making of clay figures or dolls (*pāvai*) as likenesses of the intended prey, and on which all manner of injury may be sim-

ulated to produce a similar effect on the human subjects. Thus,
a pin inserted in the stomach of the image is thought to create
abdominal pain in the person it represents. These ritual specialists are also associated with graveyards, where they are said
to obtain the skulls of eldest children (usually sons) who have
died young, from which to prepare their pernicious medicines
(*mai*). At the beginning of this century, Thurston was told that
first-born children dying in infancy were often buried near or
even inside the house lest their brains should be used in sorcery,
'a sort of ink decoction being distilled from them' (1912:
240–1). The strength (and cost) of the *mai* is said to depend
on the extent of the harm which the client wishes to inflict. The
medicine is usually given to the latter with instructions to place
it at a site where it is likely to come in contact with the quarry.
If someone else happens to touch it inadvertently, serious consequences can ensue. The daughter of a member of the CSI-
Western congregation who was taken ill suddenly was said to
have brushed up against some *mai* on her way home from
school. This had been smeared on the compound wall of a
complete stranger. It is not uncommon, therefore, for misfortune to be attributed to sorcery intended for quite different
victims.

Sorcerers are also assumed to control a number of spirits
whom they can despatch to bring a variety of afflictions to
their victims. One widely known spirit is Kutti Chatan (Little
Satan), whom Ayyar refers to as the 'imp of mischief in South
Indian demonology' (1928: 151). He creates havoc, causing
stones to fall around the house (but not on it), food to turn to
excrement, dishes to fall off shelves or people out of their beds,
etc. The Travancore Census Commissioner in 1901 wrote in
precisely these terms of Malabar beliefs about Kutti Chatan.
He concluded that, with all this annoying mischief, the 'Boy
Satan' does no serious harm, and is moreover a 'protective
sentry' for those who make him their servant and feed him.
Houses are left 'in the knowledge that no thief would dare enter
with Kutti Chatan on guard' (see Thurston 1912: 237–8). A
Keralite (Hindu) friend tells me that, when he was a child near
Cochin, the family compound contained a small shrine to Kutti
Chatan. Some Hindu households in Madras place an image in

one corner of the *puja* room where offerings are made to the spirit.

Most superhuman assistants of the sorcerers, however, are portrayed as considerably more malign, and their principal means of attacking humans is through possession. These are the *pēy* or evil spirits. These same spirits, it is believed, can also act independently and capriciously, outside the control of sorcerers.

Pēy

Oppert, writing about these baleful spirits at the end of the last century, stated that they 'persecute, seduce and destroy mankind', and that their malignity is 'unbridled' (1893: 515, 594). Later, Whitehead noted that 'every village in south India is believed by the people to be surrounded by evil spirits, who are always on the watch to inflict diseases and misfortunes of all kinds ... villagers pass through life in constant dread of these invisible enemies' (1921: 46). Their presence and their vindictiveness appear not to have diminished over time. One recent study of a Chingleput village describes the *pēy* as 'low, impure, blood-thirsty and maleficent' (Moffatt 1979: 113).

In some of the literature on south Indian popular Hinduism the *pēy* are said to be the ghosts of those who were bad characters or committed crimes in their lifetimes. But most writers, and certainly all my own informants, Hindu and Christian, suggest that they are, in the main, ghosts of persons who died untimely or inauspicious deaths, and so roam the earth in search of humans against whom to vent their anger and frustration at having been denied their full measure of life and happiness. Whereas in the rural areas of Tamilnadu—and certainly in the district which surrounds Madras—the *pēy* are said to live outside the village, in the city itself they are thought to be everywhere. I was told by one man, resident near a large washing site by the Adyar river, that for some time he was awakened at 2.00 a.m. each morning by the sound of clothes being beaten against the stones. When he finally asked a washerman (*dhobi*) why they worked during the night he was told it was not the living who did so, but the unhappy ghosts of the prematurely dead washermen and women. The concentration of *pēy* is generally said to be greatest near cemeteries and (to a lesser extent) cremation grounds, trees, wells, and railway tracks. The spirits of suicides, in particular, are thought to congregate at these latter sites.

Although it is possible to be affected simply by the nearness of a *pēy*, or to be 'slapped' or struck by one, generally it manifests itself by possession of a victim, and so must be cast out. Its identity is usually revealed in the course of an exorcism rite, by the spirit itself under the prodding of the exorcist. Sometimes the dead person was known to the family of the possessed individual but this is not invariably the case. Often, too, the physical condition which led to the death will be recreated in the victim: for example, the spirit of a person who died of TB will be thought to cause chest pain or incessant coughing in the one possessed.

Women are said to be more susceptible to attack by the *pēy*, a fact explained by their greater fear (*payam*). The term *payam* connotes a range of feeling from mild apprehension to painful emotion generated by a belief in impending danger. Numerous individuals recounted their experiences involving serious illness or other misfortune (their own or that of close relatives, usually children), attributed to the machinations of *pēy*, and some related personal encounters with such spirits. In so far as I was able to judge, such events had been extremely distressing at the time, and even the recollections were often very upsetting. A number of people I met, moreover, reported taking elaborate ritual precautions, when going out in the dark or retiring to bed, in order to obviate demonic attacks, the thought of which they found intensely frightening.

The notion of fear is frequently coupled with that of weakness, generally meaning weakness of mind (*iḷakiya maṉam*), and since women are thought to be weaker than men, they are thereby more liable to become possessed. A complementary view is that evil spirits are blood-thirsty, and therefore drawn especially to menstruating women. Some *pēy*—especially the ghosts of young unmarried women—are reputed to be attracted to pregnant women, whose unborn foetuses they want to take away. Women whose pregnancies are aborted are often thought to have been possessed by such a spirit.

Although the *pēy* form a category of unnamed ghosts of prematurely deceased persons, there are other kinds of possessory being who behave in similar ways and are equally referred to as *pēy*. These, however, are non-human or, at least, not invariably human in origin. The most widely known spirits of this kind in Madras are Katteri, Muniswaran, and Mohini.

Elmore (1915: 47), quoting a Telugu dictionary of 1903, refers to Katteri as a 'forest demon'. He also suggests that Katteri appears to be a 'kind of house-name for a group of *saktis*—or 'fallen' goddesses' (1915: 48). In one of its forms, 'Blood Katteri', it is thought by most people I met to be either the name for any female *pēy* or the spirit of women who die in childbirth. Thus, Katteri desires the blood of humans and is especially associated with aborted pregnancies. As in the village, some Hindu families in the city worship Katteri as a lineage deity (*kula teyvam*) or otherwise propitiate her in a domestic shrine, which is thought to render her less harmful (see Moffatt 1979: 183-4). But she also possesses people, and in Madras is commonly regarded as a *pēy*.

She is sometimes said to be the wife of Muniswaran, who is considered in villages near Madras as a 'low' but protective being, and so will often have a temple at the entrance to the settlement. He is also worshipped by some Hindus as a lineage god and placated as a personal or chosen god (*iṣṭa teyvam*) by others to whom he has demonstrated his power (ibid.: 224, 230). But, in the city, Muniswaran is frequently said to be the chief of the *pēy*, and is identified as a possessory evil spirit. One informant explained that the urban practice differed from the rural due to the 'influence of the films', which are sometimes responsible for re-presenting and recasting traditional ideas and practices.

Mohini is a somewhat different matter. As a female form of Vishnu, she appears in several Mahabharata myths, when Vishnu takes the guise of an enchantress—on one occasion to distract the demons and turn their minds away from capturing the ambrosia of immortality. In south India she is sometimes Siva's consort, and the mother of the popular Aiyanar. According to Shulman (1980: 311-12) Mohini is worshipped in Tamil villages, although no Hindu I met in Madras ever spoke of doing so. Here, Mohini is most commonly regarded as the spirit of females who die (sometimes by their own hand) because of disappointed love. She appears occasionally to young women of whose good fortune she is jealous, but mainly she

appears to young bachelors, most typically on their way home
from a late night film. She wears a white *sari* and flowers in
her hair, and seeks to lure the young man in order to live with
him as his wife, take his strength, and finally kill him. One
member of the CSI-Western congregation related how, when
he was a young man, on one occasion returning home after
midnight, he was called by a woman in the field below the
road. 'She was very beautiful and smelled of jasmine. She beck-
oned me to come to her. But I got frightened and ran away. I
realized it was Mohini'. Some people say she is especially attracted to those who have lustful thoughts, or who visit pros-
titutes. When she has entered the body of such a person he has
erotic dreams and loses his semen, and so his blood or strength.
In Madras, among both Hindus and Christians, she is referred
to as 'Mohini *pēy*'.[17]

The *pēy*, though amenable to the control of sorcerers, are also
able, as I have noted, to act of their own volition, and so
to trouble their victims without such guidance. Thus, while
affliction may be attributed to the evil intentions of *sūniyakāran*
acting on behalf of aggrieved clients—and so to a failure of
human relations—it is also perceived as the result of capricious
spirits, whose motivations are not accessible to ordinary human
understanding.

THAUMATURGY IN THE HINDU CONTEXT

These beliefs regarding the aetiology of affliction are widely
shared by all segments of the lower class in Madras. Hindus,
however, have access to a ritual means of coping with the
ordeals wrought by sorcerers and spirits, through appeal to
various deities in the divine hierarchy of Hinduism. Among the
more common regional gods entreated are the sons of Siva and
Parvati, i.e. Ganesh (the elephant-headed deity, known also in
south India as Vinayakar), and Murukan. They are lesser but
more popular beings among the Hindu masses, regarded as
intermediaries to the higher gods, and equally beneficent,
though liable to punish lapsed devotees. They are also seen as
able to defend them from the threats of maleficent beings.
Those who follow Murukan, for example, pray regularly for his
protection from *sūniyam* and the *pēy*. 'When we carry the Sashti

Kavasam [a book of verses praying the deity to keep watch on his votaries] the *pēy* are frightened', I was told by one devotee.

However, it is probably to the Goddess more than to any other divinity that ordinary Hindus turn for shelter from the agents of affliction, and for assistance when they have fallen victim. In south India this component of folk Hinduism probably goes back to pre-historic times (Stein 1973), and today the Goddess is still worshipped in her many forms of Amman (mother) or Sakti (spiritual and generative power or energy).[18] Moffatt refers to these deities as 'quintessentially intermediate beings', alternately benevolent and malevolent, peaceful and angry (1979: 233). Their powers are specific and concentrated, but regarded as considerable for just that reason.

There are innumerable ritual specialists in Madras who claim to have an intimate relationship with the Goddess, and through whom she communicates directly with her devotees. While a few acquire wide reputations and build large temples to which considerable numbers of people from all over the region are attracted, most mediums are only locally known, and hold regular seances in their own homes. The highlight of most such sessions comes when the medium enters a state of trance and becomes possessed by the deity. When the Goddess enters the person of the medium, she speaks through him or her to those present, giving advice, reassurance, promises, and ritual prescriptions for dealing with all manner of misfortune. When necessary, evil spirits are exorcized.

Some sorcerers also purport to draw their power from the Goddess. A Muslim *mantiravāti*, whose practice is in a busy road in north Madras, advertises his presence by a huge outdoor wall painting of the Goddess in her fierce aspect as Kali. He perceives no contradiction between his faith and his tutelary deity, but claims to bring Sakti (as he usually refers to her) into him by meditating first upon Allah.

Thus, in this divine order, lower beings are ultimately controlled by higher ones. The *pēy* can be dealt with through recourse to the deities whose powers are greater, and generally more beneficent. But these higher divinities operate only on behalf of their Hindu devotees. Protestants, by contrast, find their own religious tradition unable to provide an appropriate response to their notions about affliction. According to Diehl,

'they must either change their means of solving their problems
or trust in the old helpers' (1965: 138). In the past, some did
turn, often surreptitiously, to Hindu specialists to help them
cope with the misfortunes in their lives. But, for the most part,
devout Christians were compelled to suppress this aspect of
their traditional beliefs and inclinations.

THAUMATURGY IN THE PROTESTANT CONTEXT

While secular and missionary scholars eventually acknowledged the positive qualities of the ethical and moral themes
they discovered in the epic literature of Hinduism, the folk
tradition was dismissed out of hand. Marshall notes that
popular cults of the eighteenth century were either deemed
unworthy of study or described 'only to be condemned or
ridiculed' (1970: 20). In a letter written shortly after his arrival
in south India, Ziegenbalg describes certain popular beliefs and
apologizes to his correspondent for 'rehearsing to you so much
of this useless trash' (1718: 25). The missionaries of that period,
observes Arasaratnam, 'were opposed to all forms of Sakti worship [which they] castigated as devil worship and sorcery. They
put in this category all forms of medium cults and exorcism
ceremonies that must have been popular then' (1981: 32). Later
missionaries had no greater sympathy for such views and practices. Even the liberal scholars did not extend their tolerance
to popular Hinduism. Müller is reported to have explained
that he dwelt exclusively on the 'good' (i.e. classical philosophical) side of Hinduism, since 'the other [popular] side is so
childish that it does not seek to deserve any notice' (see Forrester 1980: 137). Farquhar similarly expressed dismay at how
the 'true motives' of Hindu religion were often betrayed in
'unclean, debasing or unworthy practices ...' (1913: 458).

By denying the existence of evil spirits and the efficacy of
sorcery, missionaries of all the major Protestant Societies effectively denied the agencies which, in the view of most people,
protected them from mystical dangers. The missionaries regarded as nonsense popular convictions about them and 'attempted to laugh the matter away' (Machin 1934: 481). They
traded stories of the more 'bizarre' episodes which came to their
attention, but wrote little in their journals and correspondence

about these matters, revealing their own bemusement and embarrassment in the face of such ideas, as well as the inability of their overseas headquarters to regard them with any seriousness. I was told by one mission worker who arrived in India some forty years ago that when she sought guidance from her home base in the USA on the grounds that in India 'evil spirits are everywhere', she was as much as told that she had better take to the hills for a rest cure, or ask for a transfer home.

There were very occasional missionary voices which sought to develop a dialogue about indigenous views on affliction. Revd Machin (1934) pleaded with colleagues to share their opinions and advice on how to deal with reported instances of demonic possession. Can missionaries in India, he asked, take the rather materialistic nineteenth-century view that all this is nonsense? A perusal of subsequent editions of the journal in which he published his plea suggests that Machin received not a single reply to his request for a pooling of experiences and an exchange of views.

For the most part, converts and their descendants looked in vain to their missionaries and their indigenous clergy for a satisfactory response to their traditional views of affliction. On the whole, these were ridiculed, rationalized, and explained away by ecclesiastics who had long since rejected their own thaumaturgical legacy. The Reformation in England saw a 'spectacular reduction' in the powers attributed to holy words and objects and took away the priest's 'magical' functions, e.g. his powers of exorcism (Thomas 1982: 304, 327). Certainly, by the era of missionary expansion throughout the Third World, such beliefs had virtually disappeared from orthodox Protestantism. Hill argues that it was the theologians rather than the scientists who banished miracles, exorcism, magic, and the like from everyday Protestant religion, assigning them to 'the distant past, to the age of Christ and the Apostles' (1983: 182-3). Such attitudes spread throughout the missionized world. Wilson, writing about Africa, observes how missionaries 'showed themselves incapable of understanding the Christian past or the African present ... The extent to which new anxieties have been caused by the Christian refusal even to countenance the idea of witchcraft is inestimable' (1973: 82).

In south India, too, Protestant leaders and churchmen turned their backs on such concerns. Neither in their theological training nor in that given to local candidates for the clergy were such ideas even considered. The CSI clergymen with whom I discussed this theme could recall no occasion during their period of training or, subsequently, as ordained ministers in a diocese, when issues of this kind were even raised. Protestants thus looked in vain to their missionaries and their indigenous clergy for a satisfactory response to these popular conceptions of adversity, and so were denied the authenticity of such forms of knowledge. A popular tradition which externalized evil and sought thaumaturgical solutions was met and opposed by a Western Protestant tradition which urged, instead, individual responsibility through self-help and prayer, what Hill calls the 'internalization of the struggle against the forces of evil' (1983: 183).

The 'official' denial of popular views and observances was and still is reinforced by other kinds of aspersions emanating from the middle class. The well-to-do, well-connected, and well-employed (who are, as it happens, less prone to the adversities of the disprivileged), on the whole regard the views of those less fortunate than themselves as 'superstition'. In the (English) words of one prosperous member of the CSI-Northern congregation:

My own understanding of it is this: it is superstition. A lot of these superstitions go hand in hand with ignorance, with lack of education. This, along with poor circumstances, creates an atmosphere for people to hold these views. With knowledge, education, and comfortable circumstances, people see that nothing like this [i.e. magic or evil spirits] really happens. In fifty-six years I have not personally come across one single case of sorcery.

The idea that magical beliefs thrive among the economically and educationally less fortunate is echoed by a CSI-Southern congregant:

These are typical Indian beliefs, prevalent among people who are lower class and not educated much. If anything goes wrong they immediately begin to think 'this is *sūṇiyam*', or 'this is a *pēy*'. People of our class, because they are well educated, do not follow these ideas. I am not attracted to this at all. My father and mother never discussed it. As far back as I can remember I never heard anyone in my family talk about such things. I have not experienced anything like it.

Others belonging to élite congregations attribute the persistence of such popular views to the machinations of cunning and unscrupulous 'witchdoctors', who 'make a lot of money out of the gullibility of the poor'. They also blame the inadequate and expensive health facilities which compel people to turn to 'bogus healers'. Some, nowadays, regard all manifestations of possession and claims of sorcery as evidence of mental illness, brought on by irrational fears. One middle-class informant even suggested that part of the 'problem' was the inadequate lighting in neighbourhoods and houses of the lower class, where it is much easier to be persuaded by ideas about evil spirits and the like.

A similar assessment of popular religious beliefs and activities in and around the city of Bangalore by a committee of the National Institute of Mental Health and Neuro-Sciences (NIMHANS) led to recommendations for (a) improved health services; (b) the holding of periodic psychiatric 'camps'; (c) legislation against magical practices (*banamathi*); and (d) the introduction of a programme to 'eradicate superstition'.[19] Clearly, the middle class do not see popular beliefs about affliction as a coherent and authentic system of thought, but as a regrettable, if understandable failure, due mainly to ignorance on the part of the uneducated masses, to comprehend and accept a world-view based, like their own, on science and 'rationality'. This is a view, Crick reminds us, which 'values achievement of goals, efficiency and control; it thus appears as the subjection of nature ... and the subjugation of man' (1982*b*: 299). Commitment to 'superstition', moreover, is seen by the middle class as clear evidence of irrational thinking. Popular notions about misfortune, therefore, constitute people as backward and subordinate.

CONCLUSION

In the context of a Christian population characterized for several decades by growing economic and social divisions, the privileged minority has, through its control of church structures, effectively determined what was to be the dominant theological emphasis within the community. The 'social gospel', which early twentieth-century Western liberal theologians introduced to south India, has remained the 'authentic' religious discourse of the ecclesiastical and community élites in the post-independence period. It features a commitment to national development and social welfare and the alleviation of poverty and hardship through charitable works, though it nowhere challenges or seeks significantly to change existing social structures which create and sustain inequalities. Involvement in the 'world' has gone hand in hand with a more considerate and ecumenical approach to Hinduism.

By contrast, the majority of ordinary Protestants pursue a sober, Bible-based faith, which promises individual salvation for the devout. The legacy of earlier conservative evangelical missionaries, it stresses the continuous exercise of piety, refuses to compromise with those who have not accepted the 'true faith', and determines to convert the latter through persistent evangelism.[20]

The religion of ordinary Protestants also accommodates a set of beliefs regarding the aetiology of affliction, some of whose basic tenets would appear to contradict—or, at any rate, sit uneasily alongside—this pietistic Christianity. Thus, for example, while one set of views may be seen as an ideology demanding acceptance of personal responsibility for adversity, the other seeks to project it on to external mystical beings. But the contradiction is never resolved, because it is not perceived as such and because it does not and is not allowed to emerge so starkly. This is itself partly attributable to the constant negation of popular ideas and practices relating to affliction on the part, first, of missionaries and, later, of the indigenous church and community leadership.

The different historical derivations of these two main components of the religion of ordinary Protestants in Madras highlights, in a striking way, the difficulty of offering unitary formulations on popular culture. One view suggests that a power bloc imposes its ideas on those whom it subordinates, so that all members of a community think in the categories of the dominant group. Bourdieu, for example, has argued that in modern industrial society there is effectively one culture, that of the dominant class, and that those outside this class have to define their own culture in terms of it (Bourdieu 1968). Returning to the more restricted context of south India, it would certainly be difficult to understand the centrality of pietism in Protestant life during the past century and a half without acknowledging the almost total dominion exercised by the missionaries over the first generations of new Christians. Theirs, after all, was a body of beliefs which had its origins in and drew its meanings from the theological history of Western Europe. Yet these doctrines and rites became, and still remain for most south Indian Protestants, a vital part of their religious discourse. This is surely an instance of a dominant religious ideology being imposed not by compulsion but by consent, what Gramsci saw as the essence of 'hegemony' (1971).

Moreover, it could be (and has been) argued that a theology which concentrates entirely on inner spirituality and personal salvation directs attention away from those 'objective structures and relations of human social existence' which establish and reproduce inequality (Thomas 1977: 28). Looked at in this way, such a theology in the embrace of a dominated class invites labelling as 'false consciousness'.

What of the popular discourse of affliction? The ideas and behaviours to which it refers are, as we have seen, generated from below, from a long-standing tradition shared by all those—Hindus and Christians—who occupy and experience a similar position in the class order. There are obvious similarities here with Keith Thomas's well-known exposition of popular beliefs in sixteenth- and seventeenth-century England, which highlighted the gap separating the magic-focused culture of the disprivileged masses from the religion-focused culture of the dominant minority (1982). This suggests that popular ideas and practices can exist, to some extent, independently of the dominant culture, and are more truly in accord with the experiences and interests of the subordinate bloc.

To preserve some degree of cultural autonomy requires a determined commitment to its authenticity in the face of intense hostility from above. At times, antagonism to popular religion can take a violent form. In south India, opposition was more subtle. We have seen how beliefs about the mystical agents of misfortune were ridiculed, condemned, and effectively denied legitimate public expression, first by the missionaries and later by the indigenous church and middle class. Autonomy also calls for resistance to the dominant discourse. The social gospel, it was shown, provides no benefits for the majority of Protestants, and has no popular appeal. Furthermore, the activities and institutions it generates have no place for those outside the circles of the élite. So it is an ideological proposition which is simply 'unconvincing despite [its] authoritative source and stamp' (Turton 1984: 64).

In brief, then, the cultural dialectic assumes several shapes, and its outcome is uncertain. It may feature incorporation, autonomy, or resistance, but it almost invariably entails a complex process of interaction and 'negotiation' between groups of unequal endowment. The dialectic, moreover, can never be entirely insulated from wider historical developments. Some of these, by introducing novel modes of discourse, roles, and institutional arrangements, reshape the terms of the struggle. The recent spread of fundamentalism in south India constitutes such a development.

8

THE MIRACLES OF FUNDAMENTALISM
Affliction, Healing, and Charismatic Renewal

INTRODUCTION

DURING the past twenty-five years, the Protestant community in Madras has been profoundly influenced by the rapid growth of new congregations and sects offering a fundamentalist version of Christianity. This is not a trend exclusive to south India, but one which has been widely reported in the Third World as, indeed, in the First World, as well. Organizationally, these bodies remain outside the World Council of Churches. Within India, they do not affiliate to the National Christian Council, to which the country's mainline churches belong. Doctrinally, they differ from the orthodox pietists and evangelicals in placing stress on the significance of the Holy Spirit in the Christian Trinity, and isolating for special emphasis the 'gifts' of the Spirit.

This chapter first traces the growth of this kind of fundamentalism in south India, and seeks the reasons for its efflorescence in terms both of indigenous understandings and particular historical trends in the wider Christian world. It also looks at the ways in which fundamentalist views and observances reinforce, subsume, and authenticate popular explanations of misfortune, and offer a means of overcoming it. The charismatic prophets, individuals believed to be selected by God to deal with human affliction, are then discussed through an examination of the ritual contexts and procedures in and by which they operate. The threat to orthodoxy offered by these charismatic figures and the religious ideologies they promote is considered and, in a final section, note is taken of the recent interest shown by certain sections within the church in appropriating elements of this fundamentalist discourse.

THE GROWTH OF FUNDAMENTALISM

Sectarian groups professing fundamentalist ideas have been reported in south India for over seventy-five years.[1] The first

Pentecostal missionaries arrived from the United States soon after the movement was 'born' (in Los Angeles) around 1906 (Harper 1965: 13).[2] After a period of sluggish growth, interrupted by the First World War, their work resumed, and a number of congregations were established, though several of them emerged as a consequence of schism within existing groups. According to George (1975: 10–11) a general convention of all Pentecostals in south India in 1924 drew representatives from twenty-four organizations, most of them concentrated among Syrian Christians in Central Travancore (now part of Kerala). In the 1930s the fundamentalist presence in Madras was increased with the establishment of several evangelical assemblies, such as the Laymen's Evangelical Fellowship and Jehovah Shamma. Although the founder of the latter sect (a Sikh convert) is said by present sympathizers to have 'shaken the city', both these groups attracted only modest followings. An increase in the number of such sects followed the Second World War and India's independence, and their principal adherents were 'won' not from Hinduism but from among 'the old Christian communities', as one disapproving source noted (*Madras Guardian*, 8 May 1947). After 1960 the expansion of such groups became significant. Thangasamy, writing at the end of the decade, remarks that the 'big do's ... in Madras in recent times have been evangelical ones' (1969: 60). As a former bishop in Madras noted, 'what had been a small trickle became a flood. Madras, with its relatively large Christian population, was the happy hunting ground for a growing multitude of [sectarian] saviours ...' (Newbigin 1972a: 12). Nelson's data suggest a figure, in the mid-1970s, of some sixty congregations to which we might attach a fundamentalist label (1975: 192). In 1981–2, when I was in Madras, I was told that there were 'hundreds' of such congregations in the city. One Pentecostal organization alone claimed nearly fifty branches, and the Evangelical Church of India thirty-five congregations. The difficulty of estimating numbers with any degree of accuracy reflects, more than anything, the frailty of such classificatory labels. It is often impossible to distinguish independent prayer cells or associations (which are too numerous to count) from small, independent, sectarian congregations. In terms of numbers, rites, and beliefs they may be virtually identical. Another difficulty is presented by the rapidity of sectarian schism and multiplication. On one occasion while I was sitting with an executive of the Bible Society a young man entered the office to request some Bibles and tracts. The conversation went like this:

OFFICIAL. Who do you represent?
VISITOR. I am from the Universal Church of Christ.
OFFICIAL. I have never heard about your assembly.
VISITOR. We are new. We started only a few months ago.
OFFICIAL. Where were you (affiliated) before?
VISITOR. Most of us were with the Church of God [*another Pentecostal group*], but we came away from there.
OFFICIAL. How many are you?
VISITOR. We are about 25 families in all.
OFFICIAL. Who is your pastor?
VISITOR. You would not know him, sir, he is not ordained.
OFFICIAL. How do you support yourselves?
VISITOR. We give tithes of 10 per cent. But we pray daily for God's help to find an organization to help us.

I was told by my host that these kinds of visits are a regular occurrence. Most such groups, he noted, do not survive for very long, for if they want to expand and acquire a building of their own, they require more resources than they can possibly raise from their own adherents. (Hence the young man's reference to a sponsor.) Notwithstanding their dramatic expansion in the city, these groups have attracted a comparatively small proportion of the Protestant population to their ranks. Nelson gives figures which indicate that about 15 per cent of the urban community are members of sectarian organizations (1975: 192). But the concept of membership itself is vague and slippery, and does not convey the extent of fundamentalist influence on those within the mainline churches. To illustrate the point, we might examine for a moment the kinds of relationships established with fundamentalist groups by adherents of the CSI-Western church.

A few are active adherents of one or other sect, to the extent of taking second baptism, in defiance of CSI ordinances,[3] and 'speaking in tongues'—thought to be a prime manifestation of the Holy Spirit—which together constitute for fundamentalists, according to Goodman, 'the entrance ticket to heaven' (1972:

87).⁴ Those so committed may also pay tithes and, of course, attend the sect's frequent rituals. Most groups are very demanding of their votaries' time, and the latter report some form of prayer activity on nearly every day of the week. Such persons also attend an occasional service in the CSI-Western church, but their ties to the parish are only nominal, and usually retained either out of sentiment for the church of their childhood or out of deference to a spouse, parent, or other senior member of the household who attends regularly. It is worth noting that as many as a fifth of households in the lower class sample contain individuals whose primary attachment is to a fundamentalist group—whether or not the latter acknowledge some link with the orthodox church as well. Moreover, a perusal of genealogies reveals that about one quarter of focal householders have at least one sibling, parent, or child whose primary affiliation is with such a group.

Some individuals, as we saw in Chapter 7, while retaining one foot firmly planted in the CSI, participate in or have even been instrumental in forming neighbourhood-based independent prayer cells or formal associations which draw their adherents from various sects and churches. Several couples affiliated to the CSI-Western congregation hold weekly meetings in their own homes, where people speak in tongues (*pala pāṣai*) and healing rites are conducted. The hosts and some of those in attendance are said to be filled with the Holy Spirit (*parisutta āvi*) on these occasions. Another congregant, who refers to herself as an 'evangelist' (*ūḻiyakkāran*), began her career by holding prayer meetings in her home and over time accumulated the capital to construct a two-storey building on an adjacent plot to house the growing activities of her burgeoning assembly. But, like the couples mentioned above, she still attends services regularly in the CSI-Western church, and takes part in its various programmes. She is fortunate in having her brother's help for her independent evangelical work, but he does not regard himself as a member of the CSI-Western or any other orthodox congregation. Several other congregants aspire to build such an enterprise, but for the moment are 'doing God's work' (*karttarūṭaiya ūḻiyam*) on their own, as freelance evangelists. They are usually asked to attend people at home, and to preach on the circuit of small independent sectarian groups and prayer cells. They also attend services at the CSI-Western church on a regular basis.

A third category comprises those congregants who have established a personal link with a charismatic sect leader or independent evangelist, generally one who has been instrumental in assisting them (or members of their households) to overcome an illness or resolve some other difficulty. Thus, one such leader was credited with the return of a missing son. The household members thereafter became supporters of his independent Pentecostal assembly, the boy's mother even removing her ornaments, in accordance with the sect's beliefs and practices, 'as witness that our prayers were answered'. The links thus established involve making 'thank offerings' of cash and other favours, and organizing prayer meetings at their home to which the evangelist is invited as guest preacher. This is one important way in which the latter's achievements are advertised, abilities demonstrated, income raised, and reputation enhanced. At least half a dozen households of CSI-Western congregants claim such an attachment to one particular sect leader who today has a growing following in the south-western area of Madras. His own church—now affiliated to a large Pentecostal organization—was built originally with the help of several grateful beneficiaries of his charismatic powers. Other CSI-Western congregants are linked to different evangelists, but on the whole they all insist on retaining their primary loyalties to the CSI. They thus resist becoming fully committed to the assemblies formed around these persons, though they may subscribe in large measure to the latters' fundamentalist views.

For many, the most crucial symbol of their fidelity to the orthodox church is a refusal to take second baptism. I was told by the couple whose missing son had returned home through the assumed intervention of the Pentecostal leader that, while they readily give money and other forms of support for his 'ministry', they consistently refuse to take second baptism. Despite his urgings, and his denial of holy communion to those who have not undergone the rite, they are adamant in their refusal. 'We were both properly baptized as children. So we have to agree to differ with him on this matter.' Others take

their stand on the question of communion, insisting on celebrating it only in a CSI church.

Finally, we have to note that the majority of members of this
CSI congregation stay well clear of any firm attachments to
such sectarian leaders and of permanent involvement in ritual
groups outside the orthodox church. But even they do not seek
to avoid exposure to fundamentalist ideas, nor could they easily
do so if they wanted to. There are numerous everyday contexts
in which these doctrines are reiterated. In its May 1980 edition,
the *Christian Focus* announced under a front-page headline—
'Flood-tides of Evangelism'—that during the first two months
of the year there were no less than twenty-three meetings advertised on city walls by various fundamentalist groups and
sects. Both indigenous and foreign evangelists hold frequent
'crusades' at which they expatiate on the Holy Spirit, and offer
assistance to those who, in one way or another are, and/or
believe themselves to be, the victims of misfortune. Several of
the better known charismatic personalities in Madras even have
regular programmes broadcast to home as well as overseas
Tamil audiences from private radio stations in Manila, the
Seychelles, Sri Lanka, etc. Some of the most popular tunes
within the community are written and sung by local charismatic figures. They are widely available for sale on record
or tape, and nowadays heard in various contexts where Protestants gather together. I attended several weddings of persons
affiliated to the CSI-Western parish at which the loudspeakers,
placed strategically around the compound in which the reception was held, offered a steady diet of popular religious
songs which contained obvious fundamentalist sentiments.

At the annual Festival of Joy (*pēriṉpa peruviḻā*) held in May
and attended by thousands who consider this to be the event
of the year in the Madras Protestant calendar, there was a
noticeable increase over the five years between my stays in
the city in the number of fundamentalist speakers on the
programme. It was evident to everyone who attended in 1982
that the latter attracted the largest crowds and received the
most enthusiastic response. Members of the CSI-Western congregation were especially impressed by the minister of a Pentecostal assembly in the neighbourhood of their own church,
who was appearing for the first time at the Festival. Many

congregants regularly attend his meetings, held on Sunday
mornings after services in their own church, and some have
relatives and friends who are full-time adherents of his
assembly.

Now the members of this CSI congregation are by no means
aberrant or unusual. Acquaintance with their kinship networks, which reach many parts of the city, suggests that lower
class Protestants throughout Madras, however much committed to the orthodox church, are nowadays familiar with
and, to a greater or lesser extent, sympathetic to fundamentalist
beliefs and practices. The growing sympathy for these ideas
within certain sections of the CSI hierarchy (see below) is, in
part, an acknowledgement of the widespread disposition of so
many of its own members to disregard the vague boundaries—
theological as well as organizational—which still exist between
sect and denomination.

THE WIDER CONTEXT OF GROWTH

The timing of this efflorescence is not wholly fortuitous, and I
think that two important contributory developments have to
be acknowledged if we are to understand the increasing attraction of fundamentalism in urban south India. The first
concerns the wider aspects of this growth which, as I have
noted, reaches into many corners of the world. This is a phenomenon which has been much commented on, though hardly,
if at all, examined. While I am not in a position to offer more
than a few observations, these may serve to draw attention to
the links between certain global politico-religious trends and
the particular context we are considering.

What is clear is that many if not most fundamentalist groups
are American-led and funded. These now devote more personnel and resources to evangelism than the orthodox churches
which had, for so long, monopolized the international Protestant mission field. Moreover, the funds available have, if
anything, increased in recent years with the emergence of a
coalition between American fundamentalists and the 'New
Right'. Thus, fundamentalism has spread with American overseas influence in much the same way as early missionary Christianity spread with colonialism.

In Madras, foreign missions based mainly in the USA provide finances and other forms of support for most of the large and successful fundamentalist churches. The local head of one of these bodies was quite candid about his organization's reliance on foreign aid now and for the foreseeable future. These missions also seek out independent groups which show signs of attracting a large following, to offer them association and assistance. Alternatively, small congregations with ambitions to expand, or evangelists convinced that they have been especially chosen to do 'God's work' are on the lookout for sponsors (see above), and so seek to interest foreign missions in their activities. The *Christian Focus* of 15 July 1975 announced the recent public début of an evangelist in the following words: 'It is reported that he is in touch with a rich American body, which has the avowed purpose of providing resources for evangelism all over the world. A shining stream of dollars, they say, has washed [his] door'. Some groups or their leaders 'shop around', forming and severing attachments with more than one sponsoring mission over time. The leader of a congregation near the CSI-Western church, who was brought up in the American Arcot Mission (which became part of the CSI) was affiliated during the 1950s to an American mission society which backs a large fundamentalist church in south India with numerous branches in the city. Following a disagreement he left it to join the Mormons, and five years later left them to join forces with another American-backed mission to which his congregation is presently affiliated. As the number of independent evangelists and their followings has grown, these foreign organizations have had to become more selective in their choice of individuals and groups to support, and consequently the competition among them is nowadays intense. The head of one small congregation complained bitterly that his negotiations with one American body had been 'poisoned' by another sect leader seeking affiliation to the same mission.

What is also clear is that the official rhetoric of these foreign missions usually includes an aggressive attack on socialism, Marxism, or, indeed, any left-wing stance. Strong criticism is, therefore, reserved for 'liberation theology' which has strongly influenced many of the clergy in Latin America and parts of Asia. The World Council of Churches, to which the CSI and most other orthodox Protestant denominations in the country are affiliated through the National Christian Council of India, is also seen in some fundamentalist quarters as a hotbed of liberalism and as even being sympathetic to 'communism' (see Hollenweger 1972: 441). In the south Indian Protestant context, where a radical theology is almost totally absent, fundamentalists add their voices to the popular critique of the church hierarchy's attachment to 'modernism' and the social gospel (see Chapter 7).

A second development which would appear to have a bearing on the advance of fundamentalism in south India relates to recent socio-economic changes, especially in and around Madras. I have discussed these in some detail in Chapter 3, and here we need only recollect the principal features. The immediate post-independence expansion of industry, commerce, and services in the metropolitan area, which encouraged a considerable migration of Christians (as well as others) to the city, had by the mid-1960s levelled out, constricting opportunities for urban employment and advancement. The circumstances of those at the lower end of the class order grew increasingly difficult as a result. The new middle class, moreover, in defending and consolidating its own recently won privileges, exacerbated the situation of the disprivileged.

Wilson, examining the phenomenon of Pentecostal growth around the world, correlates it with, among other things, the 'loss of warm associations of [the] rural communities' which people experience in the course of rapid urbanization (1970: 71–4). This has led, he suggests, to conditions of 'anomie' in the city, as large numbers of people migrating from the countryside experience 'disruptive cultural contact and social change' in their new urban environments (ibid.: 89). Similarly, in Chile, writes d'Epinay, 'Pentecostalism appears as a communal religious answer to the confusion of large sections of the population, caused by the anomic character of a society in transition' (1969: 15).

Though Madras has experienced a considerable population growth in this century—from 0.5 million in 1901 to some 3 millions in 1981—much of it the result of immigration, it must remain an open question as to whether this development has resulted in 'confusion' and 'anomie'. Studies of migration in

India have emphasized the kin and caste-based character of these population movements, which have assisted adaptation to urban environments (Rowe 1973). Moreover, as I have shown, Protestant migrants who entered Madras from the rural areas on the whole preserved their previous denominational links which provided familiar ritual surroundings. The vast majority still retain their ties to the orthodox churches. In any event, whereas Protestants of the lower class have, for the most part, a relatively long association with the city going back several generations, the interest in fundamentalism is largely a phenomenon of the recent past. The urban transition, therefore, has been largely characterized by institutional continuity. The 'disruptive' aspect lay in a quite dramatic economic reversal, during the 1960s, which most people experienced in a direct and personal way. For those in the lower class, prospects began to appear less bright than in the past; their material conditions deteriorated and were felt to have done so. It is mainly among such people, as we have seen, that fundamentalist discourse gained a ready and sympathetic hearing.

INDIGENOUS EXPLANATIONS OF FUNDAMENTALIST EXPANSION

How do Protestants within the orthodox churches understand their own as well as the general growth of interest in fundamentalism? I have heard several kinds of explanation offered by members of the CSI-Western congregation, and, not surprisingly, these reflect to some degree the extent of their own commitment to sectarian groups and ideologies. One, from the handful of congregants most persuaded and engaged by fundamentalist beliefs and practices, suggests that this proliferation is itself a manifestation of the Holy Spirit moving in the community. Therefore, in this view, the phenomenon cannot be referred to external 'causes' other than, of course, 'the mysterious ways of God'.

From the small minority of those who remain exclusively attached to the orthodox church and most adamant in their rejection of fundamentalist doctrines comes a wholly censorious view. It attributes the growth of this kind of religiosity to, on the one hand, the machinations of schismatic foreign missions with their vast resources and, on the other, the indigenous sectarian groups engaged in what is seen as an unedifying scramble to find foreign sponsorship and 'steal' members from the denominational bodies. They save their most deprecatory (and often scurrilous) remarks for the activities of popular evangelists who, as they perceive it, are concerned only to gain money from and influence over ordinary decent people who approach them in times of need.

A similar view is expressed even more widely within the Protestant middle class, for it enables the attraction of fundamentalism to be explained in terms of the gullibility of the uneducated who, in 'chasing after miracles', are 'taken in' and cynically exploited by these charismatics. They especially relish recounting the histories of several former popular evangelists whose scandalous activities were publicly exposed and who consequently left Madras in disgrace. The allure of these figures, as Gilsenan observes about a not dissimilar category of ecstatics in regions dominated by Islam, 'serve as a proof to the ... more privileged classes of the moral and ethical degradation of the lowest level of society' (1982: 90). A somewhat more sophisticated way of disdaining those who are attracted to fundamentalism is to suggest that this form of religiosity, with its 'superstitious' doctrines and practices, and its emotional ritual ambience, is more attuned to the 'Indian character'. What remains unspoken is the corollary that the educated, Westernized middle class is suited to a more controlled, dignified religious expression. Here again, as I suggested in the previous chapter, the middle class distinguishes itself from and, at the same time, constitutes those beneath it by pointing to a basic difference in 'rationalities'.

The majority of those within the CSI-Western parish (and the CSI parishes of the lower class generally) who, as we have seen, remain firmly planted within the orthodox church at the same time as they are drawn into the orbit of fundamentalist ideas and practices, offer an explanation somewhere between these 'extremes' of opinion (although some of them may acknowledge the poignancy of either or both of the above viewpoints). It is most commonly presented in terms of the 'failure' of the mainline churches to meet the 'spiritual needs' of their votaries. This is usually elaborated as the excessive formalism or 'coldness' of worship, the absence of 'strong' (i.e. evangelistic) sermons, and a dearth of pastoral care, sometimes interpreted as a lack of caring. By contrast, the fundamentalist rites experienced by these Christians are described as 'warm', for they allow scope for individual spontaneity and emotionalism. The messages heard in these assemblies provide 'spiritual food', i.e. they are didactic in intent, or as one establishment Christian paper commented, 'really lessons in Biblical teaching ... most Christians prefer this' (*Madras Guardian*, 12 March 1964). Finally, reference is invariably made to the abundant concern shown for and emotional support given to those who are in adversity by 'brothers and sisters' within the sectarian fold.

This much is, of course, familiar commentary, echoing the strongly pietistic segment within the ordinary congregations of the orthodox church and which, as we saw in Chapter 7, finds expression in their numerous prayer cells and associations. But fundamentalism taps a more crucial vein in the corpus of popular ideas, namely those which relate to affliction, for they offer a way of understanding and overcoming it.

FUNDAMENTALISM AND POPULAR BELIEFS ABOUT MISFORTUNE

Fundamentalist doctrines are consistent with popular ideas about the aetiology of affliction. These beliefs are not negated or ridiculed as they were in the early mission and later indigenous orthodox context. Rather, they are given legitimacy by incorporation in a system of knowledge based on inerrant scriptural authority. Fundamentalism acknowledges that misfortune is brought by a host of evil agents, who are identified, moreover, as in the employ of Satan. There is some disagreement about how to accommodate the widespread notion that suicides and other persons who die prematurely provide the bulk of the spirit population. One tendency is to fortify this belief by seeking scriptural justification. A well-known evangelist finds evidence in the words of Ecclesiastes (3: 1–2) that 'to everything there is a season, a time to every purpose ... a time to be born and a time to die ...'. And if the allotted time is not lived out in full, the argument goes, then a person is condemned to roam the earth as an evil spirit until the date appointed for death by the heavenly diarist (Dhinakaran 1979: 33).

Some fundamentalists find this particular argument somewhat fanciful and assimilate indigenous ideas about the *pēy* more directly to the Judeo-Christian notion of the Fall. The untimely dead, in this approach, are regarded as the victims of Satan, and the spirits they leave as his maleficent servants. To this category of evil forces are added the Fallen Angels, whose main role, in the fundamentalist view, is to deceive the majority of people in this heathen land by appearing to them in the guise of Hindu deities and demons, so keeping them from the true faith. Hinduism is, thus, a kind of 'devil worship' and the Hindu pantheon an array of malevolent spirits under the control of Satan. Such views are commonly propounded, but, for obvious reasons, seldom appear in fundamentalist literature, and when they do are left somewhat vague. For example, the leader of one large group based in Madras writes that 'the demons which we cast out . . . identify themselves as the deities which are much worshipped in neighbouring places' (Daniel 1980: xv). While I was in Madras during 1981–2, some violent incidents took place in a town about eighty miles away, following similar remarks made about Hinduism during a public meeting organized by a rapidly growing fundamentalist group.

As I have noted, the *pēy* are common to both Hindus and Christians. But the fundamentalists do not recognize the divisions within the divine hierarchy of Hinduism between the evil spirits and the various higher, more beneficent, and powerful deities who are enlisted to confront and neutralize, if not defeat the *pēy*. While in practice they appear never to name the highest embodied deities—Siva and Parvati—they make no distinctions among the lesser Hindu divinities and between them and the *pēy*. Murukan, Aiyanar, Ganesh, and the Goddess, in her various forms and especially as Kali, as well as all manner of demons, are said to possess people as evil spirits. Thus, while popular Hinduism in Madras involves the recognition of a hierarchical order of divinities with gradations of benign and malign powers, popular Christianity—as it finds expression in fundamentalism—in effect eliminates the hierarchy by regarding all non-human beings in the Hindu pantheon as undifferentiated. Like the early Christians who made demons of the gods of Greece and Rome (Russell 1977: 58), the fundamentalists absorb and relegate Hindu divinities in their own pantheon. The latter are all equal and unequivocally evil.

Just as they classify all Hindu divinities as maleficent spirits, so they dismiss Hindu exorcists—whose powers are frequently claimed to be derived from the Goddess—as tools of the devil. There are several different types of Hindu specialist using a variety of ritual techniques to deal with possessory *pēy*, one of the most common being the 'god-dancer' (*sāmiyaṭi*), a shaman-like figure who becomes a medium for the deity, and drives out the spirit either by appeasing it with a sacrifice, or threatening it with his/her superior power, or both (see Moffatt 1979: 241–2; Egnor 1977).

Since the power of the Hindu deities is regarded as satanic, the rituals these exorcists perform cannot, by definition, be protective or benign. A similar view is held in respect of the *mantiravāti*, the self-proclaimed guardians of the public against all manner of mystical attack. They are designated by fundamentalists as practitioners of harmful magic, and therefore to be counted among the legions of darkness. The ritual objects—coconuts, sacred ash, or talismans (*tāyattu*)—which these specialists give the victims of affliction to ward off further attack, say the fundamentalists, in fact contain evil spells and evil spirits—the very forces they are meant to guard against. 'The buggers', in the colourful English of one Christian charismatic 'are putting devils in the talisman itself'.

Until one accepts Jesus Christ as personal saviour, and is imbued with the Holy Spirit, it is argued, there is an 'empty space' which Satan can easily occupy. Thus, 'nominal' (*peyar*) Christians, no less than Hindus, are amenable to attack by satanic forces. The question which then arises, and it is frequently debated by fundamentalists, is whether 'true' (*ūṇmai*) Christians are also liable to mystical assault. One view is that with the Holy Spirit a person is invulnerable to the threat of such agents. But this leaves people who have apparently received the Holy Spirit, yet are ill or otherwise afflicted, open to self-doubt and to the suspicions of others that their Christian conviction is lacking in some degree. The conundrum is resolved by suggesting that someone can be tormented or troubled in some area of his/her life, yet 'still be a sincere believer' (Basham 1971: 61).

For these Christians, it is only the power of the Holy Spirit which can overcome the agents of affliction. The divine hierarchy of fundamentalism is, therefore, two-tiered. Below are the forces of Satan—which include not only ghosts but the demons and deities of, especially, popular Hinduism. Above stand the forces of good, the Holy Spirit and the Son of God. Unlike the liberal Christianity spread by the early twentieth-century missionaries of the principal denominations, and still found today within the leadership of the orthodox Protestant church and community, which denies the 'reality' of evil forces in the everyday lives of their votaries and potential converts, fundamentalism not only acknowledges their existence, but seeks continually to demonstrate the power of the Holy Spirit to vanquish them.

While all those who receive the Holy Spirit may also obtain one or more of its boons (*varam*), only those especially selected by God, it is believed, are granted all or most of its boons, and, most importantly, the gift of healing (*kuṇamākkum varam*). God's chosen few—the charismatic prophets[5]—therefore have a special role to play not only in disseminating the fundamentalist message through their preaching, but by attesting to and demonstrating how the power of the Holy Spirit confronts and overcomes the agents of human affliction.

CHARISMATIC PROPHETS

Weber applied the term 'charisma' to a quality in certain individuals who are believed to be 'endowed with supernatural, superhuman, or at least exceptional power ... regarded as of divine origin or as exemplary ...' (1964: 358–9). Today, in Madras, there are many Christians claiming and widely acknowledged to have this quality in consequence of being imbued with gifts of the Holy Spirit. The CSI-Western church is probably not untypical of orthodox congregations in lower class areas of the city in having at least a dozen members who are reputed to possess charismatic traits (though many more may claim to be filled with the Holy Spirit). The individuals themselves deny their own or other human agency in their selection.

It is God's will alone: the charismatic ministry cannot and should not be actively sought. Ideally, as Weber points out, it is conceived as a duty, which cannot be shirked but must be recognized and acted upon (ibid.: 359). Those so chosen often learn of their calling in dreams and visions. One man told me of his struggle to continue a teaching career in the face of divine insistence that he devote his life to doing 'God's work'. In the end he had to submit, resigned his job, and became a full-time evangelist.

Most such charismatic figures operate within a neighbourhood context, visiting homes and preaching to a range of independent congregations. Some, as I have intimated, establish and lead local prayer groups to which persons from different denominations and sects (or none, for they sometimes attract Hindus in the vicinity) affiliate on an informal basis. They invariably claim one or more gifts of the Holy Spirit, and almost certainly the gift of healing. This involves the ability to diagnose the causes of affliction—which can mean anything from infertility to cancer, from unemployment to examination failure—and to prescribe suitable remedies. These may include intensive fasting and prayer, the imbibing of substances (such as oil) blessed in the name of Jesus, the use of the Bible as a prophylactic talisman (kept by the bed or under the pillow), and the recitation of protective spells—the most common being 'blood of Jesus'.[6] They also deal with the effects wrought by a plethora of maleficent human and superhuman agents who are identified as the sources of misfortune.

I present below two examples of Christian healing through the power of the Holy Spirit. Both involve women from orthodox congregations (one of them the CSI-Western parish) seeking relief from distress outside the orthodox church. Each of these cases was represented to me as an encounter between a charismatic prophet and an evil spirit.

Case 1. A greedy sister causes an evil spirit to be sent

In this case the spirit was said to be under the control of a sorcerer (*sūṇiyakāraṇ*), employed by the victim's sister and the latter's husband. The couple desired to have the afflicted woman (Shanta) killed so that they could acquire her property. (The sisters were the only two children of their deceased parents.) These events were related by the prophet, Bro Jiva, who leads a small congregation in a poor and overcrowded slum in central Madras, although many of those who seek his aid, like this afflicted women, come from outside his core following and the locality.

BRO JIVA. Shanta came to me with a pain in her chest, and a lot of coughing, and asked me to pray for her. While the group was praying I walked around blessing everyone there, and as soon as I put my hand on her head she fell down. This is because for those who have an evil spirit the laying on of hands is like being beaten with a stick; this is how they feel the Holy Spirit. After prayers I told her to come again the next morning: she seemed better and went home. When she arrived the next day she was serious—wheezing and unable to breathe. Her people (husband and three children) thought it was asthma and wanted to take her to a hospital, but she had already seen a doctor, so someone said she should be brought here.

(Bro Jiva then turns on a tape recording he made of the session.)

BRO JIVA. [*Addressing the spirit possessing Shanta*]. Why have you come here? In the name of Jesus! Hallelujah! [*He speaks in tongues. There is no response. He repeats the question several times. Finally, the spirit responds*].
SPIRIT. Leave me alone. I have come to take this woman's life. I have been sent to take her head.
BRO JIVA. Who has sent you?
SPIRIT. Konar [*the name of the sorcerer*].
BRO JIVA. Who is responsible? [*i.e. who is paying the sorcerer*].
SPIRIT. Leela [*the possessed woman's sister*]. She wants her [*sister's*] property.
BRO JIVA. How long have you been inside this woman?
SPIRIT. Thirty days.
BRO JIVA. What diseases have you brought her?
SPIRIT. I climbed over her, sat on her chest and gave her TB, so that she would die of TB and no one would know it was sorcery [*sūniyam*].
BRO JIVA. She is a child of God [*i.e. a Christian*]. You cannot take her life! In the name of Jesus I bind you and send you below [*i.e. to the Abyss (pātāḷam)*]. Do you realize where you are? [*i.e. this is a house of God*].
SPIRIT. Konar [*the sorcerer*] has given me the blood of three cocks, eggs, and coconuts. I cannot leave her until I finish.
BRO JIVA. I am giving you the blood of Jesus. [*He gives the woman holy oil to drink and speaks in tongues*].
SPIRIT. It is not nice! Give me the blood of a cock and I'll go away.

BRO JIVA. I'll give you nothing. Here you get nothing! Only the blood of Jesus. [*He speaks in tongues and gives the woman more oil to drink*].
SPIRIT. [*Curses.*] The man [*Konar*] has sent me to do this, so I came. [*There are more curses but Bro Jiva has erased these from the tape*].

BRO JIVA. [*Switching off the tape*]. While we were recording this the tape suddenly stopped running. The spirit was doing this. It spoiled two cassettes. Then I repaired it, and told the spirit to stop in the name of Jesus. The rest of the tape was alright. [*He turns the recorder on again*].

BRO JIVA. You have to go, along with the TB. In the name of Jesus you are going. Tell me you are going.
SPIRIT. Please leave me alone. I'm going.
BRO JIVA. [*He speaks in tongues*]. Will you come again? [*He places a Bible on the woman's head*]. Promise not to come to her again. And take away the disease. Say the name of Jesus. You must not touch her again, nor anyone in her house. You must go down.
SPIRIT. I'll never come to her again. But if Konar sends me, then ...
BRO JIVA. Not even if he sends you. Kneel. Hallelujah! [*He speaks in tongues*].
SPIRIT. Let me alone. I'm suffocating. I've come here without knowing about you [*i.e. Bro Jiva*]. Take it [*the Bible*] off my head; it's a heavy stone. I've come to a place I should not have come. [*The congregation prays, many speak in tongues; the spirit moans*].
BRO JIVA. Go down. In the name of Jesus I'm burning you!
SPIRIT. Don't torture me. I'm going. They spent so much on me [*i.e. they gave the sorcerer a lot of money*]. They spent Rs 13,045. I'm going. Release me.

(The spirit apparently departs at this point and the woman regains her composure. Bro Jiva switches off the tape and continues the narrative.)

BRO JIVA. The magician sent another spirit—Katteri [see Chapter 7]—to Shanta. Every time I drove one out he sent another. He had arranged things so that the woman would have a spirit for forty days and then die. So I kept the woman and her family in my house, and for the whole period I took little food—water and limes mostly. The fortieth day is the most important; on that day the evil spirit is very dangerous. This was my last chance to drive it away. On that morning at 4:00 a.m. I awoke and could hear her struggling to breathe. I woke everyone in the house. We began to pray and went on a complete fast. Meanwhile the sorcerer was saying *mantra* in his own place. The woman was cold and her temperature was going down. I was frightened. If I failed to drive out the spirit, I would lose my name (*peyar*). People would think badly of me. So I prayed and wept and asked God to give me more power (*vallamai*). All of us laid hands on her, and we put Bibles on her body. The sorcerer's clients must have spent thousands on that day alone. Konar even had new clothes. I saw him in a vision. He sent a healthy new spirit, one that was not so worn down. We continued our fast and prayers. At five minutes to midnight the *eman* ['final spirit' which takes life] was in the room. We sprinkled holy water all around, and on the woman. Then I gave her a slap and said (to the spirit) 'in the name of Jesus I bind you'. It left her at exactly midnight. She came back to normal, and was completely relieved of all her chest troubles. The family gave her new clothes. She was happy. Both she and her husband decided to take water baptism, so they would get the Holy Spirit and be safe from this kind of attack in future. [*Laughing*] The sorcerer probably thought I was an ordinary *mantiravāti*. But in the end he must have realized I wasn't that but a true Christian. The power of Jesus is greater than the power of spirits.

Case 2. A jealous spirit attacks an innocent woman

This case involves Bro Prem who leads a Pentecostal congregation near Madras airport in the southwest of the city, and several members of the CSI-Western church consult him regularly when they have difficulties. One afternoon while I was interviewing him in his home (after having attended one of his prayer meetings the previous evening), a young couple arrived. The woman seemed somewhat distracted, and Bro Prem explained the circumstances of her case.

BRO PREM. This woman, Kumari, was entered by an evil spirit while she was returning home from the cinema with her husband a few months back. It was the spirit of a Muslim girl, named Sakarena, who had died by drowning herself because the man she had wanted to marry didn't want to marry her. And because Kumari loves her husband, the spirit was jealous. Her husband took her to someone—an Anglo-Indian—and for a whole month he and his group prayed for her, but could not get rid of the spirit. He was a false healer. And because of this delay an angel of light[7] came in to her and it has the power to keep the spirit inside her, so that it is difficult to cast out. The angel of light is a great deceiver. Sometimes Kumari speaks in tongues as if she is filled with the Holy Spirit, and reads the Bible. At such times you might think she is cured and has come to God. But that is the way with an angel of light. Only a Christian with the gift of discernment can tell if a person has been taken by an angel of light.

While Kumari remains silent in a corner of the room her husband sits beside Bro Prem. Realizing I have been asking about the case, he explains for my benefit:

HUSBAND. We took her to a doctor since she didn't get pregnant. But the doctor took some tests and told us we don't have any sterility problems. Only then the spirit confessed it had eaten two male children. Some days ago the spirit pretended to go away. But it is still there. When it is active my wife says she is Sakarena and wears her *sari* as if in *purdah*, just like a Muslim.

Kumari has in the meanwhile moved to the centre of the room and sat down on the floor. She moans sporadically. Bro Prem moves over to stand in front of her, and addresses the spirit inside her.

BRO PREM. How did you come into her?
SPIRIT. By the wind. I am standing on her. I am in her tongue.
BRO PREM. How many are you there?
SPIRIT. I am alone. Only me, Sakarena.
BRO PREM. You are lying. Who is that praying next to you?
SPIRIT. Someone is with me. I don't know. I am happy here.
BRO PREM. You cheating spirit! Go, in the name of Jesus. [*The woman looks at him for the first time.*] You are the only spirit which is bold enough to look at me directly. You are the angel of light, not Sakarena.
SPIRIT. [*Her voice, normally soft, becomes gruff and louder. She speaks in high Tamil*]. You know who I am. Do you know my power (*sakti*)?
BRO PREM. [*Also changing to high Tamil*]. I know your power. But with the help of Jesus I am going to fight you until you leave this woman.
SPIRIT. [*The woman resumes her soft voice again*]. If I dwell in here she will prosper and be happy. [*Laughs*] Where can I go? She has a weak mind (*manam*). That is why I have come into her.
BRO PREM. [*To me*]. The evil spirit alone would be easy to cast out. But the angel of light has a little power against us. We can still drive it out with the power of Jesus, but it takes some time.

There is a further brief exchange like the previous one. After a few minutes the woman sits up and regains her composure. She and her husband arrange to see Bro Prem again in a few days, during one of his weekly prayer and healing meetings.

These cases point to several procedures surrounding fundamentalist curing in Madras. For one thing, fasting and praying are central elements in ritual, enhancing and concentrating the prophet's divine powers. The significance of 'forty days' in Case 1, which recurs again and again in the discourse of healing is usually referred to the period spent in the wilderness by Jesus, during which time 'he did nothing eat' (Luke 4: 2).

Secondly, charismatic figures have a crucial diagnostic role, which (though it need not) ignores and overrides the self-assessments of the victims or their families, and even encourages symptoms in the patient to accord with the healer's interpretation. In Case 2 the change in Kumari's behaviour followed the discovery by Bro Prem of her possession by an 'angel of light'. This case also underlines how afflictions may be redefined during the treatment process to allow for and accord with the patient's changing condition. The fundamentalist healer, as we have seen, has a determining say in whether a spirit is acting capriciously or is under the control of a sorcerer, and is, therefore, responsible for commenting on and influencing the quality of human relationships within the community. As occurred in Case 1 the involvement of a sorcerer usually becomes the occasion for what was portrayed as a dramatic confrontation between the forces of good and evil.

Thirdly, the procedures of Christian exorcism involve casting out by the power of the Holy Spirit. There is no question of appeasement, as Bro Jiva was quick to point out when the spirit suggested a small blood sacrifice similar to that which the *sūn-iyakaran* had provided. Such an offering, which is not uncommon in popular Hindu curing rites would, in the fundamentalist view, be tantamount to treating with the devil. Instead, the spirit must be abused and confronted with the power of Jesus, which is manifest in the very name of Christ or in his word as contained in the Bible; both name and word are said to be feared by satanic agents. Sacred oil, blessed by the prophet in the name of Jesus, is given to the victim; hands of true believers and/or the Bible are placed on the latter's body; and commands to leave the victim issued in the Lord's name. All these are said to frighten the *pēy* and ultimately drive them out. The charismatic healer and congregation occasionally speak in tongues, giving evidence of the presence of the Holy Spirit.

There are no further rites to cast out the spirit, or accompany it to its place of origin, as practised by Hindu exorcists, and fundamentalists generally point out that while the *pēy* driven out by non-Christians are free to attack again, possibly even the same victim, the spirits exorcized by Christian prophets are driven 'below'—into the Abyss (*patālām*). The reference is to Revelations (20: 3) where the vision of the Last Days has Satan chained up for a thousand years, and driven into the Abyss, where he can no longer seduce the nations. Even then, however, the victim may be attacked by other maleficent forces unless baptism in the Holy Spirit takes place to effect at least partial immunity.

Finally, charismatic prophets have a range of explanatory devices and elaborations to deal with recalcitrant symptoms or apparent failures. The gift of discerning deceptive spirits is claimed by many specialists who are, like Bro Prem, thereby enabled to identify angels of light, which seek to confuse and trick the healer and victim alike. Parenthetically, as Wilson remarks, the gift of discernment is ideally monopolized by sectarian leaders, since 'no one is more dangerous to the group than the lay person who claims divine power to evaluate the charismatic utterances of his fellows' (1967: 146). Another gift, the interpretation of tongues, also assists prophets to distinguish those who are truly filled with the Holy Spirit from others who would mislead the faithful. They can also attribute stubborn conditions to the incompetence of specialists who treated the victims before them, and again, like Bro Prem, underline the near fatal consequences of putting oneself in the hands of a 'false healer'. This is an accusation which can, of course, be thrown at virtually anyone claiming to do God's work. Overall, then, like Zande witch beliefs, there is here a self-enclosing system which is not falsifiable.

Charismatics are intensely competitive, as I have already noted, and their evaluations of one another are rarely generous. The bitterest remarks I ever heard about prophets were made by other prophets, and their sharpest criticisms were reserved for the most prominent figures. They are especially caustic about those known to have health problems, for this is clear evidence, they suggest, that they are unable to heal themselves, let alone others.

Bro Jiva's comment about fearing not only for his patient but his own 'name' expresses the concern of these evangelists for their reputation. A few charismatic figures gain prominence beyond their own congregations, and attract followings from outside their immediate neighbourhoods. The more miraculous their achievements, the wider their notoriety. Some develop 'specializations', i.e. they become known for dealing effectively with particular kinds of problem: certain prophets in Madras are thought to have a special gift for finding lost property, others for identifying thieves, exorcizing spirits, or predicting the outcome of a marriage proposal. One charismatic leader, whose songs are much admired and sung in south India, attributes her compositions to the heavenly choirs of angels she hears in her dreams. Another reveals at public gatherings the names of afflicted persons and announces their imminent cure. He explains his gift as follows:

As I complete my message and enter the time of intercession, my heart is filled with compassion. I feel that the sorrows and illnesses of all those listening to me are my own. When, therefore, I close my eyes and pray with great groanings and tears, without being conscious of so doing. I see at times before my mind's eye, through the power of God, the names of certain persons revealed to me by God. I am able to visualize the places where they are located. I see their needs. I repeat them as I see them. Since, at such times, I am completely engulfed by the presence of the Lord Jesus Christ, I am completely governed and dominated by Him. I do not think that there is anything surprising in that the Lord God, who called by name Zaccheus whom He never knew before, should call people by name even today, through the medium of a man.

Those who achieve supra-local fame do so because they are seen to stand above the innumerable local healers in terms of their charismatic powers. They are also usually acknowledged to be strong orators, able to hold an audience for (sometimes) hours at a time, to present the 'word of God' in a compelling and convincing way. There are a handful of prophets whose reputations extend throughout the city and even beyond, in certain cases to other parts of the world (e.g. South East Asia, Sri Lanka) where there are large numbers of Tamil-speakers. Though the core of their adherents may be found in a particular congregation, their popularity ensures a much more widely based support. Some, in fact, do not have an established congregation at all, and are, therefore, not closely associated with any particular sectarian organization, though the ideology they foster is no less fundamentalist.

The attainment of this level of recognition requires a strong public persona, one which is not simply established in the context of regular interaction with, and validated in terms of experiences within a small group of followers. The achievement of such a status seems to require evidence of a special and ongoing relationship with the divine. Because such prophets are removed to a very great extent from those who seek their assistance, their links with the supernatural must be reiterated continually. The biographies of these prophets, which become public knowledge through print as well as by word of mouth, emphasize not only the acquisition of charismata, but the dramatic circumstances in which these are obtained. The literature they issue recounts their life histories, with special emphasis on miraculous events. What is also stressed is the contrast between their lives before and after receiving the Holy Spirit. In the period immediately prior to this experience these prophets portray themselves as being at the brink of spiritual if not physical death. In the case of one prophet, the official biography has her actually summoned back from the dead. The relevant portion reads as follows:

After my marriage and the birth of my two sons bad things stormed into my life. My husband and his sister wanted to kill me so that he could marry her daughter. They paid a sorcerer and he sent *sūniyam*, so I was unable to move my limbs or speak. I was in bed for six months. With the help of some Christian friends who prayed for me I regained the use of my hands and my speech. Still, I was not happy. I wanted to die and I bought some poisonous fruits. I thought my husband would try to prevent me from taking them, but instead he encouraged me. So I ate them, and became unconscious. My friends rushed me to the Government Hospital. After a few hours the doctors said I was dead. They covered me with a white cloth. My friends prayed at my side all night, and the next morning when the staff came to take me to a post-mortem my limbs began to move and they rushed to call the doctors. I realized then that God did not want me to die.[8]

(Later she tries suicide again, but this time Jesus personally intervenes to save her; she is 'converted' and receives the Holy Spirit.)

Other prophets similarly write and speak of being plagued

by incurable illness, long and hopeless unemployment, in a state of total despair and near suicide, and frequently engaged in a life full of 'sin' (drinking, smoking, cinema-going, and political activity). Conversion changes their lives totally and brings them into regular contact with Jesus, who thereafter guides them in all their undertakings, and channels his power through them. They portray the malignant activities of the devil in the starkest, most dramatic terms, and in consequence their struggles with satanic forces are hair-raising in the extreme, taking on mythic dimensions. Their victories, and so their power, seem all the more amazing for it.

Prophets also seek to reinforce conviction among the public of their selection by illustrating the dire consequences for those who cast doubt on the authenticity of their charismatic gifts. Their literature and, occasionally, their sermons refer to how sceptics are struck down, not by the prophet, but by an angry God. Thus, Daniel reports how when someone in an orthodox congregation he was addressing protested at his being given the pulpit, the man was soon paralysed and bedridden and never recovered: 'His death became a warning to the ungodly, not to play around where God is at work' (1980: 167).

The main contexts within which the public encounters these popular prophets are 'crusades' or 'conventions'. These take the form of open meetings (*kūṭṭam*) which may extend over a period of several evenings, and which can attract thousands. The ubiquitous wall posters around Madras announcing the five-day crusade of a popular female prophet, in February 1982, advertised her 'visions of God' (*tēvatarisaṇam*), and invited members of the public to bring along those who are 'possessed by evil spirits', or 'in the grip of sorcery', since Jesus heals them 'irrespective of caste (*jati*) or religion (*matam*) '.

The first part of each evening's programme included entertainment by a group of well-known gospel singers, interspersed with prayers and brief sermons by lesser personalities. When the meeting ground was full to capacity (it holds 3–4,000 people) and the last light had faded, the prophet appeared under a single spotlight, alone in a white *sari*, all of which gave a striking effect. She demanded that the evil spirits in the audience identify themselves and come forward (some twenty persons moved to the stage); she announced that two magicians had come to witness her healing; that nine members of the audience had cancer and that two were being healed at that moment; that twelve others were under the influence of sorcery (people stood); that ninety-three young men were unemployed (many men—women are never said to be unemployed—stood up); and so on. After inviting all those who acknowledged their misfortune to stay on for the healing session at the end of the evening, the prophet spoke for ninety minutes, with short breaks for a few songs and Bible readings. The healing ritual consisted mainly of collective prayer, the laying on of hands and Bibles, and the abuse of malignant forces. The drama of the occasion produced a few cures and conversions, demonstrating yet again the power of the Holy Spirit (and, of course, the prophet). There was, as is usually the case, a hierarchy of officials on hand, trained by the prophet, to deal with those individuals who underwent such an experience.

The evangelical potential of this demonstration is overtly acknowledged in fundamentalist writings and statements. Divine healing campaigns, writes George, 'will attract many people ... [and] when people get healing ... some of them accept Christ as their personal saviour. The divine healing ministry has helped the growth of the Pentecostal churches all over the world' (1975: 51; see also Harper 1965: 109).

The most successful prophets travel throughout the south, and, increasingly, to other parts of Asia, where the local Tamil communities organize crusades. The best-known prophet in south India has established an organization employing some twenty-five people to handle his many activities. It deals with upwards of five hundred letters daily (usually asking for help and advice), produces a monthly magazine, and runs a twenty-four hour telephone service which, in reply to the supplicant's stated problem, plays an appropriate recording of the prophet's voice. It also produces and distributes his sermons and songs on records and tapes. People report that if hands are placed on the radio set during the prophet's broadcasts, his curative powers reach the afflicted.

THE CHALLENGE OF CHARISMA

Charisma, as Weber (1964) pointed out, challenges orthodoxy and the traditional socio-religious order. It threatens to undermine ecclesiastical structures, such as that of the CSI, based on an authoritative, episcopally ordained ministry. In the Madras Protestant context the charismatic prophet very clearly emerges as the opponent of hierocratic institutions. The majority of ordinary members of the church readily compare their priests—'the bishop's employees', as I have often heard them called—with the prophets chosen by God to do his work. An explicit contrast is drawn between the kinds of knowledge invested in these two figures. Protestants from the orthodox churches, who flock in their hundreds and thousands to hear the word of God from the prophets, frequently stress how awesome are the insights conferred by the Holy Spirit as against the insignificance of the formal theological training undergone by their own priesthood.[9] Referring to a quite different ethnographic context (Tanna in Melanesia), Lindstrom makes the point that no amount of priestly knowledge can equal the knowledge of healing power monopolized by charismatics (1984: 300).

In Madras, people are aware that no educational, birth (caste), or gender qualifications are necessary for divine selection, not even a Christian commitment. Indeed, if any particular set of qualities appears to count more than anything else, it is—as the public biographies of the prophets suggest—poverty, unhappiness, despair, even a life of sin and godlessness. The association of prophecy with the dispriviledged and the dominated within the Protestant community is evident. The strong representation of women among the category of charismatics also illustrates the careful separation made between these two forms of knowledge.[10] The insistence on a male monopoly within the orthodox clergy contrasts sharply with the gender blindness exhibited by those who seek prophetic inspiration or assistance. The very people who oppose the ordination of women in the orthodox church might with equal ardour submit themselves to and sing the praises of a female charismatic.

So, while these prophets are perceived, in one sense, as extraordinary figures, since they are divinely chosen, in another sense they are quintessentially ordinary individuals, who simply love and serve God as best they can—in the way that all true Christians should do. The Holy Spirit and the charismatic gifts are, therefore, within the grasp of everyone, and the prophets are a constant reminder of this possibility. Furthermore, in as much as the doctrines and practices it professes are wholly in accord with widely held theodicies, fundamentalism has become the favoured religious discourse of the Protestant masses in Madras. While encouraging the common piety of the majority, it also encompasses and authenticates traditional ideas about misfortune. From several perspectives, then, fundamentalism may be seen as a form of popular protest against the religious preferences of the dominant segment within the church and community.

In so far as the gifts of the Holy Spirit—especially those which bestow miraculous competences—remain outside the control of the institutional churches, they constitute an insidious and pervasive threat to existing authority. The miracle is, after all, a manifestation of power on the part of individuals who are not fitted by their place in the social order, nor designated by human authority, to hold and exercise it. As Gilsenan observes, the miracle is a 'weapon or refuge of the dominated, an essential part of the discourse, hopes, expectancies and creations of the poor' (1982: 77). It is no surprise, therefore, that miracles have, for long, been suspect and downgraded within the missionary fold and ecclesiastical structures, for they suggest the possibility that God may be revealing himself through alternative agencies. There are signs, however, that the church hierarchy now seeks to assimilate such powers and bring them within its purview. I conclude this chapter with a brief account of 'charismatic renewal' within the CSI.

THE APPROPRIATION OF CHARISMA

This development became evident to me on my return to Madras in 1981 after an absence of six years. When I was first in the city it was still very much the practice of the mainline churches to refuse their pulpits and premises to fundamentalist preachers of whom they were generally contemptuous.[11] Prophets were frequently ridiculed—'Johnies jumping for Jesus' is one epithet I heard—stigmatized, and denied any official hearing in CSI parishes.

By 1981, there was evidence of a growing tolerance of, even interest in, fundamentalist discourse within the hierocracy of the orthodox church. A CSI clergyman who had been in Europe during much of the same period, and returned to Madras shortly before I did, commented that he had found a growing move towards 'emotionalism' and 'spirituality' in the upper echelons of the diocese. The bishop in Madras during this period had declared himself in favour of the charismatic movement, a somewhat more respectable and accommodative, less enthusiastic and divisive form of Pentecostalism. It does not emphasize second baptism, nor regard speaking in tongues as a necessary proof of being filled with the Holy Spirit. It is a world-wide movement which has spread from the USA,[12] and reached south India—including the Catholic church there (see Thamburaj 1982)—only in the last few years. The CSI bishop in Madras nowadays preaches and lectures on the Holy Spirit, and invites church members to let the Spirit enter them as it has entered him.[13] A special department of 'spiritual renewal among the laity' has been established within the diocese, and its declared aim is that every member should be a genuinely converted, 'born again' Christian. The hope is also expressed that charismatic gifts will be employed in the rituals of the orthodox church; and there is increasing use of healing services in CSI congregations. One church historian with fundamentalist leanings remarks with evident surprise and delight that 'today the anointing and gifts of the Holy Spirit, once despised and rejected by the larger churches in south India, are more and more respected . . .' (George 1975: 1).

Gone are the offensive references to those within the CSI who associate with sectarian groups. Charismatic prophets who were once banned from church premises are now welcomed to its pulpits and CSI clergy are to be found among the sponsors and organizers of healing crusades featuring these prophets. The most important of them now appear alongside bishops and preachers from the mainline churches on a variety of platforms, including the popular Festival of Joy, as I noted above.

In conversations with diocesan officials and clergymen who are instrumental in encouraging these developments, two main themes seem to recur. The first indicates a pragmatic concern about the need to revitalize the commitment of CSI members

to their 'traditional' congregations. The feeling is widespread that most people only remain anchored in their orthodox par-
·ishes in order to be married in a 'proper' church, and buried in a decent cemetery, or for some other, not entirely appropriate, reason. But for their 'spiritual needs', and especially for 'help in their suffering and illness', to quote one minister, 'they run elsewhere. So we must bring the charismata into our own church, or we will lose all our members sooner or later.'

The second touches on the tendency to centre Christianity once again in the conflict between good and evil, to see Christ as the one who saves devotees from the power of the devil, objectified in the malevolent forces which inhabit the everyday world. One of those involved in organizing and promoting the diocesan 'renewal' programme expressed it in this way:

A Hindu friend once complained to me that the trouble with Christianity is that it is all about forgiveness and love. 'The Christian God', he said, 'has no power (*sakti*)'. So Christians must exalt their God, and show everyone that he is a living saviour, who can help them, now, to solve their problems. He can heal them, and relieve their suffering. The proof of his divinity is in the gifts of the Holy Spirit. The charismatic movement is all about power.[14]

In brief, then, some leading ecclesiastics within the CSI have reacted to the challenge of charisma, which they see as threatening not only their authority, but the very integrity of their constituency. Their response to the religious predilections of ordinary Protestants is not, however, as in the past, to interdict and excommunicate, demote or ridicule, but to appropriate—in a suitably modified form—the very ingredients of this popular culture.

This recent trend is by no means unopposed within the CSI hierarchy and ministerial ranks, nor does it appear to find much favour among Protestant intellectuals in the city. The latter draw attention to the foreign organizations (again, mainly from the USA) which provide encouragement for charismatic renewal in the form of funds, literature, and even personnel training. Some of these organizations finance trips overseas for CSI ministers to enable them to take special courses at institutes providing a strong fundamentalist version of Christianity. Nor does the conservative political stance of most 'charismatic' theologians from the West escape their attention.

I quote a few extracts from one article reprinted in the monthly
News and Notes of the Madras diocese:

It would seem that the theology which finds expression in the World
Council of Churches and in much radical theology is based on a false
view of the kingdom, identifying it far too simplistically with the here
and now [and] not profoundly enough with either the future or with
the present reality of the church ... In many parts of the church there
is a retreat from spirituality, the vacuum being filled with work or
social and political action ... The fact remains that the growing [i.e.
fundamentalist] churches of the world have not imbibed the spirit of
humanism but stand firmly on the basics of the faith ... Nor have
they time to indulge in much sociopolitical activity (Harper 1981).

Voices within the clergy note, in addition, that serious and
complex theological issues are being trivialized by supporters
of the charismatic movement and made to appear overly
simple. This is in part due, they complain, to the fact that,
nowadays, CSI pulpits are being made available to 'anyone
who preaches anything'. There is also a feeling that in looking
increasingly to healing as a way of keeping congregations loyal,
the CSI is 'promising too much'.

Finally, although there is a growing interest in the charismatic movement within some segments of the middle class,
most are disdainful of what is regarded as the excessive emotionalism of charismatic rites. They see this movement as only
a slightly laundered version of Pentecostalism, which is as much
despised for its association with the lower class as for its beliefs
and practices. And, like many senior clergy, they still remain
committed to liberal theology and its active expression in the
social gospel.

CONCLUSION

In this and the previous chapter I have attempted to outline
the nature of changing religious trends within the Protestant
fold in Madras. In Chapter 7 I showed how, until around the
turn of the present century, under the influence of European
missionaries and notwithstanding differences of doctrinal emphasis among denominations, the overall character of Protestantism was conservative evangelical. This was portrayed as

centred in the belief in scriptural inerrancy and in individual salvation through appropriate spiritual exercises.

In this culture of piety, Hinduism was regarded as idolatry, to be confronted by persistent if not aggressive evangelism. The spread of liberalism in the early part of the twentieth century introduced new cultural possibilities, and threatened the existing religious consensus. Its more accommodative attitudes to at least certain aspects of non-Christian faiths, coupled with the appearance of the social gospel, which blurred the careful distinctions between the 'world' and the realm of the 'spirit', found support first among intellectuals in the theological institutes and mission colleges of south India, and, in time, the emerging indigenous middle class and church leadership.

Thus, the conservative evangelicalism of the early missionaries, which had become the favoured discourse of the Protestant majority, was gradually superseded by the 'modernist' tendency within the dominant sector of the church and community. The beliefs and usages of ordinary people were, in effect, downgraded and overtaken by a confident, socially conscious and development-oriented gospel-in-action. Views on the aetiology of affliction, widely shared by Hindus and Christians within the lower class, constituted another aspect of popular Protestantism. Based as they are on a conception of the universe as rife with hostile occult forces, these notions have, for the most part, been disdained, though for somewhat different reasons, by mission, church, and middle class alike. This aspect of popular culture, perhaps even more than that focused on piety, was consistently ridiculed and, to all intents and purposes, became what Foucault calls a 'subjugated knowledge' (1980: 81). It was seen, on the one hand, as having affinity to an extremely outmoded version of Christianity, and as being much influenced, moreover, by degraded forms of Hinduism. On the other hand, it was regarded as an inferior and not quite rational mode of thought. From the perspective of the dominant element within the Protestant fold, adherence to such beliefs, as to pietistic doctrines, provided sufficient evidence of social and cultural inferiority.

The recent arrival of fundamentalist Protestantism in south India has threatened the established religio-cultural hierarchy. In this chapter I have traced the expanding influence of fundamentalism and examined the circumstances which are thought by both its supporters and detractors to have encouraged this growth. Whatever importance it may have as a contributory factor to this efflorescence, what is clear is that fundamentalist knowledge accords with and in an important sense authenticates popular theodicies. This has been noted in a number of Third World contexts. Ackerman, for example, observes that among Catholics in Malaysia there is a close 'affinity' between newly introduced fundamentalist and traditional folk beliefs (1981: 92–4). Among the Tannese in Melanesia the loss of confidence in orthodox missionary knowledge came relatively early in this century. Lindstrom attributes the loss of 'interpretive control' by the Presbyterians to the 'emergence of alternative and competing systems of interpretation by John Frum movement cognoscenti' (1984: 300).

Fundamentalism can, thus, be seen as a system of knowledge which incorporates indigenous interpretive understanding; which provides everyday knowledge with an authoritative status, both in intellectual terms (as a theology) as well as through being associated with a global, expanding, and powerful religious movement. Furthermore, ordinary individuals whose participation in discourse is limited and constrained by the formalization of orthodox rites—the victims, if you will, of 'restrictive ideological practices' (Turton 1984: 46)—find themselves enfranchized within a fundamentalist setting. They are engaged, heard, listened to, and given support, in many instances rediscovering a new sense of 'self'.

This is not to deny the significance of the considerable financial and ideological resources exported to south India from abroad. But, whatever the international interests and aims of fundamentalist organizations in the West, their impact can ultimately only be fully understood and assessed in the complex histories of particular cultural contexts.

9

CONCLUSIONS

IN this book I have examined certain religious changes within
the Protestant community of south India, especially that part
resident in Madras city. Other observers would, no doubt, have
described and understood these events in quite different ways.
Some would probably have concerned themselves with problems of meaning: with the rituals and beliefs as symbolic complexes, perhaps, or as intellectual systems. The approach
adopted here has situated religious views and practices in the
everyday contexts of social life, and represented them as part
of a wider dynamic in which dominance and resistance to
dominance are as much a cultural as a material process.

Such a dialectic characterized the relationship between missionaries and their 'target' populations almost from the moment
of the formers' arrival in south India. Beidelman suggests that
the mission was a 'quintessential colonial organization', in as
much as it aimed 'at the most far-reaching domination, attacking the most deeply-held traditional beliefs and values'
(1982: 29). Comaroff and Comaroff similarly see the missionaries as implicated in the subjugation of indigenous populations through the 'subtle colonization ... of indigenous
modes of perception and practice' (1986: 2). The objects of
missionary evangelism in south India, however, were seldom
wholly passive or subjected. The vast majority, as we saw,
simply rebuffed all efforts to convert them. Those who did
accept the proffered faith did so selectively, one might almost
say, creatively. Certain elements were accommodated, but by
no means all; some indigenous notions were superseded, others
were zealously guarded in the face of threat and ridicule. People
occasionally rejected one mission suitor, but allowed themselves
to be persuaded by a second, even relinquished an existing
affiliation to seek out another, and, in time, moderated if they
did not altogether abandon their commitment to the denominational structures introduced by their European
benefactors.

This latter development was itself partly a consequence of the mission impact on the lives of their adherents. The provision of education, employment, and assistance of various kinds enabled a small proportion of converts to take advantage of growing economic opportunities in south India during the latter part of the nineteenth century. This led to the emergence of differentiation within what had previously been a near-uniformly indigent body of converts. Industrialization, infrastructural growth, the advent of independence, the exit of European élites, and the increasing success of the anti-Brahmin movement in Tamilnadu encouraged migration to urban centres, deepening the nascent distinctions within the community. By the time of my field-work in Madras, stark inequalities were evident in terms of housing, education, occupation, income, and property ownership.

Such differentiation has encouraged and, in turn, been encouraged by cultural disparities. Distinctive modes of consumption now exist within the Protestant community. One, associated with the majority belonging to the lower class, concentrates expenditure on subsistence goods and on the intensification of existing relationships among kin and neighbours. Middle-class householders, by contrast, direct resources to the purchase of luxury goods which not only lighten the burdens and enhance the comforts of everyday living, but make visible statements about their pre-eminent place in the social order. Less apparent, though perhaps more significant, are the implications of investment in 'information goods' (Douglas and Isherwood 1978). Through English education in select private institutions, 'social work' in diocesan and other organizations, affiliation to élite congregations, and the pursuit of 'clubbism', wide-ranging links are established throughout the extent of the dominant class, transcending barriers of caste, region, language, and even religion.

The cultural divide also reveals itself in the practices and ideas surrounding Protestant marriage. The emphasis on intensification of bonds among ordinary householders, and on the elaboration of links among élites in the consumption sphere is replicated and reinforced in the matrimonial domain. There are other distinctions as well: in marriage arrangements, the siting of rituals, the flavour of festivities, the dimension, direction, and sources of marriage prestations—all of which point to distinctive matrimonial sub-cultures. Even where there are common institutions and terminology, there are significant contrasts of organization and perception. These should not be seen simply as symbols of class difference, but as serving to constitute persons as occupants of separate levels within the urban hierarchy. While marriage strategies blur distinctions between the various 'fractions' or status circles within each class, they are part of a process whereby the dominant group conserves its privileges and its pre-eminent place in the community by refusing affinity with those whom it designates as inferior.

The process of winning and maintaining hegemony involves more than the tactics of closure and the securing of boundaries. As Lukes puts it, 'the supreme and most insidious exercise of power' consists in 'shaping ... perceptions, cognitions and preferences in such a way that [people] accept their role in the existing order of things ...' (1974: 24). This includes rendering vital forms of knowledge inaccessible to the dominated. Take again the question of consumption. Unlike the luxury products which are a visible reminder of inequality, the knowledges controlled by members of the dominant class through their virtual monopoly of 'information goods' are largely invisible to the majority of their co-religionists. These remain outside their awareness, and inevitably must constrain their appreciation of the extent and quality of their disprivilege, as well as their ability to act upon it.

The consciousness of human subjects is also moulded and transformed through continuous exposure to innumerable discourses, official and unofficial, operating as ideologies (Therborn 1980). Consciousness of class must struggle to emerge against a range of other subjectivities. While caste is far from being an integrated or consistent discourse, it can, in appropriate circumstances, drown out other voices which urge a more heightened class awareness.

There are other ways in which consciousness of their situation among ordinary people is deflected and muted by the dominant segments within the community and church, though this is not to imply intentionality or conspiracy on their part. By constantly drawing attention to its national 'responsibilities', the middle class not only maintains pressure on the State for a greater share of national resources, and fosters its own unity and common cause, but diverts attention away from attempts by those beneath them to speak about their own disadvantages. The ecclesiastical leadership, perhaps unwittingly, further restrains the development of such a consciousness in two main ways: first, by hinting at the divine endorsement of inequality, and second, by representing any divisions within the community as those of caste.

The class divide has not been excluded from the religious domain. The existence of diverse religious tendencies within a social group or formation is, of course, unexceptional. Anthropologists of south Asia, like most European scholars and missionaries who sought to understand the religions of the subcontinent, were for years fascinated, one might almost say obsessed, with locating dichotomous 'levels' within Hinduism, as within (though perhaps to a lesser extent) Buddhism and Islam. All-India and Local, Sanskritic and non-Sanskritic, Transcendental and Pragmatic, Orthodox and Heterodox, Great and Little traditions were some of the dualisms identified. These 'fragmentary' approaches, as they were to be labelled by Sharma (1970), pointed not only to differences but to continual interchanges between the levels. In Marriott's familiar terminology, features of the Great Tradition were 'parochialized', while those of the Little Tradition were 'universalized' (1955).

This approach has been criticized on a number of grounds, and raises several issues which are relevant to the present discussion. The first concerns the widespread association of the higher level with a literate tradition and its opposition to a lower, pre-literate or non-literate tradition. Tambiah, in my view rightly, points out that in a complex society 'various kinds of written sacred literature have a referential basis for the whole society, even for the unlettered masses' (1970: 373). Certainly, in a comparatively well-educated community like the Protestants of Madras, the notion of popular religion cannot and does not imply an absence of literacy or literary sources. Quite the contrary, it connotes familiarity with and ability to explicate sacred texts.

A second issue relates to the query raised initially by Harper (1964) and reiterated by Sharma (1970). It is whether the apparent diversity of the different levels is in fact integrated by an underlying purpose or rationale. Sharma's reply is that this rationale may be found 'in the constant application of the rules of purity and pollution to the relationship between man and the forces which he reveres as divine'. The purity/pollution principle 'is applied in the conduct of religious rituals of all types in exactly the same manner' (ibid.: 17, 21). Another argument put forward for dissolving the distinctions is that from the point of view of the villager 'there are not two traditions but simply one ...' (Tambiah 1970: 369). Thus, the early dualistic models have been replaced by monistic ones. So, what may have been wholly appropriate objections to a widespread predilection for finding substantive religious divergence where there is structural consistency has led to an opposite predisposition for seeing unity where there may in fact be important distinctions. Within south Indian Protestantism there is an integrated set of doctrines and rites based on a core of fundamental principles and a common inspirational text to which all believers subscribe. Yet we are able to identify significant differences of theology and practice within the church and community.

To appreciate the nature of this division we have to refer to yet a third difficulty with some of the earlier anthropological formulations. It is that the criteria on which the distinctions were based were 'culturological', as Sharma observes (1970: 2). The processes considered, therefore, involved the conceptualization and comparison of 'disembodied elements of religion' (Tambiah 1970: 368). One alternative to this form of analysis would be a sharper focus on religious divergences in terms of distinctive social categories. Some Indianists have attempted to understand the divine hierarchy in terms of the caste system, seeing the one mirrored in the other. Few students of religion in south Asia, or elsewhere for that matter, would be content nowadays to represent the latter as simply a reflection of the former.

However, it is one thing to exaggerate the social determinations of religious views and practices, it is quite another to ignore the social dimension altogether. This tension has for some time plagued anthropological attempts to interpret certain kinds of popular religiosity. The ecstatic, millenarian, cargo, or other cults found in many parts of the world have frequently been labelled 'religions of the oppressed', and their emergence attributed to a variety of factors in the surrounding environment. Colonialism, anomie, insecurity, deprivation, stress, or intolerable material circumstances are a few of the rationales which have been offered for the proliferation of these cultic activities. There is little point in joining the chorus of criticism which has found such exegeses wanting on the grounds that they seek their understandings of ritual phenomena primarily in the inadequacy of social conditions.

A more recent attempt to understand the proliferation of independent—mainly charismatic—churches in (especially) southern Africa has viewed these groups as positive responses to the urban environment in which most of them have arisen. They are seen, moreover, as offering 'solutions' to 'urban problems' (see Kiernan 1981: 142). Certainly, the religious proclivities of ordinary Protestants in Madras cannot be divorced from their material and social circumstances, and I have described these in some detail. However, religious beliefs and observances cannot be adequately comprehended by setting them apart and examining them in isolation: they become more fully intelligible when seen in relation to the views and practices of Protestant élites. Hence, religious distinctions within the community may be regarded as different cultures or part-cultures, related to (though not necessarily determined by) quite separate experiences of the world. More importantly, these cultures are not merely dissimilar, but are unequal, for one is part of the 'authoritative' discourse of the dominant class, the other an 'alternative' discourse of the popular class (see Asad 1979: 621). Neither is autonomous of nor explicable without reference to the other. They articulate, engage, and negotiate with one another in what, borrowing a phrase from Stuart Hall (1981a: 233), can be called a 'cultural struggle'.

This conception allows for the recognition that religious movements 'can be as much challenges to the existing order as escapes from it' (Firth 1981: 593). Thus, Sufi activities in Turkey may be seen, according to Gilsenan, as 'a kind of populist opposition to the ruling "them" ...' (1982: 261). In south India, the Tamil *bhakti* or 'devotional' tradition in Hinduism is characterized by Egnor as 'populist anti-authoritarian', which claims 'the moral superiority and greater religious fitness of those who suffer' (1980: 21). Similarly, Protestant fundamentalism in Madras, with its stress on piety, the Holy Spirit, and the doctrine of miracles, validates previously disqualified popular knowledges—'le savoir des gens', as Foucault (1980: 82) phrases it—and constitutes a challenge to the dominant liberalism of the middle class and ecclesiastical hierarchy.

Thus, religion cannot but be implicated in the processes of winning (and resisting) hegemony. For it is within the religious arena that certain crucial discourses are entitled and others disallowed, definitions sanctioned or denied, truths contested, and so forth. It seems appropriate to ask, with Asad (1983: 252), how power creates religion.

While fundamentalism, in the particular conditions we have been considering, appears as an appropriate class culture, which appeals to and strikes a responsive chord in the Protestant 'masses', we cannot thereby conclude that fundamentalism *per se* can be deemed an authentic folk or popular mode of religiosity. In other contexts, it may be identified with—constitute an apposite body of cultural knowledge for—a different segment of the populace. In Haiti, for example, where Catholicism and voodoo retain a grip on those situated at opposite poles of the class order, the 'rising middle class' is reported to be mainly Protestant Evangelical and Pentecostal (see Gerlach 1974). Nor is there a need to rehearse the close links between fundamentalist churches and the particular middle-class constituency of the New Right in the United States (see Crawford 1980). Thus, we have to guard against any essentialist view which argues for an a priori relationship between a class and a particular religious mode or world-view. In Madras, we have seen how charismatic beliefs and practices have quite recently begun to engage the interest of the orthodox church hierarchy, which hitherto disdained altogether such predilections.

The extent of foreign influence on developments in south Indian Protestantism is difficult to gauge precisely. For the 'true believer' such influence is irrelevant. God always moves in mysterious ways and the individual is predisposed to accept if not anticipate the unexpected. The opinion is not infrequently expressed that spiritual revivals have occurred spontaneously in south India from time to time and that the present out-pouring of the Holy Spirit on the community—though perhaps more pronounced and sustained than in the past—is but one in a long series of such divinely inspired occurrences. How far should we privilege such explanations? What do anthro-pologists know, asks Crick, which entitles them to offer in-terpretations utilizing frameworks not provided by the actors themselves (1982*a*: 228)?

Part of the answer must lie in the recognition that certain kinds of knowledge—in this case about, for example, the fund-ing agencies for or international aims of Western-based fun-damentalist organizations—are simply not available to most people. There is now a substantial amount of comment about the operations of fundamentalist groups, especially in parts of the world where the established church, or much of its clergy, has committed itself on the 'side' of the poor and oppressed. Not surprisingly, none of my informants among the Protestant lower class in Madras were (or had the opportunity to become) appraised of any of these activities, or of the developing dis-course around them. What would they make, I wonder, of an attack by a recent BBC Reith Lecturer on all varieties of 'liberation theology', and his observation that in its place, re-ligion ought to provide 'a sense of the ultimate worthlessness of human expectations of a better life on earth' (Norman 1979: 19–20). Absence of awareness obviously limits the range of indigenous frameworks available.

The other part of the answer resides in the fact that different actors provide different frameworks, and these may be, to an important extent, socially situated. The notion of class culture recognizes the possibility of distinctive cultural products outside the precincts of the dominant class, while allowing for a degree of cultural heterogeneity among those who share a similar loc-ation in the hierarchy. When we ask whose representations, therefore, it may be less a matter of theirs or ours, and much more a matter of *which of theirs*. The (etic?) notion of a cultural struggle has proved useful in understanding the relation be-tween alternative (emic?) religious ideologies. The image of negotiation has replaced one of ineluctable domination, though it is by no means negotiation between equals. Popular culture,

as Hall points out, can never escape 'the field of force of the
·relations of cultural power and domination' (1981a: 232). Thus,
we may understand the growing sympathy of senior figures in
the CSI for the charismatic movement as, in part, an attempt
to appropriate fundamentalist knowledge and so restrict the
extent of its autonomous power among those groups and assemblies which appeal so strongly to the lower class.

The fundamentalist efflorescence throws into relief the somewhat ambiguous relationship between popular Hinduism and
Christianity. Ayrookuzhiel (1979) suggests that, in a country
like India, to speak of a religious divide, in the sense of a distinct
conception and experience of god, may not be tenable. This is
a difficult proposition to interrogate in the abstract although, in
the specific domains of belief and action concerning affliction, it
acquires a certain credence. Despite what some scholars might
regard as a wide ontological chasm between them, and the
extremely harsh judgements of Hinduism by Protestant pietists
and fundamentalists alike, at the phenomenological level, at
least, there would appear to be a wide measure of overlap. For
people of both 'faiths' the world is populated by a host of
maleficent forces—human or superhuman—which must either
be avoided, or against which the protection of more powerful,
benign beings must be sought. In accord with this conception,
both traditions have recourse to a divine hierarchy, though one
(the Hindu) consists of a number of subtle gradations, while
that of Protestantism is starkly dualistic, with Jesus opposed to
all the forces of malignancy. There is, thus, also a place in both
for the prophet, the divinely inspired worker of miracles who is
set apart from and may be seen to undermine the authority of
the priestly specialist operating within prescribed textual or
traditional systems of knowledge. Those who hold to such beliefs
see the prophet as a mediator for the divinity, engaged on
behalf of the helpless against the agents of misfortune and
disorder. Thus, while an investigation of spirit possession and
similar mystical phenomena reveals much about the tensions
in inter-personal relationships, and the cultural understandings
which predispose particular categories of person to manifest
symptoms of affliction, it also tends to expose certain local
conceptions of power (see Ackerman 1981).

The whole notion of power in world religions has received relatively little attention from anthropologists. Several south Asianists have recently sought to rescue it from its 'encompassment' by ritual status in the Dumontian model of Hindu society (Dumont 1970). Wadley, for example, has argued that 'the basic characteristic of any god, demon or ghost is the power which it controls and represents, the fact that it is, in essence, power' (1977: 138). Unlike Dumont, she sees power and purity as 'inseparable factors of any ideas of being or action in Hindu thought' (ibid.: 154).

Fundamentalism draws attention to the significance of power in early Christianity. The conflict between good and evil, it may be argued, constitutes a central theme of the New Testament. The figure of the devil, suggests Russell, is comprehensible only when it is seen as the counter principle of Jesus Christ. The latter, by exorcizing the demons and curing diseases sent by the former, makes war upon the kingdom of Satan. Thus, the saving mission of Christ can be understood in terms of its opposition to the power of the devil (Russell 1977: 221-49).

A fundamentalist reading of scriptures similarly underlines God's dominion over satanic forces. Athyal proposes that although Western Christians—this can be extended to include *Westernized* indigenous middle-class Protestants belonging to the orthodox church in Madras—find this emphasis 'quite irrelevant today', Asian Christians regard it as expressing precisely 'what they would want to say' (1980: 70). While fundamentalists might balk at portraying the saviour primarily as a miracle worker, as Smith (1978) has recently done, attention is explicitly focused on the notion of a power encounter. Charismatics operating with the gifts of the Holy Spirit, like the ritual specialists with mediatory links to the divinities of Hinduism, offer the prospect of overcoming the evil forces in the lives of ordinary people. In both popular traditions, therefore, at the phenomenological level, power confronts power.

Such a cosmology cannot depend on a too rigid separation between the spheres of the 'natural' and 'supernatural', the 'human' and the 'divine'. This is frequently stressed by students of Hinduism. Thus, Wadley underlines the point that 'there is no native Hindu conception of a bounded domain of religion

or of the spiritual' (1977: 140). While, doctrinally, fundamentalists distinguish the 'world', the mundane activities
of everyday life, as a sphere set apart from and potentially
contaminating to the 'spiritual' realm, experientially they
differentiate little between them. Human and superhuman
agents—such as the *pēy* or the *mantiravāti*—regularly traverse
the dividing line and partake of both. Popular prophets, too,
despite theological interdiction and personal protestations to
the contrary, are sometimes divinized by their followers, and
become objects of worship. Moreover, they must continually
attest to the power of the Holy Spirit, and give proof of their
own divine selection and favour, by public demonstrations of
their miraculous abilities. These charismatic gifts have to be
renewed not only by prayer and the performance of stipulated
ritual exercises, but through direct communication with God,
effected by means of heavenly journeys, visions, and dreams.

A recognition of boundaries as permeable is encouraged by
and, in turn, encourages a conception of power as belonging
no less to the spiritual than to the material realm. To the extent
that many if not most everyday problems and misfortunes are
attributed by fundamentalists to the operations of occult evil
forces, it should not surprise us that the appropriation and
control of supernatural power becomes a paramount concern
(see also Ackerman 1981: 92).

We do not contribute to an anthropological understanding
of such notions of power by labelling them 'irrational', priv-
ileging, as this does, Western scientific knowledge about the
material world, and thereby invalidating other forms of cultural and social knowledge (Overing 1985: 5). For one thing,
the dramatic emergence of charismatic forms of Christianity in
the West during the past few decades should compel us to
question the notion of uniformity in Western thought. Pen-
tecostalists in Britain and the USA 'never weary of debunking
worldly social status and of emphasizing the unqualified significance of election by the Holy Ghost as the only status which
really matters' (Wilson 1967: 154). Such power, Wilson tells
us, they call 'real' power, and since its source is supernatural,
it is 'seen as greater than the power of the rich and worldly'
(1970: 70). The growing belief in biblical inerrancy and the
authenticity of miracles—in all the paraphernalia of fun-

damentalist religiosity—should lead us to ask whether we can any longer (if indeed we ever could) assume a universal Western commitment to 'scientific' thought.

For another, the rationality debate which has been waged on the frontier between anthropolgy and philosophy for over a decade has, in its concern to contrast Western modes of thought with those found in 'traditional' societies, tended to overlook the growing complexity and heterogeneity of many Third World civilizations. The transformations which they have undergone, partly a result of incorporating certain Western epistemologies (educational, scientific, bureaucratic), have too often been ignored in the interests of proposing a somewhat simplistic opposition. So, in Madras, as we have seen, popular theodicies and recipes for dealing with misfortune were and still are designated as 'superstitious/irrational' by the superordinate elements within the Protestant mission, church, and community. This datum emphasizes how, in the pursuit and reproduction of domination, certain Western notions are appropriated to disqualify and render inferior particular modes of thought. This is familiar grist for the anthropological mill. But it should be no part of *our* enterprise to nominate certain knowledges as 'rational' or 'true' or 'logical', and thus to predetermine hierarchies within the very cultures we are seeking to comprehend. It is its employment in the political discourses of those we study that the question of 'rationality' might most fruitfully be investigated, as one among many techniques of power.

NOTES

NOTES TO CHAPTER I

1. Throughout the book 'community', unless otherwise specified, will refer to the Protestant population of Madras, and not to any particular caste, which is how the term is often employed in common usage.
2. By making reference to determination 'in the last instance' by the forces and relations of production, they can, to recall Thompson's barbed comment, pay 'pious lip service to the theory and take out a license to ignore it . . . in practice' (1977: 263).
3. There is a body of opinion which argues that 'the colonial state was a decelerator, not an accelerator of industrialization in India' (Saberwal 1978: 9).
4. Driver found that perceptions of the social class structure in Madras varied according to the position of his respondents. Most in the lower class saw it as a dichotomous order; most in the middle class as a three-tiered structure (1981: 248).
5. I follow my informants who frequently use the (English) term 'élite' when referring to the dominant class. Although 'elite theory' was developed to 'repudiate class analysis' (Giddens 1982: 158), Ganguli suggests that in the Indian context 'it is precisely [the] elites that form the dominant class' (1977: 29).
6. A recurring theme in writings by economists on India is the concentration of ownership of the means of production. Sau estimates that the 'big bourgeoisie'—both rural and urban—constitute no more than 1.5 per cent of the population (1981: 71). Misra also notes the concentration of company directorships within the country's major business houses (1961: 252).
7. While the terms bear some resemblance to those used by anthropologists of India in their earlier discussions of 'levels' of Hinduism, the epistemological starting-points are significantly different. I discuss this in the concluding chapter.
8. There are several good studies of Syrian Christians (Brown 1956; Mathew and Thomas 1967). Lewandowski's work on Kerala migrants in Madras city (1980) also includes important data on these Christians. Luke and Carman (1968) have studied Protestants in a rural area of Andhra Pradesh, while Diehl (1965)

organized and directed a survey among Lutherans in Tamilnadu
mainly to ascertain the extent of Hindu beliefs among them.
Godwin's study (1972) of Catholics in Salsette, a suburb of
Bombay, is the only full-length work on urban Christians by a
sociologist that I am aware of.

9. According to McGavran's figures for 1977 of Christians in the
whole of India, Roman Catholics account for 50.5 per cent, Protestants for 32.4 per cent, Orthodox and other Keralite churches
for 10.6 per cent, while 'other Christians' make up six per cent
(McGavran 1979: 186–8).

10. There was apparently some dispute as to whether several chapels
built before 1820 (and not consecrated) were intended for 'native'
Christians or Europeans and Eurasians (see Penny 1904 (vol. 2):
259–60).

11. In one issue alone (1919) a knighthood, and several OBE (Officer
(of the Order) of the British Empire), MBE (Member (of the
Order) of the British Empire), OIE (Officer (of the Order) of the
Indian Empire), and Kaisar-i-Hind awards were announced.

NOTES TO CHAPTER 2

1. The character of this 'colonial context', of course, altered considerably during the period of European presence in India.

2. Niyogi, an avid opponent of Western missionaries, chaired an
investigation into their activities after independence. The Niyogi
Report (1956) caused great consternation among Christians, but
did not result in any specific legislation.

3. By 'conversion' I mean the transition from one religious community to another. (See Frykenberg 1980: 129, for a more detailed 'working definition'.) In certain contexts it can also refer,
following local usage, to being 'born again', the acceptance of
Jesus as personal saviour (see Chapters 7 and 8). Comaroff and
Comaroff have recently suggested that conversion can imply not
so much a 'commitment to Protestant ideology, but ... a subtle
internalization of its categories and values' (1986: 15).

4. While some missionaries and mission historians employ 'evangelism' to mean the 'sympathetic penetration of a culture and
society with the spirit of Christ', others use the term in the more
accepted sense of 'propagating Christianity' (Forrester 1980:
144). Throughout the book I use the term in this latter way.

5. The Boden chair of Sanskrit at Oxford was established in 1832 to
promote knowledge of the sacred language of the Brahmins, so
that, according to the wishes of Colonel Boden, 'my Countrymen

[can] proceed to the Conversion of the Natives of India to the Christian Religion ...' (Gombrich 1978: 5).

6. Missionaries themselves sometimes differentiated between 'diffuse' and 'concentrated' conversion strategies, which have as their 'targets' whole communities or individuals, respectively (see Mylne 1908; Heise 1967). However, mission strategies do not invariably bring the intended results. Etherington, referring to the southern African setting, notes that 'success in making converts appears to have been totally unrelated to the strategies of missionaries' (1977: 35).

7. There has been a considerable amount written on mission education. A few of the more useful sources are Frykenberg 1986; Manickam 1929; Mitra 1971; Satthianadhan 1894; P. J. Thomas 1939.

8. In Oceania, the administration relied on missions to provide educational services because the latter had the necessary personnel and organizational structures. However, according to Boutilier, this became an 'institutionalized excuse for its unwillingness or inability to tackle educational problems more resolutely' (1978: 87).

9. In the Madras Presidency at this time there were only three government and a few 'native' institutions (McCully 1966: 124). By contrast missions supported 1,185 schools with over 38,000 pupils (Satthianadhan 1894: 39). The SPG operated 186 institutions with 5,000 children in the south. The CMS maintained 317 elementary vernacular schools with 8,000 pupils in Tinnevelly alone, and in 1867 Bishop Caldwell reported that the district contained 450 mission educational establishments with 13,500 pupils, over a fifth of them girls. Indeed, the missionaries placed a great deal of emphasis on the education of females. The movement began around 1820 and 50 years later there were over 6,500 female pupils in the Presidency. The first high school for girls in the south was established by the CMS in Tinnevelly in 1836 (see Raj 1958: 125).

10. Writing of the Dinka of north-east Africa, Lienhardt observes how the 'road to Christianity, or at least to a Christianised way of thought ... came with the acceptance of the idea of progress through education ...' (1982: 81).

11. W. Taylor, Secretary of the Madras District Committee of the LMS, in a letter to the Treasurer and Secretaries of the LMS, Madras, 17 March 1831. For mention of specific disadvantages suffered by Christians, see also Ingham 1956: 17; Sherring 1875: 330–1; Penny 1904 (vol. 1): 348–9; Forrester 1980: 55.

12. In India, as elsewhere, no comity obtained between Protestants and Catholics, nor did sectarian groups later accept such constraints.

13. In the Tonga Islands where comity apparently did not exist, Dektor Korn reports the existence of seven major denominational representatives in a single village (1978: 399).

14. To give several examples from south India: (a) in 1820, a number of stations belonging to the Lutheran mission at Tranquebar were handed over to the Anglican SPCK; (b) in 1857, the Anglican SPG transferred most of its stations in Madurai district to the recently established American Madura Mission (Congregationalist); (c) about the same time, the SPG's stations in North Arcot were given to the Arcot Mission of the Dutch Reformed Church in America; and (d) in 1865 the LMS and SPG agreed that thereafter the former were to be restricted to Travancore and the latter to the neighbouring Tinnevelly district. In consequence, six stations belonging to the (Congregationalist) LMS in Tinnevelly were transferred to the (high) Anglican SPG mission (see Estborn 1961: 14; Sharrock 1910: 58; Sherring 1875: 365).

15. See 'An Appeal on Behalf of the I.M.S.', Church World Archives (London), Box 7, Folder 1, Jacket B.

16. Letter from the Revd J. A. Sharrock to the Lord Bishop in Madras, Trichinopoly, 24 April 1901 (SPG Archives, London).

NOTES TO CHAPTER 3

1. According to a recent study on migration to Madras, 60 per cent of migrants originating in Tamilnadu still come from the same three districts (see Blomkvist 1983: 6).

2. In 1946, approximately 20 square miles of inhabited territory were incorporated within the city's limits, bringing them near to their present (1981) extent of some 50 square miles.

3. By 1882 Madras already had a university, five Arts colleges, three for professional training, as well as a medical and an engineering college.

4. In 1975 there were over 100 companies based in Madras in which there was British capital investment (*Hindu*, 24 May 1975). According to Sau (1981: 57) the 'dominant foreign investor' in India is the UK, closely followed by the USA.

5. The exodus of foreign personnel did not, of course, imply the exodus of foreign capital or influence.

6. The presence of Christian girls in educational establishments was

very pronounced. In 1871 about four-fifths of all girls under instruction were Christians. By the end of the nineteenth century one in ten Christian females of school-going age were in educational institutions, as against one in 509 females belonging to all other categories of the population (Satthianadhan 1894: 75–6).

7. To teach in elementary school (grades 1–5) requires a minimum of 8th standard and two years of training; for middle school (grades 5–8) the School Leaving Certificate, followed by two years of training. A graduate with one year of training may teach in secondary school; to teach at the recently introduced 'plus 2' (pre-university level), a post-graduate qualification (M.Sc./MA) is demanded along with a year's training.

8. In 1981–2 scheduled castes and tribes were allocated 18 per cent of places in state-aided institutions of higher education, while 'backward' communities had 50 per cent, leaving only 32 per cent to the 'Forward' groups.

9. In a recent study of a small town Protestant parish, in North Arcot district, Burkhart was struck by the high proportion of working women who are teachers (1985: 101).

10. The demand for skilled labour in the oil-rich Gulf countries increased enormously after 1973, and, for many workers, landing a job there represents the British equivalent of a win on the 'pools'. The main recruiting centres are on the west coast (mainly Kerala), and Muslims are said to be favoured, so that few Madras Protestants of this class have managed to obtain such employment.

11. In the private sphere they work for firms such as Shaw Wallace, Brooke Bond, Burmah-Shell, Bayer and Co., ICI, and Binny's; in the public category, for corporations like Madras Port Trust, Indian Railways, Tamil Nadu Housing Board, All-India Radio, Madras Refineries, Indian Airlines, and various state-owned banks.

12. Breman rightly points out that this dichotomy sometimes applies to 'separate economic circuits' and at other times to 'distinctive employment situations' (1976: 1871). It is the latter to which this discussion mainly refers.

13. Settlements which have been taken under the wing of one or other of the political parties, however, can be well-maintained and serviced. They often manifest a strong sense of community pride (see Wiebe 1975; Lynch 1974).

14. Exchange rates fluctuated between Rs 15 and Rs 18 per £1 (sterling) during periods of field-work. The most consistent rate was approximately Rs 16.50 per £1.

15. Figures on the middle class were gathered principally in 1974-5. Those on the lower class were collected in 1981-2. For the purposes of comparison, therefore, the former had to be adjusted. In the absence of official figures on average income I have utilized the Consumer Price Index for Urban non-manual Employees in Tamilnadu (December 1980) which indicate an increase of approximately one-third during the period 1975-81, and may be seen to reflect, though crudely, the extent of growth in incomes of persons in this category (see Tamilnadu Statistical Handbook 1980: 353). This seems to accord roughly with my own data on salary rises earned by householders in the middle-class sample.

16. According to Kurien (1974: 53) the top 20 per cent of the urban population accounted for 73 per cent of total wealth held in the form of owner-occupied houses, while the bottom 10 per cent owned only one per cent of house property.

NOTES TO CHAPTER 4

1. During the Emergency (1975-7) the output of beer rose by 66.2 per cent, cars by 67.6 per cent, toothpaste by 56.3 per cent, motor scooters by 39 per cent, domestic refrigerators by 34.9 per cent, and room air-conditioners by 108.4 per cent (Shetty 1978: 199-200).

2. For example, the *Hindu* of 23 July 1981 carried advertisements for the following products: televisions sets, washing machines, mixer-grinders, pressure cookers, radio-cassette recorders, refrigerators, records, clothes irons, electric kettles, hi-fi equipment, stereo decks, car stereos, and video-cassette recorders.

3. The television service in Madras began in 1975. To purchase a set, in 1981, cost in the region of Rs 3,000.

4. Bottled gas is extremely difficult to obtain in the city. It is the preferred cooking medium because it is fast and clean. The initial outlay for the cooker and the cylinder rental is high, although the actual cost of the gas is not radically greater than for other fuels.

5. Whereas daily servants who do 'top work' are usually paid Rs 25-75 per month (along with coffee and a snack), cooks and drivers must be given at least Rs 150 and in some cases well over that amount.

6. In 1979, in a population of some 3 millions, there were only 30,500 registered cars in Madras city (Tamilnadu Statistical Handbook 1980: 274). In 1981, a decent second-hand car could not be

bought for less than Rs 25,000. A new scooter could be purchased for around Rs 5,000–8,000.

7. Most Protestant homes have framed mottoes nailed on their walls. 'I am the Way' and 'Christ is the Head of this Household' are two of the most popular aphorisms.

8. Many state government leaders can speak only Tamil, and even the few who know English are loath to employ it on public occasions.

9. With the rise of nationalism and the approach of independence, many Christians increasingly adopted what they felt were more suitable Indian names, though they still sought to avoid those associated with Hindu deities. I was told by one woman that when her grandfather lent his sympathy to the nationalist struggle, he 'dropped Burton and became Ragaviah'.

10. It is no small irony that the Europeans with whom these Christians identified, if anything, detested their 'pretensions', and there are numerous references in church and missionary literature to the divide between the two groups. One clergyman at the time wrote of the 'pernicious *race-feeling*' towards Indian Christians on the part of many Europeans (Lord 1896: 88–9, my emphasis).

11. In Tamilnadu there are nine medical colleges with approximately 10,000 student places (two-thirds are filled by men and one-third by women). There are also thirteen engineering and technical institutes with about 17,000 places—all but 700 of them filled by male students (Tamilnadu Statistical Handbook 1980: 253).

12. Of the Madras Club—the oldest of its kind, founded in 1831— one member wrote: 'I do not know whether any Indian has ever been admitted to membership, but I think not ... in the evening, after a day's work is over, men need to relax in the company of their own kind' (Slater 1936: 47).

13. European women—save on special 'ladies nights'—were also not admitted to the club. I would also assume that European men without either adequate status in the occupational hierarchy or financial wherewithal would not have been found in the more select associations.

14. Part of this life-style involved a form of transhumance. After 1840 the Madras government established its summer headquarters in the hill station of Ootacamund, so that during May and June each year the 'cream' of European society went *en masse* to the hills. Only a handful of the most senior Indian bureacrats could or would accompany the move.

15. The DMK (Dravida Munnetra Kazhagam) and ADMK (Anna Dravida Munnetra Kazhagam) are the two Dravidian parties which have held office in Tamilnadu since 1967. The latter is a

breakaway from the former. In 1974–5, during my first field trip the former was in power, and in 1981–2 the latter.

16. Several churches originally built to serve Europeans—especially those in the older parts of the city—were, after some time, Indianized (and 'Tamilized') simply because the Europeans who had worshipped there moved to the suburbs leaving only an indigenous congregation.

17. Posting to an élite church in Madras usually implies comfortable accommodation (perhaps in a manse), the likelihood of good schools in the neighbourhood, adequate living allowances, perhaps even a motor vehicle, and generous gifts from the congregation.

18. The educational qualifications demanded of candidates for the ministry have been rising of late, and it is unlikely nowadays for someone without a university degree to be accepted.

19. One minister estimated that 90 per cent of the Madras clergy are of Harijan background.

NOTES TO CHAPTER 5

1. The widespread notion that hypergamy is the general pattern in north India has been somewhat overstated, it appears. Fruzzetti has recently pointed out that the Bengali system is not hypergamous (1982: 34).

2. Letter dated 17 March 1841 from Miss Emily Lewis of the Female Orphan Asylum in Coimbatore (Tamilnadu) to the LMS (see Church World Mission Archives).

3. The proportion of scheduled castes in the northern districts of Tamilnadu, from which most lower class Madras Protestants originate, is consistently higher than in the general population of the state. The 1981 Census gives the figure for Chingleput as 27.5 per cent, for North Arcot as 22 per cent, and for South Arcot as 27 per cent, against 19 per cent in the whole of Tamilnadu.

4. The Syrian Christian community is today divided among adherents of the traditional Jacobite, Mar Thoma (a breakaway reformist movement), Protestant, and (the largest segment) Catholic churches. Until the British period, Jacobites and Catholics had regularly intermarried but this became rare in the course of the 19th century (Kaufmann 1979: 330).

5. The CSI discourages, but does not ban, such marriages.

6. A generation or two ago this list might have included clergymen and school teachers, then among the most prominent careers to which Christians could aspire. Many focal householders within the middle-class sample are the children of clerics and teachers.

7. Vatuk notes a distinction made by her informants between 'love marriages', which are akin to elopement, and those which are initially proposed by the couple themselves but effected by their parents 'with the decorum of an arranged union'. The former are called 'real love marriages' (1972: 89).

8. *Parisam*, among some groups in Tamilnadu, is a term for what anthropologists usually refer to as 'bridewealth' (Miller 1980).

9. *Biriyani* is a rich, highly flavoured and coloured *pulao* rice, cooked together with a high proportion of vegetables, fish, or meat. In Madras, Muslim cooks, who are regarded as specialists in preparing this dish, are generally hired to prepare the feast.

10. There seems to be no such stigma attached to this practice among rural households in those parts of north India described by Sharma—where the mother-in-law takes charge of a new daughter-in-law's 'dowry' goods, and even distributes them among the other women in the household (1984). Elsewhere, there appears to be more ambiguity regarding the rights of in-laws to these goods (see Madan 1975).

11. Households in the middle-class sample earn an annual average income from employment of approximately Rs 37,000 (see Chapter 3). In addition, they have other earnings from investments and savings, as well as access to credit from a variety of sources.

12. Kapadia (1955: 128) notes how a girl's physical beauty or educational qualifications may reduce the amount of *dowry* her parents must pay, 'but often this reduction is very meagre'.

13. Catherine Hall, referring to 19th-century Birmingham, notes that among the wealthier bourgeoisie 'it was common practice to have a marriage settlement which protected the wife's property whereas amongst the petit bourgeoisie this would have been very unusual' (1981: 167).

14. Watson notes that Chinese landlord-merchants in the New Territories of Hong Kong take wives from a larger area than peasants (1981: 605).

NOTES TO CHAPTER 6

1. Caste and class are not the only kinds of subjectivity of course. Regional/linguistic and religious affiliation are significant to these Protestants as well.

2. Sudra Christians, according to Mullens, 'would not drink at the Lord's supper with [the outcastes] or after them ...' (1854: 87).

3. Eichinger suggests that various practices found within the Christian community which may be linked to pollution concepts are probably observances of the prescriptions of Leviticus (1974:

150). I never heard any of my informants make such an observation.

4. Obsequies among rural Protestants are, in some places and among certain groups, very nearly fully in accord with those of Hindu caste counterparts (see Diehl 1965: 122–5; Raj 1958: 176–9). Writing about rural Catholic funerals Good (1978: 492) observes: '... it seems ... a case of the Christians retaining both their former behaviour and, more or less overtly, the previous justifications for it.'

5. Eichinger (1976: 591–2) finds it difficult to accept Fuller's findings, on the grounds that the Tamil Christians she studied (who observe various forms of pollution) are neighbours of the Keralites. In his response, Fuller notes the considerable differences in historical circumstances between the ancient Syrian community and the relatively new Christian groups created by Western missionaries (1977: 528–9).

6. Several mission Societies were, during the first decades of their presence in south India, reluctant to antagonize their converts, especially members of the higher castes among them, and so tolerated various manifestations of caste prejudice (see Richter 1908; Frykenberg 1976; Forrester 1980).

7. At a meeting of Christian leaders in Madras (2 Feb. 1981) the following resolution—probably not untypical of the many agreed over the years—was passed: 'We, the Christians of Madras ... appeal to the Prime Minister to remove the disabilities of Christians of Scheduled Caste origin'.

8. When Bishop Sargent was near the end of his term of office in Tinnevelly, during the last quarter of the nineteenth century, there was talk of choosing an indigenous cleric as successor, but, according to Hudson, 'neither the Vellalars nor the Nadars would tolerate a bishop from the other caste' (1970: 431). Kaufmann also makes clear that conflict between these groups over ceremonial privileges within the Catholic church in various parts of the south was a 'feature of the 19th century' (1979: 238).

9. The Anglican communion in what is now southern Tamilnadu was regarded as a 'one-caste' (Nadar) church; Lutherans of the Danish mission in Tranquebar were predominantly Vellalars; the American Arcot Mission of the Dutch Reformed Church in America consisted almost entirely of (Palli and Paraiyan) Harijans; and so on.

10. The first Indian bishop was only consecrated in 1912, and even in 1947 eight of the fourteen bishops of the newly formed CSI were Europeans. In missionary establishments a similar situation obtained. Of the Principals of mission colleges in the Madras

Presidency in 1927, not one was an Indian (Manickam 1929: 102). Indian Christians frequently complained loudly of missionary 'imperialism' (Orr 1967: 36).

11. According to informants, he received approximately 290 of the 340 votes cast.

12. The North Arcot area was the geographical focus of the 'western region', one of the five into which the Madras diocese had been divided. There was widespread agreement that the diocese had become too large and administratively unwieldy.

13. Safa has recently argued for the need to take account of gender consciousness in assessing the degree of class awareness. She notes that 'shanty town women [in Puerto Rico] share a greater sense of sexual subordination than of class oppression' (1970: 455).

14. See 'Why the Indian white collar is angry' (*Express*, 21 Feb. 1982); 'Hospitals for middle class proposed' (*Hindu*, 15 Nov. 1981); 'Disaffected middle class' (*Hindu*, 13 Dec. 1981); 'Case for higher limit for estate duty exemption' (*Hindu*, 25 Dec. 1981); 'Urban land ceiling act to be amended' (*Express*, 28 Dec. 1981).

15. Any labour agitation 'however small, brings the police directly into factory premises ... police are known to side with employers ...' (Iyer 1982: 12).

16. It should be pointed out that there were several Christian organizations, and numerous individuals, who came out strongly against the Emergency, at no small risk to themselves.

17. Records of the CSI-Northern congregation.

18. For more details of the CMCH strike and a comprehensive bibliography of sources see Caplan 1981.

19. After initial attempts at conciliation, which the management rebuffed, the state government embarked on a programme of harassment: the hospital's power and water supplies were tampered with; demands for taxes owing on the sales of medicines suddenly arrived; and senior hospital personnel, including the associate director—a prominent neuro-surgeon—were arrested.

20. For some years prior to these events, the DMK and the Congress party (at state and central levels) had been sworn rivals. This came to a head in the pre-Emergency links forged between the DMK and Mrs Gandhi's opponents in other parts of the country. During the Emergency the Congress dismissed the DMK ministry and imposed Presidential rule. The Chief Minister was placed in detention for a time. The strike may thus be seen as part of an ongoing struggle between these two political forces.

21. Although CMCH had been troubled by sporadic labour problems for at least a decade, this strike seems to have had its genesis in June 1974, when a doctor and four non-medical personnel were

accused of falsifying the College entrance examination results of two candidates applying for admission to the MB/BS course. Following investigations it was decided to terminate the services of the five. Because the doctor involved was a local Vellore man (one of the few who has risen beyond the menial ranks), and the brother of a top union official, the decision aroused strong hostility and led to agitation and violence by a number of employees.

22. The Congress-affiliated Indian National Trades Union Congress (INTUC) and the CPI-linked All-India Trades Union Congress (AITUC) took no part in these demonstrations of support for the strikers.

23. Syrian Christians enjoy a pre-eminent place within the hospital. They hold half the headships of departments and comprise three-quarters of other senior medical staff. Further, they provide approximately 90 per cent of nursing staff and 70 per cent of technical personnel.

24. There are numerous instances of strikes which purportedly fail for lack of support from workers whose caste ties coincide with those of the firm's owners or managers.

NOTES TO CHAPTER 7

1. During his term as Governor-General Warren Hastings encouraged and commissioned translations of classics from Sanskrit by H. B. Halhed (Code of Hindu Law), Charles Wilkins (*Bhagavadgita*), Sir William Jones (Kalidasa's *Sakuntula*), and others. These works reached a wide European audience for the first time, and established an awareness of Hinduism which was entirely new (see Marshall 1970).

2. 'Hinduism' was presented by Western (and nationalist) thinkers in this period as a unitary 'religion', to be compared with and opposed to Christianity and other monotheistic traditions.

3. Converts were not usually permitted to attend non-Christian weddings or other socio-ritual occasions (*Madras Guardian*, 19 Aug. 1956).

4. While the CSI inherited a number of training colleges for the clergy from its previous denominational constituents, each with its own quite distinctive tradition, the most important of them nowadays emphasize what are regarded as radical theologies. One conservative clergyman remarked to me that the CSI's 'greatest evil' is to be found in its ministerial training institutes.

5. In November 1974 there were 319 licensed lay preachers and another 116 probationers in the CSI's Madras diocese.

6. In the case of the MIPF a large proportion of its members also belong to the CSI.

7. Several prayer groups with which I am familiar are focused on a married couple, who share the organizational and ritual tasks.

8. It is interesting that while informal prayer cells are largely the domain of women, those which are formally organized are run by men, even if the participants remain predominantly women. The association's executive committee has only two women among its fourteen members.

9. The association grew despite this official disapproval.

10. A similar élite congregation in Bangalore draws attention to the fact that 'every year we raise nearly Rs 25,000 ... and this money is normally spent on deserving and needy organisations irrespective of religious affiliation' (Clarke 1973: 4).

11. These Christians also belong, as we saw in Chapter 4, to various secular organizations, many of which support welfare activities.

12. During the period I was in Madras, the CSI-Southern congregation did take part in a few welfare projects, but most of its energies and financial resources were directed to the erection of a new church building (see Chapter 1).

13. Pat Caplan (1985) analyses a number of such 'welfare rituals' among women's organizations in Madras, and shows how they mark the middle class off from those beneath them.

14. Theological colleges are frequently accused of turning out 'social workers' who are unable to relate to their parishes.

15. Other common terms for sorcery are *pilli sūṇiyam* or *sey viṇai*. Obeyesekere defines sorcery in the Sri Lankan context as 'a technique of killing or harming someone, deliberately and intentionally, generally by homeopathic or contagious magic, accompanied by spells, charms or incantations' (1975: 1). While this is largely applicable to the situation I am describing, it omits the manipulation of evil spirits by the practitioners of sorcery in Madras.

16. *Pēy* are also sometimes referred to as *pisasu, pēy-pisasu,* or *keṭṭāvi*. In biblical Tamil they are *asutta āvi*.

17. Mohini is also a spirit in Sri Lanka. Stirrat refers to her as a *peretayo*, whose victims 'act in a very lascivious manner' (1977: 139 n. 10).

18. See Egnor (1980) for a detailed discussion of the concept of *sakti* in Tamilnadu.

19. A series of articles in Bangalore newspapers, 1980-2, detailed and commented upon the *banamathi* practices found in the area, and on the conclusions of NIMHANS. I am grateful to A. M.

Abraham Ayrookuzhiel of the Christian Institute for the Study of Religion and Society for drawing my attention to these articles.

20. This kind of conservative evangelicalism has been termed 'fundamentalism' by Barr (1977) and others. I have avoided using this label so as to distinguish such beliefs and practices from more recent forms of fundamentalist religiosity which have entered South India. See Chapter 8.

NOTES TO CHAPTER 8

1. I should reiterate that I subsume under the label 'fundamentalist' a variety of groups which, while holding disparate and sometimes antagonistic doctrines, tend to emphasize the importance of the Holy Spirit and the gifts it confers.

2. There is a view that Pentecostalism was not brought by American missionaries but was an 'indigenous outpouring' in 1905, when young women at a Christian orphanage founded by the Brahmin convert Pandita Ramabai 'manifested the Holy Spirit and spoke in tongues' (Johnson 1971: 8).

3. Second baptism is often referred to as 'water' or 'immersion' baptism. The CSI teaches that the baptism of infant children of believers is valid, that baptism is unrepeatable, and that second baptism is contrary to the precepts of the Bible (see Newbigin 1973).

4. There is a considerable literature on the gifts of the Holy Spirit and, as we might expect, many differences of opinion. Lesslie Newbigin, who was bishop in Madras until 1974, disagreed profoundly with fundamentalist ideas about the importance of tongues, arguing that glossalalia was not highly regarded by Paul who stressed, rather, that 'love is supreme' (1972*b*: 25).

5. A prophet in the sense of a person who is a medium of the power of the Holy Spirit, and chosen by God for a special charismatic ministry is most likely to be referred to by the same term as is an evangelist—*ūḻiyakkāraṇ*. I use the English terms interchangeably.

6. Hollenweger writes that in 'hundreds and thousands of [Pentecostal] prayers the blood of Jesus is called down to sprinkle the meeting room and purify the hearts and minds of those present' (1972: 313). Barr notes that for conservative evangelicals sin is a fearful horror 'which only the blood of Christ can dissipate' (1977: 25).

7. 'Satan himself is transformed into an angel of light' (2 Cor. 11: 14). The arch-enemy, writes Penn-Lewis, 'can fashion himself as an "angel of light" to allure those he desires to win for his par-

ticular use'. Hence, 'they profess to be what they are not' (1973: 24).

8. Hollenweger notes that 'accounts of raisings from the dead ... are not rare in the Pentecostal movement' (1972: 369).

9. Wilson (1967: 154) notes the contrast made by Pentecostals between divine election of their own ministers and the 'futile book-learning and schooling' of denominational ministers.

10. Female prophets were not unknown in the past. Daniel refers to a 'flaming woman preacher' in the Andhra region of south India during the 1930s (1980: 47).

11. In the pre-independence period, the members of denominational churches who associated with fundamentalist groups were threatened with dire consequences. In a letter to several congregations in south Madras in November 1915, the Anglican bishop informed members that they could not remain communicants of the church if they had anything whatever to do with the Pentecostal mission which had recently appeared on the scene.

12. The charismatic movement within Protestantism is said to have begun in 1958 in California when 'in a wealthy and respectable congregation of the American Episcopal church some individuals, led by their priest, began to speak in tongues' (Wilson 1976: 34). O'Connor (1975: 145) suggests that within modern Catholicism the first manifestations occurred in 1967 at the University of Notre Dame in Indiana.

13. In his opening address at a CSI Renewal conference in February 1982, the bishop advised his audience 'not to be ashamed of speaking in tongues. It doesn't mean you are Pentecostals.'

14. Christians tend to use the term *vallamai* and not *sakti* because of what they regard as the latter's 'Hindu' connotations.

REFERENCES

Abercrombie, N. and B. S. Turner 1978. The Dominant Ideology Thesis. *British Journal of Sociology* 29, 149–70.

Ackerman, S. E. 1981. The Language of Religious Innovation: Spirit Possession and Exorcism in a Malayasian Catholic Pentecostal Movement. *Journal of Anthropological Research* 37, 90–100.

Ahmad, I. 1973 (ed.). *Caste and Social Stratification among the Muslims.* Delhi: Manohar.

—— 1976 (ed.). *Family, Kinship and Marriage among Muslims in India.* Delhi: Manohar.

—— 1981 (ed.). *Ritual and Religion among Muslims in India.* Delhi: Manohar.

Althusser, L. 1970. *Reading Capital.* London: New Left Books.

—— 1971. Ideology and Ideological State Apparatuses. In *Lenin and Philosophy and Other Essays.* London: Monthly Review Press.

Arasaratnam, S. 1981. Protestant Christianity and South Indian Hinduism 1630–1730: Some Confrontations in Society and Beliefs. *Indian Church History Review* 15, 7–33.

Asad, T. 1979. Anthropology and the Analysis of Ideology. *Man* (NS) 14, 607–27.

—— 1983. Anthropological Conceptions of Religion: Reflections on Geertz. *Man* (NS) 18, 237–59.

Athyal, S. P. 1980. Toward an Asian Christian Theology. In *Asian Christian Theology: Emerging Themes* (ed.) J. D. Elwood. Philadelphia: The Westminster Press.

Ayrookuzhiel, A. M. A. 1979. The Living Hindu Popular Religious Consciousness and Some Reflections on it in the Context of Hindu–Christian Dialogue. *Religion and Society* 26, 5–25.

Ayyar, K. K. V. 1928. Chathan: A Devil or Disease? *Man* 28, 151–3.

Azariah, V. S. and H. Whitehead 1930. *Christ in the Indian Villages.* Madras: Christian Literature Society.

Baago, K. 1966. The Post Colonial Crisis of Missions. *Int. Review of Mission* 55, 322–32.

Baker, C. J. 1975. Facts and Figures: Madras Government Statistics 1880–1940. In *South India: Political Institutions and Political Change 1880–1940* (eds.) C. J. Baker and D. A. Washbrook. Delhi: Macmillan.

Ballhatchet, K. 1961. Some Aspects of Historical Writing on India by Protestant Christian Missionaries during the 19th and 20th

Centuries. In *Historians of India, Pakistan and Ceylon* (ed.) C. H. Philips. London: OUP.

Barnett, M. R. 1976. *The Politics of Cultural Nationalism.* Princeton: Univ. Press.

Barnett, S. 1970. The Structural Position of a South Indian Caste. Ph.D. thesis, Univ. of Chicago.

—— 1973. Urban is as Urban does: Two Incidents on one Street in Madras City, South India. *Urban Anthropology* 2, 129–60.

Barr, J. 1977. *Fundamentalism.* London: SCM Press.

Barrett, M., P. Corrigan, A. Kuhn, and J. Wolff 1979 (eds.). *Ideology and Cultural Production.* London: Croom Helm.

Basham, D. W. 1971. *Can a Christian have a Demon?* Monroeville, Penn.: Whitaker House.

Baskaran, S. T. 1970. A Mass Movement in the 'Mass Movement' Area. *South India Churchman* (Aug.), 11–12.

Beck, B. E. F. 1972. *Peasant Society in Konku: A Study of Right and Left Subcastes in South India.* Vancouver: Univ. of British Columbia Press.

Beidelman, T. O. 1982. *Colonial Evangelism: A Socio-historical Study of an East African Mission at the Grassroots.* Bloomington: Univ. of Indiana Press.

Bennett, T., G. Martin, C. Mercer, and J. Woollacott 1981 (eds.). *Culture, Ideology and Social Process.* London: Batsford.

Berger, P. L. and T. Luckmann 1971. *The Social Construction of Reality: A Treatise in the Sociology of Knowledge.* Harmondsworth: Penguin.

Berreman, G. D. 1967. Stratification, Pluralism and Interaction: A Comparative Analysis of Caste. In *Caste and Race: Comparative Approaches* (eds.) A. de Reuck and J. Knight. London: Churchill.

—— 1972. Social Categories and Social Interaction in Urban India. *American Anthropologist* 74, 567–87.

Béteille, A. 1964. A Note on the Referents of Caste. *European Journal of Sociology* 5, 107–24.

—— 1969. *Castes: Old and New.* Bombay: Asia.

—— 1974. *Studies in Agrarian Social Structure.* Delhi: OUP.

Biggs, W. W. 1965. *Introduction to the History of the Christian Church.* London: Edward Arnold.

Bloch, M. 1983. *Marxism and Anthropology: The History of a Relationship.* Oxford: Univ. Press.

Blomkvist, H. 1983. *Housing the Poor in a Great City: The Madras Experience.* Mimeo.

Bourdieu, P. 1968. Outline of a Sociological Theory of Art Perception. *Int. Social Science Journal* 20, 589–612.

—— 1977. *Outline of a Theory of Practice* (trans. R. Nice). Cambridge: Univ. Press.

Boutilier, J. A. 1978. Missionization in Historical Perspective (Introduction to Part 2). In *Mission, Church and Sect in Oceania* (eds.) J. A. Boutilier *et al*. Ann Arbor: Univ. of Michigan Press.

Boutilier, J. A., D. T. Hughes, and S. W. Tiffany 1978 (eds.). *Mission, Church and Sect in Oceania*. Ann Arbor: Univ. of Michigan Press.

Boyd, R. 1969. *An Introduction to Indian Christian Theology*. Madras: Christian Literature Society.

Breman, J. 1976. A Dualistic Labour System?: A Critique of the 'Informal Sector' Concept (3 parts). *Economic and Political Weekly* 11, 1870–5; 1905–8; 1939–44.

Brown, C. W. 1956. *The Indian Christians of St Thomas*. Cambridge: Univ. Press.

Brown, H. 1948. *The Sahibs*. London: William Hodge.

Bujra, J. M. 1978/9. Proletarianization and the 'Informal Economy': A Case Study from Nairobi. *African Urban Studies* 3, 47–66.

Burghart, R. 1978. Hierarchical Models of the Hindu Social System. *Man* (NS) 13, 519–36.

—— 1983. From Pioneers to Settlers: Recent Studies of the History of Popular Culture: A Review Article. *Comp. Studies in Society and History* 25, 181–7.

Burke, P. 1976. Oblique Approaches to the History of Popular Culture. In *Approaches to Popular Culture* (ed.) C. W. E. Bigsby. London: Edward Arnold.

—— 1983. From Pioneers to Settlors: Recent Studies of the History of Popular Culture: A Review Article. *Comp. Studies in Society and History* 25, 181–7.

Burkhart, G. 1985. Mission School Education and Occupation among Lutherans in a South Indian Town. *South Asian Social Scientist* 1, 97–118.

Caplan, L. 1976. Class and Urban Migration in South India: Christian Elites in Madras City. *Sociological Bulletin* 25, 207–24.

—— 1977. Social Mobility in Metropolitan Centres: Christians in Madras City. *Contributions to Indian Sociology* (NS) 11, 193–217.

—— 1980. Class and Christianity in South India: Indigenous Responses to Western Denominationalism. *Modern Asian Studies* 14, 645–71.

—— 1981. Morality and Polyethnic Identity in Urban South India. In *Culture and Morality: Essays in Honour of Christoph von Fürer-Haimendorf* (ed.) A. C. Mayer. Delhi: OUP.

—— 1984. Bridegroom Price in Urban India: Class, Caste and 'Dowry Evil' among Christians in Madras. *Man* (NS) 19, 216–33.

Caplan, P. 1978. Women's Organizations in Madras City, India. In *Women United, Women Divided: Cross-cultural Perspectives on Female Solidarity* (eds.) P. Caplan and J. Bujra. London: Tavistock.

—— 1985. *Class and Gender in India: Women and Their Organizations in a South Indian City.* London: Tavistock.

Chandrasekhar, S. 1964. Growth of Population in Madras City: 1639–1961. *Contributions to Indian Sociology* (NS) 8, 3–45.

Clarke, S. 1973. St. Mark's Cathedral, Bangalore, as a Giving Church. *South India Churchman* (July), 4–5.

—— 1980. *Let the Indian Church be Indian.* Madras: Christian Literature Society.

Clarke, S., T. Lovell, K. McDonnell, V. J. Seidler, and K. Robins 1980 (eds.). *One-dimensional Marxism: Althusser and the Politics of Culture.* London: Allison and Busby.

Cohen, A. 1969. *Custom and Politics in Urban Africa.* London: Routledge and Kegan Paul.

—— 1971. The Politics of Ritual Secrecy. *Man* (NS) 6, 427–48.

—— 1977. Symbolic Action and the Structure of Self. In *Symbols and Sentiments* (ed.) I. M. Lewis. London: Academic.

—— 1981. *The Politics of Elite Culture: Explorations in the Dramaturgy of Power in a Modern African Society.* Berkeley: Univ. of California Press.

Comaroff, J. and J. Comaroff 1986. Christianity and Colonialism in South Africa. *American Ethnologist* 13, 1–22.

Conlon, F. F. 1977. *A Caste in a Changing World: The Chitrapur Saraswat Brahmans, 1700–1935.* Berkeley: Univ. of California Press.

Crawford, A. 1980. *Thunder on the Right: The 'New Right' and the Politics of Resentment.* New York: Pantheon.

Crick, M. 1982a. Anthropological Field Research, Meaning Creation and Knowledge Construction. In *Semantic Anthropology* (ed.) D. J. Parkin. London: Academic.

—— 1982b. Anthropology of Knowledge. *Annual Review of Anthropology* 11, 287–313.

Cunningham, H. 1982. Class and Leisure in Mid-Victorian England. In *Popular Culture: Past and Present* (eds.) B. Waites, T. Bennett, and G. Martin. London: Croom Helm.

Daniel, J. 1980. *Another Daniel.* Madras: The Laymen's Evangelical Fellowship.

David, I. 1983. God's Messengers: Reformed Church in America Missionaries in South India, 1839–1938. Doctor of Theology thesis, Lutheran School of Theology, Chicago.

Dektor Korn, S. R. 1978. After the Missionaries Came: Denominational Diversity in the Tongo Islands. In *Mission, Church and Sect in Oceania* (eds.) J. A. Boutilier *et al.* Ann Arbor: Univ. of Michigan Press.

Devadason, E. D. 1974. *Christian Law in India: Law Applicable to Christians in India.* Madras: DSI Publications.

Devanesan, C. D. S. 1980. Young Christian Dancer's Arangetram. *Christian Focus* 21, 7–8.

Devapackiam, M. 1963. The History of the Early Christian Settlements in the Tirunelveli District. MA thesis, Univ. of Madras.

Devasundaram, A. 1975. The Cathedral as a Centre of Communication. *Indian Journal of Theology* 24, 16–20.

Dhinakaran, D. G. S. 1979. *Healing Stripes* (rev. and ed. by D. S. G. Muller). Madras: Christian Literature Society.

Diehl, C. G. 1956. *Instrument and Purpose: Studies on Rites and Rituals in South India.* Lund: Gleerups.

—— 1965. *Church and Shrine: Intermingling Patterns of Culture in the Life of some Christian Groups in south India.* Uppsala: Hakan Ohlssons Boktryckeri.

Douglas, M. and B. Isherwood 1978. *The World of Goods: Towards an Anthropology of Consumption.* Harmondsworth: Penguin.

Driver, E. D. 1981. Social Class in South India: A Cognitive Approach. *Journal of Asian and African Studies* 16, 238–60.

—— 1982. Class, Caste and 'Status Summation' in Urban India. *Contributions to Indian Sociology* (ns) 16, 225–53.

Dumont, L. 1970. *Homo Hierarchicus: The Caste System and its Implications* London: Weidenfeld and Nicolson.

Egnor, M. 1977. A Tamil Priestess (paper presented at the Amer. Anthrop. Assn meeting, Houston, Tex.).

—— 1980. On the Meaning of Sakti to Women in Tamil Nadu. In *The Powers of Tamil Women* (ed.) S. S. Wadley. Syracuse: Maxwell School of Citizenship and Public Affairs, Syracuse Univ.

Eichinger Ferro-Luzzi, G. 1974. Women's Pollution Periods in Tamilnadu (India). *Anthropos* 69, 113–61.

—— 1976. Indian Christians and Pollution. *Man* (ns) 11, 591–2.

Elmore, W. T. 1915. Dravidian Gods in Modern Hinduism: A Study of Local and Village Deities of Southern India. *University Studies* 15, 1–49.

Epinay, C. L. d' 1969. *Haven of the Masses: A Study of the Pentecostal Movement in Chile.* London: Lutterworth.

Epstein, A. L. 1978. *Ethos and Identity: Three Studies in Identity.* London: Tavistock.

Estborn, S. 1961. *The Church among Tamils and Telugus.* Nagpur: National Christian Council.

Etherington, N. 1977. Mission Station Melting Pots as a Factor in the Rise of African Black Nationalism. *Int. Journal of African Historical Studies* 9, 592–605.

Evans-Pritchard, E. E. 1956. *Nuer Religion.* Oxford: Univ. Press.

Farquhar, J. N. 1913. *The Crown of Hinduism.* London: Humphrey Milford, OUP.

Firth, R. 1981. Spiritual Aroma: Religion and Politics. *American Anthropologist* 83, 582–601.

278 *References*

— Forrester, D. B. 1980. *Caste and Christianity: Attitudes and Policies on Caste of Anglo-Saxon Protestant Missionaries in India*. London: Curzon.

Foucault, M. 1980. *Power/Knowledge: Selected Interviews and Other Writings 1972–1977* (ed.) C. Gordon. Brighton: Harvester.

Fox, R. 1967. Resiliency and Change in the Indian Caste System: The Umar of U. P. *Journal of Asian Studies* 26, 575–87.

—— 1977. *Urban Anthropology: Cities in their Cultural Settings*. Englewood Cliffs, NJ: Prentice-Hall.

Fruzzetti, L. M. 1982. *The Gift of a Virgin: Women, Marriage and Ritual in a Bengali Society*. New Brunswick, NJ: Rutgers Univ. Press.

Frykenberg, R. E. 1976. The Impact of Conversion and Social Reform upon Society in South India during the Late Company Period: Questions Concerning Hindu–Christian Encounters with Special Reference to Tinnevelly. In *Indian Society and the Beginnings of Modernisation c.1830–1850* (eds.) C. H. Philips and M. D. Wainwright. London: SOAS.

—— 1980. On the Study of Conversion Movements: A Review Article and a Theoretical Note. *Indian Economic and Social History Review* 17, 121–38.

—— 1985. Caste, Morality and Western Religion under the Raj. *Modern Asian Studies* 19, 321–52.

—— 1986. Modern Education in South India, 1784–1854: Its Roots and its Role as a Vehicle of Integration under Company Raj. *American Historical Review* 91, 37–65.

Fuller, C. J. 1976. Kerala Christians and the Caste System. *Man* (NS) 11, 53–70.

—— 1977. Indian Christians, Pollution and Origins. *Man* (NS) 12, 528–9.

—— 1979. Gods, Priests and Purity: On the Relation between Hinduism and the Caste System. *Man* (NS) 14, 459–76.

Gandhi, M. K. 1964. *The Collected Works of Mahatma Gandhi* (vol. 28). Delhi: Publications Division, Ministry of Information and Broadcasting, Government of India.

Ganguli, B. N. 1977. Conceptualising the Indian Middle Class. In *Society and Change: Essays in Honour of Sachin Chaudhuri* (eds.) K. S. Krishnaswamy *et al.* Bombay: OUP.

Geertz, H. 1975. An Anthropology of Religion and Magic. *Journal of Interdisciplinary History* 6, 71–89.

Gehani, T. G. 1966. A Critical Review of the Work of Scottish Presbyterian Missions in India, 1878–1914. Ph.D. thesis, Univ. of Strathclyde.

— George, T. C. 1975. The Growth of Pentecostal Churches in South India. MA thesis in Missiology, Fuller Theological Seminary, Pasadena.

Gerlach, L. P. 1974. Pentecostalism: Revolution or Counter-revolution? In *Religious Movements in Contemporary America* (eds.) I. I. Zaretsky and M. P. Leone. Princeton: Univ. Press.

Giddens, A. 1982. Class Structuration and Class Consciousness. In *Classes, Power and Conflict: Classical and Contemporary Debates* (eds.) A. Giddens and D. Held. Berkeley: Univ. of California Press.

Gilsenan, M. 1982. *Recognizing Islam: An Anthropologist's Introduction.* London: Croom Helm.

Ginzburg, C. 1983. *The Night Battles: Witchcraft and Agrarian Cults in the Sixteenth and Seventeenth Centuries* (trans. J. and A. Tedeschi). London: Routledge and Kegan Paul.

Gist, N. 1954. Caste Differentials in South India. *American Sociological Review* 19, 126–37.

Godwin, C. J. 1972. *Change and Continuity: A Study of Two Christian Village Communities in Suburban Bombay.* Bombay: McGraw-Hill.

Gombrich, R. 1978. *On Being Sanskritic: A Plea for Civilized Study and the Study of Civilization* (inaugural lecture, Oxford, Oct. 1977). Oxford: Clarendon.

Good, A. 1978. Kinship and Ritual in a South Indian Macro-region. Ph.D. thesis, Durham Univ.

—— 1980. Elder Sister's Daughter Marriage in South India. *Journal of Anthropological Research* 36, 474–500.

Goodman, F. D. 1972. *Speaking in Tongues: A Cross-cultural Study of Glossalalia.* Chicago: Univ. Press.

Goody, J. R. 1973. Bridewealth and Dowry in Africa and Eurasia. In *Bridewealth and Dowry* (eds.) J. R. Goody and S. J. Tambiah. Cambridge: Univ. Press.

Gough, K. 1956. Brahman Kinship in a Tamil Village. *American Anthropologist* 58, 826–53.

Gould, H. 1970. Occupational Categories and Stratification in the Achievement of Urban Society. In *Urban India: Society, Space and Image* (ed.) R. Fox. Durham: Duke Univ. Press.

Grafe, H. 1969. Benjamin Schultze and the Beginnings of the First Indian Protestant Church in Madras. *Indian Church History Review* 3, 35–54.

Gramsci, A. 1971. *Selections from the Prison Notebooks of Antonio Gramsci* (eds.) Q. Hoare and G. Nowell-Smith. London: Lawrence and Wishart.

Grant, J. W. 1959. *God's People in India.* Toronto: Ryerson Press.

Guiart, J. 1970. The Millenarian Aspect of Conversion to Christianity in the South Pacific. In *Millenial Dreams in Action* (ed.) S. L. Thrupp. New York: Schocken Books.

Hall, C. 1981. Gender Divisions and Class Formation in the Birmingham Middle Class, 1780–1850. In *People's History and Socialist Theory* (ed.) R. Samuel. London: Routledge and Kegan Paul.

Hall, S. 1981*a* Notes on Deconstructing 'the Popular'. In *People's History and Socialist Theory* (ed.) R. Samuel. London: Routledge and Kegan Paul.

—— 1981*b*. Cultural Studies: Two Paradigms. In *Culture, Ideology and Social Process* (eds.) T. Bennett *et al.* London: Batsford.

Hannerz, U. 1980. *Exploring the City: Inquiries Toward an Urban Anthropology.* New York: Columbia Univ. Press.

Hardgrave, R. L. 1969. *The Nadars of Tamilnad: The Political Culture of a Community in Change.* Berkeley: Univ. of California Press.

Harper, E. B. 1964. Ritual Pollution as an Integrator of Caste and Religion. In *Religion in South Asia* (ed.) E. B. Harper. Seattle: Univ. of Washington Press.

Harper, M. 1965. *As at the Beginning: The Twentieth Century Pentecostal Revival.* London: Hodder and Stoughton.

—— 1981. The Lukewarming of the Church. *Madras Diocesan News and Notes* (June), 19–25.

Heise, D. R. 1967. Prefatory Findings in the Sociology of Missions. *Journal for the Scientific Study of Religion* 6, 49–58.

Hill, C. 1983. Science and Magic in Seventeenth Century England. In *Culture, Ideology and Politics* (eds.) R. Samuel and G. Stedman Jones. London: Routledge and Kegan Paul.

—— 1984. Good Walkers (Review of Ginzburg 1983) *New Statesman*, 27 November.

Hodgson, G. H. 1939. Three Hundred Years of Madras Commerce. In *Madras Tercentenary Commemoration Volume.* Madras: Humphrey Milford, OUP.

Hollenweger, W. J. 1972. *The Pentecostals* (trans. R. Wilson). London: SCM Press.

Hollis, A. M. 1962. *Paternalism and the Church: A Study of South Indian Church History.* London: OUP.

Holmstrom, M. 1976. *South Indian Factory Workers: Their Life and Their World.* Cambridge: Univ. Press.

—— 1984. *Industry and Inequality: The Social Anthropology of Indian Labour.* Cambridge: Univ. Press.

Hopkins, N. S. 1977. The Emergence of Class in a Tunisian Town. *Int. Journal of Middle East Studies* 8, 453–91.

Houghton, G. 1981. The Development of the Protestant Missionary Church in Madras, 1870–1920: The Impoverishment of Dependency. Ph.D. thesis, Univ. of California.

Hudson, D. 1970. The Life and Times of H. A. Krishna Pillai (1827–1900). Ph.D. thesis, Claremont Graduate School, Ann Arbor.

Ifeka-Moller, C. 1974. White Power: Social–Structural Factors in Conversion to Christianity, Eastern Nigeria, 1921–1966. *Canadian Journal of African Studies* 8, 55–72.

Ingham, K. 1956. *Reformers in India, 1793-1833.* Cambridge: Univ. Press.

Iyer, R. 1982. Industrial Strife: Workers' Paradise Lost. *Madras Diocesan News and Notes* 16, 9-18.

Jain, R. 1977. Classes and Classification among the Peasantry in Central India: Relations of Production in Village Parsania, Madhya Pradesh. *Sociological Bulletin* 26, 91-115.

Johnson, I. C. 1971. A Study of Theories and Practices of the Pentecostal Movement in India in the Light of Lutheran Understanding of the Christian Faith. BD thesis, Gurukal Lutheran Theological College, Madras.

Johnson, R. 1979. Histories of Culture/Theories of Ideology: Notes on an Impasse. In *Ideology and Cultural Production* (eds.) M. Barrett *et al*. London. Croom Helm.

Kapadia, K. M. 1955. *Marriage and Family in India.* London: Geoffrey Cumberlege, OUP.

Kaufmann, S. B. 1979. Popular Christianity, Caste and Hindu Society in South India, 1800-1915: A Study of Travancore and Tirunelveli. Ph.D. thesis, Cambridge.

Kiernan, J. P. 1981. Themes and Trends in the Study of Black Religion in Southern Africa. *Journal of Religion in Africa* 12, 136-47.

Kurien, C. T. 1974. *Poverty and Development.* Bangalore: Christian Institute for the Study of Religion and Society.

—— 1981. *Mission and Proclamation: The Church in India Today and Other Pieces.* Madras: Christian Literature Society.

L'Armand, K. and A. L'Armand 1978. Music in Madras: The Urbanization of a Cultural Tradition. In *Eight Urban Musical Cultures* (ed.) B. Nettle. Urbana: University of Illinois.

Lewandowski, S. 1975. Urban Growth and Municipal Development in the Colonial City of Madras, 1860-1900. *Journal of Asian Studies* 34, 341-60.

—— 1980. *Migration and Ethnicity in Urban India: Kerala Migrants in the City of Madras, 1870-1970.* Delhi: Manohar.

Lewis, I. M. 1971. *Ecstatic Religion: An Anthropological Study of Spirit Possession and Shamanism.* Harmondsworth: Penguin.

Lienhardt, R. G. 1982. The Dinka and Catholicism. In *Religious Organization and Religious Experience* (ed.) J. Davis. London: Academic.

Lindstrom, L. 1984. Doctor, Lawyer, Wise Man, Priest: Big-men and Knowledge in Melanesia. *Man* (ns) 19, 291-309.

Lloyd, P. 1982. *A Third World Proletariat?* London: George Allen and Unwin.

Lord, J. H. 1896. How to Develop a Greater Sympathy between Indian and European Christians. *Indian Church Quarterly Review* 9, 85-100.

Luke, P. Y. and J. B. Carman 1968. *Village Christians and Hindu Culture: Study of a Rural Church in Andhra Pradesh, South India.* London: Lutterworth.

Lukes, S. 1974. *Power: A Radical View.* London: Macmillan.

Lynch, O. 1974. Political Mobilization and Ethnicity among Adi-Dravidas in a Bombay Slum. *Economic and Political Weekly* 9, 1657–68.

McCully, B. T. 1966. *English Education and the Origins of Indian Nationalism.* Gloucester, Mass.: Peter Smith.

McDonnell, K. and K. Robins 1980. Marxist Cultural Theory: The Althusserian Smokescreen. In *One-dimensional Marxism: Althusser and the Politics of Culture* (eds.) S. Clarke *et al.* London: Allison and Busby.

McGavran, D. 1979. *Understanding the Church in India.* Bombay: Gospel Literature Service.

Machin, W, 1934. Evil Spirits. *National Christian Council Review* (NS) 54, 481–3.

Madan, T. N. 1975. Structural Implications of Marriage in North India: Wife-givers and Wife-takers among the Pandits of Kashmir. *Contributions to Indian Sociology* (NS) 9, 217–43.

Manickam, R. B. 1929. *Missionary Collegiate Education in the Presidency of Madras, India.* Lancaster: Conestoga Publishing Co.

Marriott, M. 1955. Little Communities in an Indigenous Civilization. In *Village India: Studies in the Little Community* (ed.) M. Marriott. Chicago: Univ. Press.

—— 1968. Multiple Reference in Indian Caste Systems. In *Social Mobility in the Caste System in India* (ed.) J. Silverberg. Paris: Mouton.

Marshall, P. J. 1970. *The British Discovery of Hinduism in the Eighteenth Century.* Cambridge: Univ. Press.

Mathew, C. P. and M. M. Thomas 1967. *The Indian Churches of Saint Thomas.* Delhi: ISPCK.

Matsuo, T. 1979. The Japanese Protestants in Korea, Part Two: The 1st March Movement and the Japanese Protestants. *Modern Asian Studies* 13, 581–65.

Mauss, M. 1979 (1950). *Sociology and Psychology: Essays* (trans. B. Brewer). London: Routlege and Kegan Paul.

Mencher, J. 1974. The Caste System Upside Down, or the Not-so-mysterious East. *Current Anthropology* 15, 469–78.

Merquior, J. G. 1979. *The Veil and the Mask: Essays on Culture and Ideology.* London: Routledge and Kegan Paul.

Michaelson, K. 1973. Class, Caste and Network in Suburban Bombay: Adaptive Strategies among the Middle Class. Ph.D. thesis, Univ. of Wisconsin.

Miller, B. D. 1980. Female Neglect and the Costs of Marriage in Rural India. *Contributions to Indian Sociology* (NS) 14, 95–129.

Misra, B. B. 1961. *The Indian Middle Classes: Their Growth in Modern Times*. Delhi: OUP.

Misra, V. 1962. *Hinduism and Economic Growth*. Bombay: OUP.

Mitra, S. K. 1971. Education and Missionaries in the Presidency of Madras, 1793–1833. *Indian Church History Review* 5, 117–24.

Moffatt, M. 1979. *An Untouchable Community in South India: Structure and Consensus*. Princeton: Univ. Press.

Moisa, M. A. 1983. Fourteenth-century Preachers' Views of the Poor: Class or Status Group? In *Culture, Ideology and Politics* (eds.) R. Samuel and G. Stedman Jones. London: Routledge and Kegan Paul.

Mullens, J. 1848. *Brief Sketch of the Present Position of Christian Missions in Northern India and of their Progress during 1847*. Calcutta: Baptist Missionary Press.

—— 1854. *Missions in South India*. London: W. H. Dalton.

Murdoch, J. 1895. *Indian Missionary Manual: Hints to Young Missionaries in India*. London: James Nisbett.

Mylne, L. G. 1908. *Missions to Hindus: A Contribution to the Study of Missionary Methods*. London: Longmans, Green and Co.

Nader, L. 1974. Up the Anthropologist: Perspectives Gained from Studying up. In *Reinventing Anthropology* (ed.) D. Hymes. New York: Vintage Books.

Nambiar, K. K. G. 1982. Taxation and Inflation: Middle Class Faces Double Squeeze. *Madras Diocesan News and Notes* (March), 6–8.

Neill, S. 1964. *A History of Christian Missions*. Harmondsworth: Penguin.

—— 1972. *The Story of the Christian Church in India and Pakistan*. Madras: Christian Literature Society and ISPCK.

Nelson, A. 1975. *A New Day in Madras: A Study of Protestant Churches in Madras*. South Pasadena, Calif.: William Carey Library.

Nelson, J. 1970. The Urban Poor: Disruption or Political Integration in Third World Cities? *World Politics* 22, 393–414.

Newbigin, L. 1972a. Twenty-five Years in Madras Diocese. *South India Churchman* (March), 11–13.

—— 1972b. *The Holy Spirit and the Church*. Madras: Christian Literature Society.

—— 1973. Our Practice of Infant Baptism (an address given to the Madras city clergy, Aug. 16). Madras: Diocesan Press.

Niyogi, M. B. 1956. *Report of the Christian Missionaries Activities Enquiry Committee* (2 vols.). Government of Madhya Pradesh.

Norman, E. 1979. *Christianity and the World Order*. Oxford: Univ. Press.

284 *References*

Obeyesekere, G. 1975. Sorcery, Premeditated Murder, and the Canalization of Aggression in Sri Lanka. *Ethnology* 14, 1–23.

O'Connor, D. 1975. *Charismatic Renewal*. London: SPCK.

Oddie, G. A. 1977. Christian Conversion among Non-Brahmans in Andhra Pradesh, with Special Reference to Anglican Missions and the Dornakal Diocese, c. 1900–1936. In *Religion in South Asia: Religious Conversion and Revival Movements in South Asia in Medieval and Modern times* (ed.) G. A. Oddie. New Delhi: Manohar.

—— 1978. Brahmans and Christian Conversion in the Kaveri Delta, South India, 1800–1900. Paper read at the Sixth European Conference on Modern South Asian Studies, Paris, 8–13 July.

—— 1981. Christianity in the Hindu Crucible: Continuity and Change in the Kaveri Delta, 1850–1900. *Indian Church History Review* 15, 48–72.

Oppert, G. 1893. *On the Original Inhabitants of Bharatavarsa or India*. Westminster: Constable.

Orr, J. M. 1967. The Contribution of Scottish Missions to the Rise of Responsible Churches in India. Ph.D. thesis, Univ. of Edinburgh.

Overing, J. 1985. Introduction. *Reason and Morality* (ed.) J. Overing. London: Tavistock.

Parkin, D. J. 1978. *The Cultural Definition of Political Response: Lineal Destiny among the Luo*. London: Academic.

—— 1982. Introduction. *Semantic Anthropology* (ed.) D. J. Parkin. London: Academic.

—— 1984. Political Language. *Annual Review of Anthropology* 13, 345–65.

Parkin, F. 1972. *Class Inequality and Political Order: Social Stratification in Capitalist and Communist Societies*. London: Paladin.

—— 1982. Social Closure and Class Formation. In *Classes, Power and Conflict: Classical and Contemporary Debates* (eds.) A. Giddens and D. Held. Berkeley: Univ. of California Press.

Parry, J. P. 1970. The Koli Dilemma. *Contributions to Indian Sociology* (NS) 4, 84–104.

Patankar, B. and G. Omvedt 1977. The Bourgeois State in Postcolonial Social Formations. *Economic and Political Weekly* 12, 2165–77.

Pathak, S. M. 1967. *American Missionaries and Hinduism*. Delhi: Munshiram Manoharlal.

Paul, B. 1973. Women and Church Administration. *South India Churchman* (Oct.), 11–12.

Paul, R. D. 1958. *The First Decade: An Account of the Church of South India*. Madras: Christian Literature Society.

Peace, A. 1980. Structured Inequalities in a North Indian City. *Contributions to Indian Sociology* (NS) 14, 239–60.

Penn-Lewis, J. 1973. *The Warfare with Satan* (based on addresses given in 1897). Poole: The Overcomer Literature Trust.

Penny, F. 1904. *The Church in Madras* (3 vols.). London: Smith, Elder and Co.

Pickett, J. W. 1933. *Christian Mass Movements in India: A Study with Recommendations.* Lucknow: Lucknow Publishing House.

Pocock, D. J. 1960. Sociologies: Urban and Rural. *Contributions to Indian Sociology* 4, 63–81.

—— 1972. *Kanbi and Patidar.* Oxford: Clarendon.

Ponniah, J. S. 1938. *An Enquiry into the Economic and Social Problems of the Christian Community of Madurai, Ramnad and Tinnevelly Districts.* Madurai: American College.

Pouchedapass, J. 1982 (ed.). Caste et classe en Asie du sud. *Collection Puruṣārtha* 6.

Prabhakar, M. E. 1981. *Caste-class and Status in Andhra Churches and Implications for Mission Today.* Revised version of a paper presented to the Biennial Council of CISRS, Bangalore, November. Unpublished mimeo.

Pro Mundi Vita: Dossiers 1980. *Christians and the Emergency in India. Asia–Australasia Dossier* 14.

Raj, H. 1958. Persistence of Caste in South India—an analytical study of the Hindu and Christian Nadars. Ph.D. thesis, American Univ., Washington, DC.

Rajaraman, I. 1983. Economics of Bride-price and Dowry. *Economic and Political Weekly* 18, 275–9.

Ransom, C. W. 1938. *A City in Transition.* Madras: Christian Literature Society.

Richter, J. 1908. *A History of Missions in India* (trans. S. H. Moore). Edinburgh: Oliphant, Anderson and Ferrier.

Ross, A. 1961. *The Hindu Family in its Urban Setting.* Toronto: Univ. Press.

Rosser, C. 1966. Social Mobility in the Newar Caste System. In *Caste and Kin in Nepal, India and Ceylon* (ed.) C. von Fürer-Haimendorf. Bombay: Asia.

Rowe, W. L. 1973. Caste, Kinship and Association in Urban India. In *Urban Anthropology* (ed.) A. Southall. London: OUP.

Russell, J. B. 1977. *The Devil: Perceptions of Evil from Antiquity to Primitive Christianity.* Cornell: Univ. Press.

Saberwal, S. 1978. Introduction. Indian Urbanism: A Sociological Perspective. In *Process and Institution in Urban India: Sociological Studies* (ed.) S. Saberwal. New Delhi: Vikas.

Safa, H. I. 1979. Class Consciousness among Working Class Women in Puerto Rico. In *Peasants and Proletarians: The Struggles of Third*

World Workers (eds.) R. Cohen, P. Gutkind, and P. Brazier. London: Hutchinson.

Satthianadhan, S. 1894. *History of Education in the Madras Presidency.* Madras: Srinivasa, Varadachari and Co.

Sau, R. 1981. *India's Economic Development: Aspects of Class Relations.* New Delhi: Orient Longman.

Selbourne, D. 1982. *Through the Indian Looking-glass: Selected Articles on India 1976–1980.* Bombay: Popular Prakashan.

Sharma, U. M. 1970. The Problem of Village Hinduism: 'Fragmentation' and Integration. *Contributions to Indian Sociology* (NS) 4, 1–21.

—— 1980. *Women, Work and Property in North-west India.* London: Tavistock.

—— 1984. Dowry in North India: Its Consequences for Women. In *Women and Property: Women as Property* (ed.) R. Hirschon. London: Croom Helm.

Sharpe, E. 1965. *Not to Destroy but to Fulfil: The Contribution of J. N. Farquhar to Protestant Missionary Thought in India before 1914.* Uppsala: Gleerup.

Sharrock, J. A. 1910. *South Indian Missions.* Westminster: Society for the Propagation of the Gospel in Foreign Parts.

Sherring, M. A. 1875. *The History of the Protestant Missions in India from their Commencement in 1706 to 1871.* London: Trubner.

Shetty, S. L. 1978. Structural Retrogression in the Indian Economy since the Mid-sixties. *Economic and Political Weekly* 13, 185–244.

Shiri, G. 1969. The Indian Government Policy on Missionary Activities since 1947. BD thesis, Union Theological College, Bangalore.

Shulman, D. D. 1980. *Tamil Temple Myths: Sacrifice and Divine Marriage in the South India Saiva Tradition.* Princeton: Univ. Press.

Singer, M. 1972. *When a Great Tradition Modernizes: An Anthropological Approach to Indian Civilization.* London: Pall Mall.

Slater, G. 1936. *Southern India: Its Economic and Political Problems.* London: George Allen and Unwin.

Smith, M. 1978. *Jesus the Magician.* London: Victor Gollancz.

Smith, M. W. 1953. Structured and Unstructured Class Societies. *American Anthropologist* 55, 302–5.

Souza, S. D' 1966. Some Demographic Characteristics of Christianity in India. *Social Compass* 13, 415–30.

Srinivas, M. N. 1942. *Marriage and Family in Mysore.* Bombay: New Book Co.

Stein, B. 1973. Devi Shrines and Folk Hinduism in Medieval Tamilnad. In *Studies in the Language and Culture of South Asia* (eds.) E. Gerow and M. D. Lang, Seattle: Univ. of Washington Press.

Stirrat, R. L. 1977. Demonic Possession in Roman Catholic Sri Lanka. *Journal of Anthropological Research* 33, 133–57.

—— 1982. Caste Conundrums: Views of Caste in a Sinhalese Catholic Fishing Village. In *Caste Ideology and Interaction* (ed.) D. McGilvray. Cambridge: Univ. Press.

Sundkler, B. 1954. *Church of South India: The Movement towards Union, 1900–1947*. London: Lutterworth.

Synod of the Church of South India 1959. *Guidance Concerning Marriage Law: Rules and Regulations for Ministers of the Church of South India*. Madras: Christian Literature Society.

Tambiah, S. J. 1970. *Buddhism and the Spirit Cults in North-east Thailand*. Cambridge: Univ. Press.

—— 1973. Dowry and Bridewealth and the Property Rights of Women in South Asia. In *Bridewealth and Dowry* (eds.) J. R. Goody and S. J. Tambiah. Cambridge: Univ. Press.

Thamburaj, Fr. 1982. Charismatic Renewal in the Catholic Church. *Madras Diocesan News and Notes* (May), 23–5.

Thampan, K. M. 1968. A Study of Factionalism in the Church with Special Reference to the CSI Dioceses in Kerala. BD thesis, Union Theological College, Bangalore.

Thangasamy, D. A. 1969. Some Trends in Recent Theological Thinking in Madras City. *Indian Church History Review* 3, 55–74.

Therborn, G. 1980. *The Ideology of Power and the Power of Ideology*. London: Verso.

Thomas, K. 1975. An Anthropology of Religion and Magic, II. *Journal of Interdisciplinary History* 6, 91–109.

—— 1982 (1971). *Religion and the Decline of Magic*. Harmondsworth: Penguin.

Thomas, M. M. 1977. *Towards an Evangelical Social Gospel*. Madras: Christian Literature Society.

Thomas, P. J. 1939. History of Education in Madras. In *Madras Tercentenary Commemoration Volume*. Madras: Humphrey Milford, OUP.

Thompson, E. P. 1977. Folklore, Anthropology and Social History. *Indian Historical Review* 3, 247–66.

Thurston, E. 1912. *Omens and Superstitions of Southern India*. London: T. Fisher Unwin.

Turton, A. 1984. Limits of Ideological Domination and the Formation of Social Consciousness. In *History and Peasant Consciousness in South East Asia* (eds.) A. Turton and S. Tanabe. Osaka: National Museum of Ethnology.

Van Binsbergen, W. M. J. 1981. *Religious Change in Zambia: Exploratory Studies*. London: Kegan Paul International.

Vatuk, S. 1971. Trends in North Indian Urban Kinship: The

'Matrilateral Asymmetry' Hypothesis. *Southwestern Journal of Anthropology* 27, 287–307.

—— 1972. *Kinship and Urbanization: White Collar Migrants in North India*. Berkeley: Univ. of California Press.

—— 1975. Gifts and Affines in North India. *Contributions to Indian Sociology* (NS) 9, 155–96.

Wadley, S. S. 1977. Power in Hindu Ideology and Practice. In *The New Wind: Changing Identities in South Asia* (ed.) K. David. The Hague: Mouton.

Warren, M. 1965. *The Missionary Movement from Britain in Modern History*. London: SCM Press.

Watson, R. S. 1981. Class Differences and Affinal Relations in South China. *Man* (NS) 16, 593–615.

Weber, M. 1964. *The Theory of Social and Economic Organization*. London: Collier-Macmillan.

Westcott, A. 1897. *Our Oldest Indian Mission: A brief History of the Vepery (Madras) Mission*. Madras: Madras Diocesan Committee of the SPCK.

Whitehead, H. 1921. *The Village Gods of South India*. Calcutta: Association Press.

Wiebe, P. 1975. *Social Life in an Indian Slum*. New Delhi: Vikas.

—— 1981. *Tenants and Trustees: A Study of the Poor in Madras*. Delhi: Macmillan.

Wilson, B. R. 1967. The Pentecostal Minister. In *Patterns of Sectarianism* (ed.) B. R. Wilson. London: Heinemann.

—— 1970. *Religious Sects: A Sociological Study*. London: Weidenfeld and Nicolson.

—— 1973. *Magic and the Millenium*. London: Paladin.

—— 1976. *Contemporary Transformations of Religion*. London: OUP.

Wirth, L. 1938. Urbanism as a Way of Life. *American Journal of Sociology* 44, 1–24.

Worsley, P. 1981. Social Class and Development. In *Social Inequality* (ed.) G. D. Berreman. London: Academic.

Zachariah, M. 1981. *The Christian Presence in India: Editorials in the N.C.C.* [National Christian Council] Review. Madras: Christian Literature Society.

Ziegenbalg, B. 1718. *Propagation of the Gospel in the East: Being an Account of the Success of Two Danish Missionaries Lately Sent to the East Indies for the Conversion of the Heathens in Malabar. In Several Letters to their Correspondents in Europe* (trans. from the Dutch). Pt. 1. London.

INDEX OF NAMES

INDEX OF SUBJECTS